LYLE

Price Guide
to Uncommon Antiques
and Oddities

LYLE

Price Guide
to Uncommon Antiques
and Oddities

Anthony Curtis

A Perigee Book

A Perigee Book
Published by The Berkley Publishing Group
A division of Penguin Putnam Inc.
375 Hudson Street
New York, New York 10014

First edition: June 2000

Published simultaneously in Canada.

The Penguin Putnam Inc. World Wide Web site address is
http://www.penguinputnam.com

Library of Congress Cataloging-in-Publication Data

Curtis, Tony, 1939–
    Lyle price guide to uncommon antiques & oddities / Anthony Curtis.
      p. cm.
    Includes index.
    ISBN: 0-399-52606-4
      1. Antiques—Catalogs. 2. Collectibles—Catalogs. I. Title: Price guide to uncommon
antiques & oddities. II. Title
    NK1125.C8873 2000
    745.1'075—dc21   00-27104

Printed in the United States of America

10 9 8 7 6 5 4 3 2 1

Academy Auctioneers, Northcote House, Northcote Avenue, Ealing W5 3UR
Anderson & Garland, Marlborough House, Marlborough Crescent, Newcastle upon Tyne NE1 4EE
Auction Team Köln, Postfach 50 11 19, D-50971 Köln, Germany
Bearne's, St. Edmund's Court, Okehampton Street, Exeter EX4 1DU
Black Horse Agencies, Locke & England, 18 Guy Street, Leamington Spa
Bonhams, Montpelier Street, Knightsbridge, London SW7 1HH
Bonhams Chelsea, 65–69 Lots Road, London SW10 0RN
Bonhams West Country, Dowell Street, Honiton, Devon
Bosleys, The White House, Marlow, Bucks SL7 1AH
Bristol Auction Rooms, St Johns Place, Apsley Road, Clifton, Bristol BS8 2ST
Butterfield & Butterfield, 220 San Bruno Avenue , San Francisco CA 94103, USA
Butterfield & Butterfield, 7601 Sunset Boulevard, Los Angeles CA 90046, USA
Canterbury Auction Galleries, 40 Station Road West, Canterbury CT2 8AN
H.C. Chapman & Son, The Auction Mart, North Street, Scarborough
Cheffins Grain & Comins, 2 Clifton Road, Cambridge
Christie's (International) SA, 8 place de la Taconnerie, 1204 Genève, Switzerland
Christie's France, 9 avenue Matignon, 75008 Paris
Christie's Monaco, S.A.M, Park Palace 98000 Monte Carlo, Monaco
Christie's Scotland, 164–166 Bath Street, Glasgow G2 4TG
Christie's South Kensington Ltd., 85 Old Brompton Road, London SW7 3LD
Christie's, 8 King Street, London SW1Y 6QT
Christie's East, 219 East 67th Street, New York, NY 10021, USA
Christie's, 502 Park Avenue, New York, NY10022, USA
Christie's Australia Pty Ltd., 1 Darling Street, South Yarra, Victoria 3141, Australia
The Cotswold Auction Co., Chapel Walk Saleroom, Chapel Walk, Cheltenham, Glos. GL50 3DS
Palais Dorotheum, A-1010 Vienna, Dorotheengasse 17, Austria
Dreweatt Neate, Donnington Priory, Newbury, Berks.
Dreweatt Neate, Holloways, 49 Parsons Street, Banbury
Hy. Duke & Son, 40 South Street, Dorchester, Dorset
Eldred's, Box 796, E. Dennis, MA 02641, USA
R H Ellis & Sons, 44/46 High Street, Worthing, BN11 1LL
Fidler Taylor & Co., Crown Square, Matlock, Derbyshire DE4 3AT
Finarte, 20121 Milano, Piazzetta Bossi 4, Italy
The Goss & Crested China Co., 62 Murray Road, Horndean, Hants. PO8 9JL
Greenslade Hunt, Magdalene House, Church Square, Taunton, Somerset TA1 1SB
Andrew Hartley Fine Arts, Victoria Hall, Little Lane, Ilkley
Muir Hewitt, Halifax Antiques Centre, Queens Road/Gibbet Street, Halifax HX1 4LR
G A Key, Aylsham Saleroom, Palmers Lane, Aylsham, Norfolk, NR11 6EH
George Kidner, The Old School, The Square, Pennington, Lymington, Hants SO41 8GN
Kunsthaus am Museum, Drususgasse 1–5, 5000 Köln 1, Germany
Lawrence Fine Art, South Street, Crewkerne, Somerset TA18 8AB
Lawrence's Fine Art Auctioneers, Norfolk House, 80 High Street, Bletchingley, Surrey
Onslow's, The Depot, 2 Michael Road, London, SW6 2AD
Ian Pendlebury, Manchester 0161 747 2017
Phillips Manchester, Trinity House, 114 Northenden Road, Sale, Manchester M33 3HD
Phillips Son & Neale SA, 10 rue des Chaudronniers, 1204 Genève, Switzerland
Phillips West Two, 10 Salem Road, London W2 4BL
Phillips, 65 George Street, Edinburgh EH2 2JL
Phillips, Blenstock House, 7 Blenheim Street, New Bond Street, London W1Y 0AS
Phillips Marylebone, Hayes Place, Lisson Grove, London NW1 6UA
Phillips, New House, 150 Christleton Road, Chester CH3 5TD
Pieces of Time, 26 South Molton Lane, London W1Y 2LP
Russell, Baldwin & Bright, The Fine Art Saleroom, Ryelands Road, Leominster HR6 8JG
Skinner Inc., Bolton Gallery, Route 117, Bolton MA, USA
Sotheby's, 34–35 New Bond Street, London W1A 2AA
Sotheby's, 1334 York Avenue, New York NY 10021
Sotheby's, 112 George Street, Edinburgh EH2 2LH
Sotheby's, Summers Place, Billingshurst, West Sussex RH14 9AD
Sotheby's, Monaco, BP 45, 98001 Monte Carlo
G E Sworder & Son, 14 Cambridge Road, Stansted Mountfitchet, Essex CM24 8BZ
Tennants, Harmby Road, Leyburn, Yorkshire
Tool Shop Auctions, 78 High Street, Needham Market, Suffolk IP6 8AW
Wallis & Wallis, West Street Auction Galleries, West Street, Lewes, E. Sussex BN7 2NJ
Woolley & Wallis, The Castle Auction Mart, Salisbury, Wilts SP1 3SU

While every care has been taken in the compiling of information contained in this volume, the publisher cannot accept liability for loss, financial or otherwise, incurred by reliance placed on the information herein.

All prices quoted in this book are obtained from a variety of auctions in various countries and are converted to dollars at the rate of exchange prevalent at the time of sale. The images and the accompanying text remain the copyright of the contributing auction houses.

The publishers wish to express their sincere thanks to the following for their involvement and assistance in the production of this volume.

ANTHONY CURTIS (Editor)

EELIN McIVOR (Sub Editor)

ANNETTE CURTIS (Editorial)

CATRIONA DAY (Art Production)

ANGIE DEMARCO (Art Production)

NICKY FAIRBURN (Art Production)

Contents

CONTENTS

8

Introduction

Anyone who regularly leafs through antiques auction catalogs will know that it very seldom happens that they do not contain at least one object which causes the reader to pause, arrested either by its unusual nature or the ingenuity of its design or decoration.

These are not necessarily freaks, and are just as valid items as the more everyday lots in the rest of the catalogs. Yet they have an added dimension of interest. Some, like a Japanese mancatcher, a Southern States slave badge or collar, or a French model guillotine, reflect a way of life very different to our own. Others, such as barbed wire, dinosaur droppings, drizzling machines, hair, false teeth or mousetraps, cause one to wonder why anyone would want to make a collection of such items in the first place. (However, from the surprising amounts which they fetch, it would seem that an equally surprising number of people do!) Yet others, such as the chair in the form of a lobster, the sewing machine modeled as a clown or the slightly risqué corkscrews in the form of a pair of lady's legs, are basically conventional items with an extra dash of humor or ingenuity. One of the most entertaining of all in this category must surely be the Scandinavian cabinet on stand in the form of an army officer, his flies opening to reveal, as the catalog coyly puts it, 'a mechanical curiosity'.

Such pieces are in no way inferior to their more conventional counterparts - just the reverse, in fact. Usually beautifully made, it could be said that there is even more of the craftsman in them than usual, being made not just with professional competence, but with a large investment of the maker's own ingenuity, humor and character, often, one feels, for his own personal gratification. This was certainly the case with Tramp Art, made out of discarded cigar boxes not just by tramps but by anyone who had a penknife and liked to whittle. The pieces produced were certainly not intended for sale, but like so much else they caught someone's eye, and, well, the maker could always sell that piece and make another....

A rare 'Clown' sewing machine, German, third quarter 19th century.
(Bonhams) **$6,000**

A carved and painted chair in the form of a lobster, early 20th century.
(Christie's) **$34,960**

9

So these offbeat items are prized objects, and, because of their interest, quality and unusual nature, they can command large premiums. They are beloved of the trade and private collector alike, as eyecatching items for stock or conversation pieces for the living room. Imagine being able to tell your friends that that lump of stone in the corner was in fact a dinosaur dropping for which you'd paid $20,000, or a nest of Sauropod eggs at $77,924, or even a microscopic fragment of lunar meteorite, which would have set you back almost $15,000. However you look at it, they add much to the pleasure and interest of buying and selling antiques.

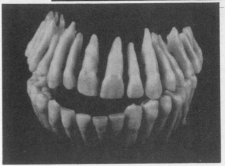

A complete set of upper and lower human teeth bound with brass wire.
(Christie's) **$800**

The Lyle Price Guide to Unusual Antiques and Oddities is a book that can be enjoyed on many different levels. It is certainly an entertaining browse, but it is also an instructive and authoritative tool of the trade, which will draw the attention to the value of many fascinating items which, because of their unusual nature, are difficult to categorize and seldom appear in more conventional price guides.

A rare nest of ten sauropod eggs, embedded, each egg 5½in. diameter.
(Bonhams) **$77,924**

In the past, these items would be scattered through catalogs of many different types. Now, for the first time, a selection has been gathered together in this book, which reveals the full extent of what it is possible these days to buy and sell successfully at auction. On every page there is something to surprise and delight, from a leather key basket at $41,400 to a silver rabbit tape measure with a wind-up tail ($160), a rather sinister life-size seated mannequin - having her in the corner of your bedroom would be guaranteed to give you nightmares - ($3,200) to a collection of teeth extracted from Royalty and other worthies ($2,636), a carved head of John the Baptist ($23,000) to a Mouse chess set ($24,000), a butterfly chandelier ($7,720) to a 'girl skipping rope' clockwork bank ($24,000).

A rare Ferdinand Gaultier life-size mannequin, French, circa 1880.
(Bonhams) **$3,200**

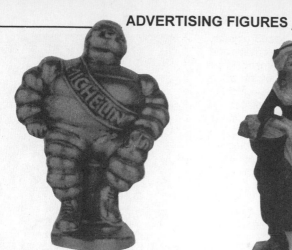

A nickel-plated seated figure of Bibendum with Michelin sash, 4¾in. high.
(Christie's) **$745**

'Yardley's Lavender' ceramic counter figure made by Dresden, early 20th century.
(Lyle) **$720**

'Moorland Tablets Make Eating a Real Joy', papier mâché counter figure, 19in. wide.
(Lyle) **$280**

Brentleigh ware plaster advertising plaque, modelled as black and white Scottie dogs, with raised inscription Scotch *'Black and White'* Whisky to oval base, 9in. high.
(Lyle) **$120**

'Euthymol Tooth Paste', a vulcanised rubber shop counter figure made by Hancock, Corfield, and Waller Ltd., 8in. high.
(Lyle) **$130**

Shop window display sign for Invicta Underwear, plaster, 20in. high.
(Lyle)   **$160**

Fyffes 'Ripe And Ready' Banana Man papier mâché counter display figure, 20in. high.
(Fidler & Taylor)   **$1,240**

A carved and painted pine cigar store Indian, attributed to Samuel Robb, New York, circa 1880, the standing figure of a small Indian Chief, carved in the round with feathered head-dress and hide cloak over a red and yellow costume, holding blocks of tobacco and bunches of cigars along with a dagger, standing on a rectangular pedestal base, 66in. high.
(Sotheby's)   **$17,250**

Sifta Sam, Jolly Good Salt, vulcanised rubber counter display figure, 16in. high. *(Lyle)* **$200**

▶

A large polychrome carved wood cod liver oil sign, mid 19th century, modelled in relief as a fisherman with side whiskers and hat, carrying a massive cod over his shoulder, 61½in. high. *(Christie's)* **$6,256**

A Dunlop golf ball man, 39cm. and a Penfold man, 51cm., 1935. *(Bearnes)* **$830**

Carved polychrome wooden cigar store figure, America, circa 1900, of a seated man carved in the full round, 52in. high. *(Skinner)* **$700**

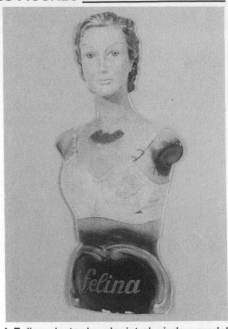

A Felina plaster handpainted window model, wearing contemporary bra, 81cm. high, circa 1950. *(Auction Team Köln)* **$334**

Tubby Trex, Better Cooking, vulcanised rubber counter display figure by Bibby & Sons, 16in. high. *(Lyle)* **$195**

Carved polychrome Turk's head tobacconist's counter figure, probably America, late 20th century, the fully carved head of a Turk with red turban, with beard and mustache and open mouth showing his tongue, mounted on blue painted base, 20in. high. *(Skinner)* **$1,725**

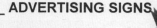

Carved and gilded pine trade sign, American late 19th/early 20th century, carved in the half round and painted black with gilding, in the form of a man's hand, inscribed *Dentist* on the front, 11in. long. *(Sotheby's)* **$920**

Painted tin trade sign, America, 19th century, painted ocher and green (paint loss), 8in. high. *(Skinner)* **$1,100**

Carved and painted wood sign of the English Foxhound Darby, signed *A.B. MacGregor/Norfolk Hunt Medfield, Mass,* on the reverse, the dog carved in relief against a fair weather sky and grass at his feet, 13½in. wide. *(Skinner)* **$4,600**

Carved and painted wood shaving trade sign razors, American, late 19th/early 20th century, inscribed *WADE AND BUTCHER* on blade, with a hinged and folding blade, painted black and silver, 19in. long. *(Sotheby's)* **$300**

A carved and painted pine fish trade sign, American, late 19th/early 20th century, the solid, boxy fish with open jaws and carved in, length 32in. *(Sotheby's)* **$4,313**

Carved and giltwood shoe trade sign, 19th century, on contemporary stand, 17½in. *(Skinner)* **$2,500**

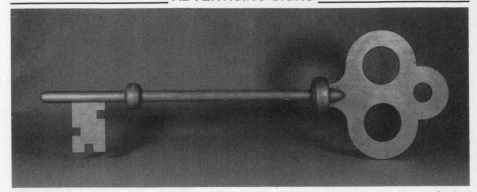

A carved and gilded wood trade sign, American, early 20th century, in the form of a key, with rectangular notched front, cylindrical collared shaft and pierced clover terminus. *(Christie's)* **$3,000**

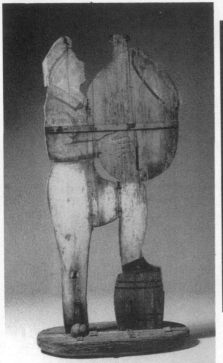

A painted pine sailor with bottle of grog: Ship's chandler's sign, probably New England, 19th century, the flat, planked form, depicted wearing a blue uniform and cap with one foot raised on a keg outlined with metal banding, on a planked base. Painted on both sides, 62in. high by 27in. wide. *(Sotheby's)* **$10,000**

A fine *ELEY'S SPORTING AMMUNITION* cartridge display board, the cartridges arranged attractively around the central 'Eley Bros.' trade-mark and comprising approximately eighty assorted brass and paper-case proprietary cartridges including 'Pegamoid', 'Sporting Ballistite', 'Amberite' 'Diamond' and 'Empire', with various other cartridge components, framed and glazed 31in. x 25¼in. overall. *(Christie's)* **$7,500**

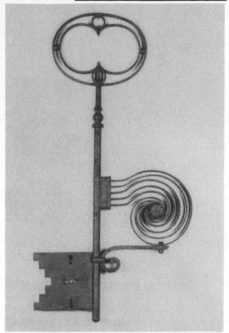

A painted sheet metal figure of a blacksmith, American, 20th century, in silhouette, a man with a black-painted cap, highlighted face, blue coat with buttons and dark trousers holding an anvil and leaning over a forge, similarly painted on reverse, 13¾in. high, 18in. wide. *(Christie's)*   **$1,500**

A wrought iron locksmith's shop sign, possibly French, 19th century, modelled as a key, with elaborate scrollwork to the shaft and pierced openwork handle, 41½in. long. *(Christie's)*   **$800**

An American leather shoe shop sign or model, early 20th century, the brown leather brogue with gilt signature to the inside *FIELD AND FLINT CO. BROCKTON. MASS.*, 25¾in. long. *(Christie's)*   **$3,160**

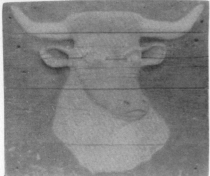

Important carved wood trade sign, in the form of a bull's head with antique swirl glass marble eyes, carved by John Bent, Edgartown, Massachusetts, 35¾ x 40in. *(Eldred's)* **$4,675**

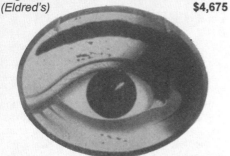

A reverse-painted on glass optometrist's trade sign, American, late 19th century, with chain hanging attachment, 17¾in. wide. *(Christie's)* **$1,725**

Whale fin bone tobacconist's sign, New Bedford, Massachusetts, late 19th century, lettered in black *FIN BONE OF A WHALE W.E. WALSH, TOBACCONIST EST. 1864,* mounted on a black painted metal base, 48in. wide. *(Skinner)* **$2,530**

A painted and carved wood boot maker's shop sign, 19th century, inscribed to one side *T. BALL MILITARY & EQUESTRIAN BOOT MAKER EST. 1804,* 46in. high. *(Christie's)* **$3,200**

A carved black painted wood sperm whale trade sign, probably New England, mid to late 19th century, the body fashioned from a single piece of wood with applied open mouth with nail teeth, the fins and flue of leather, a metal d-hoop on the back for hanging, painted black, 41in. long. *(Sotheby's)* **$3,450**

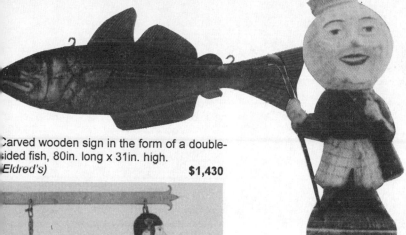

Carved wooden sign in the form of a double-sided fish, 80in. long x 31in. high. *(Eldred's)* **$1,430**

Silver King advertising man in papier mâché, circa 1920. *(Lyle)* **$720**

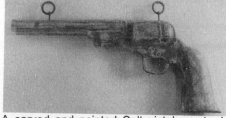

polychrome iron and tin shop sign, early 20th century, modelled with a semi-naked male bust holding a lantern with eagle to the rear and plate inscribed *BROCANTE*, with a wall mounting bracket, 32in. high. *(Christie's)* **$1,097**

A carved and painted Colt pistol gun trade sign, American, 20th century, carved in the round, a realistic depiction of a Colt pistol, suspended from wrought-iron ring hangers, 41in. long. *(Sotheby's)* **$4,312**

An Italian bronze and parcel-gilt alabaster group of a young woman riding a camel, by S. Romano, circa 1900, on a naturalistically cast oval base and green marble plinth 19¼in. wide. *(Christie's)* **$6,400**

An alabaster and gilt bronze figure, modelled as a naked young woman seated on a tapestry covered stool, her legs raised up and gazing down at a small mouse, 22.8cm. high. *(Christie's)* **$1,280**

A sculpted alabaster figure of a boy, probably Italian, late 19th century, shown seated in an armchair, 11¾in. high. *(Christie's)* **$3,68**

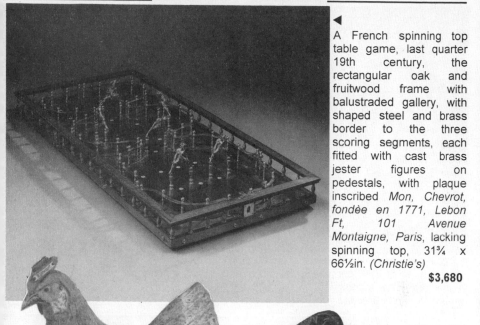

◄
A French spinning top table game, last quarter 19th century, the rectangular oak and fruitwood frame with balustraded gallery, with shaped steel and brass border to the three scoring segments, each fitted with cast brass jester figures on pedestals, with plaque inscribed *Mon, Chevrot, fondèe en 1771, Lebon Ft, 101 Avenue Montaigne, Paris*, lacking spinning top, 31¾ x 66½in. *(Christie's)*

$3,680

'Egg-laying hen' early stamped metal vending machine made by C.F. Schulze & Co., Berlin. The hen sits on an oval basket and on insertion of 10pfg in her comb and turning of the handle a 12 part container for 9 eggs is moved so that an 'egg' containing confectionery) is laid. Fully operational, circa 1900.
(Auction Team Köln)   **$3,958**

'War Eagle' gaming machine produced by Mills, U.S.A, circa 1932.
(Lyle)   **$2,250**

A pair of cast iron Indian andirons, American, early 20th century, each molded in the form of a standing figure holding a tomahawk and dressed in fringed cape, pants and skirt with moccasins and ornamented head-dress, 19in. high. *(Christie's)* **$2,000**

A pair of patinated bronze firedogs, 1940s, wrought iron dogs in the shape of cats, 8in high. *(Christie's)* **$2,505**

Gilbert Poillerat, pair of fire irons, circa 1930, wrought iron, each with a design of intertwined loops surmounted by a highly stylized crest, 13in. high. *(Sotheby's)* **$23,046**

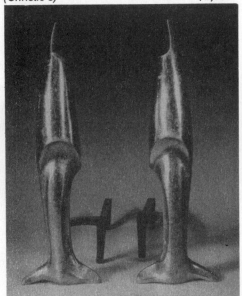

Pair of French Art Deco bronze andirons, each in a stylized form of a fish standing on its tail, lacquered bronze finish, hinged wrought iron support, 20in. high. *(Skinner)* **$3,000**

A pair of Regency black-painted cast iron firedogs, after a design by Thomas Hope each in the form of a griffin on a molded plinth base, 26¼in. high. *(Christie's)* **$12,10**

A table with glazed, brass framed hide top supported on elephant feet, 27in. wide. *(Christie's)* **$704**

A stuffed moosehead hunting trophy mounted on an oak backboard. *(Christie's)* **$1,280**

Whimsical Sheffield plate mounted ram's horn pipe rack, late 19th/early 20th century, with horse form finial on a hinged top and well, twelve pipe rests and two match wells, 17in. high. *(Skinner)* **$747**

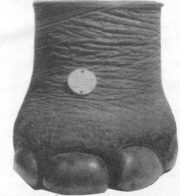

A 19th century stuffed young male lion, head and shoulders only, in glazed case, 30¼in. wide. *(Andrew Hartley)* **$400**

An elephant's foot waste-paper basket with rosewood rim and ivory plaque, 11in. high. *(Christie's)* **$697**

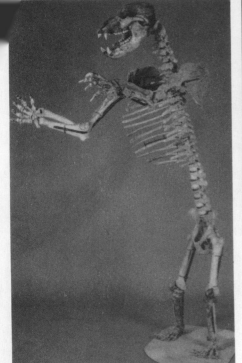

An Anglo Indian porcupine quill veneered workbox, early 19th century, of rising rectangular form and on bun feet, the lobed horn finial above panels of alternating ivory and horn veneers, with trailing foliate penwork to the borders, the interior with some fittings, 8½in. wide.
(Christie's) **$6,624**

A fully mounted prehistoric cave bear skeleton, Pleistocene, Ursus spelaeus, Austria, circa 80,000 years old, 108in. high.
(Bonhams) **$21,252**

A cased display of flamingos, late 19th century, mounted in a naturalistic setting, 3ft.8½in. x 5ft.1¾in.
(Sotheby's) **$4,609**

A large polychrome tortoiseshell, 19t century, emblazoned with a gilt painted cres and scroll inscribed *H.M.S. St. Vincent*, 47ir long. *(Christie's)* **$1,60**

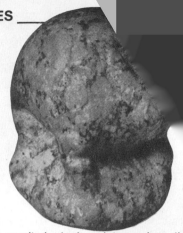

A rose granite hedgehog, late predynastic to early dynastic period, circa 3200-3000 B.C. the globular figure on four articulated legs, which, together with the rounded body, join to the integral base, the stylized head protruding with minimally modeled eyes, ears, and snout, 4½in. high. *(Christie's)* **$2,300**

A Roman terracotta twin-headed grotesque, circa 2nd century A.D., the hunchbacked figure with pronounced spine and ribs, the twin heads each with a double knot of hair on the top of the head, each with a prominent ear, large nose, bulging brows, and protruding lips, each hand originally holding a now-missing phallus, red pigment preserved on the body, yellow for the sandals, 28.9cm. high.
(Christie's) **$4,000**

A Roman purple mold-blown glass grape flask, realistically molded in the form of an asymmetrical bunch of grapes, with a mis-formed cylindrical neck and infolded rim on a flaring mouth. Eastern Mediterranean, A.D. 150-200, 11.5cm.
(Bonhams) **$4,500**

An ithyphallic fecundity figure, late Period, Dynasty XXVI-XXX, 664-343 B.C. The nude male figure sculpted from bitumen, depicted with his arms held to his sides, wearing a striated tripartite wig and false beard, 10½in. high. *(Christie's)* **$3,450**

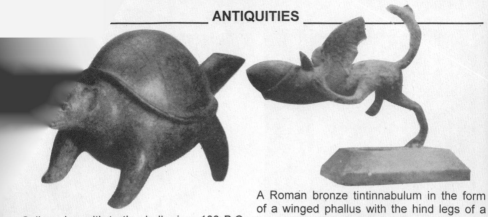

Colima dog with turtle shell, circa 100 B.C.-250 A.D., redware with black paint in geometric bands on shell, standing on four legs, 7¼in. high.
(Butterfield & Butterfield) **$546**

A Roman bronze tintinnabulum in the form of a winged phallus with the hind legs of a lion, circa 1st century A.D., 5¼in. high. *(Bonhams)* **$5,481**

A Persian pottery rhyton styled as a lower leg pierced at the toe, with a handle at the back, part of the foot glazed orange/brown, early 1st Millennium B.C., 9½in. high. *(Bonhams)* **$960**

A Celtic stone head of a male with clearly defined features, his hair delineated by vertical grooves, set on a rectangular base, the top of the head hollowed out for libation purposes, 11¾in.
(Bonhams) **$2,400**

Roman brown basalt relief of an erotic scene, 2nd-3rd century A.D., the naked copulating couple carved in high relief, 9½in. high.*(Butterfield & Butterfield)* **$3,300**

26

erner Panton, Denmark. An early rare eart chair, designed 1958, manufactured y Plus Linje, tangerine orange cloth fabric oholstered sensuous heart form cone ised on chromed metal 'X' base each point ith inserted black plastic glide foot. *3onhams)* **$4,404**

A dark stained armchair, designed by Gerrit Rietveld, circa 1918, made by G.A. Van de Groenekan. Angular construction of thirteen square section wooden units supporting a solid wood rectangular angled seat and back-rest, 34in. high.

The prototype of this chair was produced in 1917/18 and seemed to encapsulate the principles of abstraction recently espoused by the newly formed De Stijl group. A commentator in the Hollandsche Revue wrote *Where modern furniture designers only simplify the old forms into more or less straight shapes, and therefore only make variations...within the boundaries of traditional conception, here out of space, function and material a new shape, according to the demands of modern times, has emerged.*

The simplicity implied in this description is captured perfectly in this chair which is one of the first three to have been made. It predates the colored versions, an innovation suggested by Bart van der Leck (another of the De Stijl group), to whom this chair was given by Rietveld.

19th century mahogany framed adjustable ading wing armchair, with green leather holstery and studded decoration, having djustable rake to the back, the arms hinged d opening outwards for access, one with tached and adjustable reading stand and ass rest, the base with turned supports ousing an adjustable foot rest.
'hillips) **$2,400**

The use of standardized single components, in addition to a visual uniformity, also suggested the possibilities of mass production and in doing so, prefigured the developments of Bauhaus designers such as Breuer.
(Christie's) **$216,270**

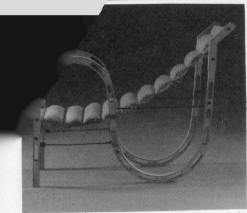

Eileen Gray, the 'S' folding terrace chair, circa 1932-34, made for her home 'Tempe A Pailla' at Castellar, the frame constructed of strips of bent wood separated by rectangular block spacers, white painted, metal hinges, stretchers and props, allowing the chair to be folded back on itself, upholstered cream canvas sling seat with padded strips, 78cm. (Sotheby's)   **$140,246**

An American horn armchair, 19th centur with rounded rectangular back and arm above a shaped rectangular padded sea on wavy legs, upholstered in brow leatherette. (Christie's)   **$1,84**

Gerald Summers for Makers of Simple Furniture, armchair, designed 1933-34, single sheet cut and bent cream tinted French polish finish plywood.
Only 120 examples of this chair, constructed from a single piece of bent plywood, were produced by Summer's company Makers of Simple Furniture. With its smooth surface and lack of metal connectors, it was originally designed for use in the tropics to withstand humidity.
(Sotheby's)   **$23,926**

Kristian Vedel; Denmark, a plywood chil chair, designed 1957, for Torben Ørsk the curving birch plywood shell v adjustable red-lacquered seat. (Christie's)   **$8**

, dark stained oak armchair, designed by
harles Rennie Mackintosh, circa 1900, for
e billiard room and smoking room of the
rgyle Street Tea Rooms, Glasgow.
haped seat above arched apron on turned
gs, 33in. high.
Christie's)   **$252,000**

George J. Snowden for Memphis,
'Mamounia' armchair, designed 1985,
lacquered wood, colored plastic laminate
and velvet, the fabric is designed by
Nathalie du Pasquier, 39in. high.
(Sotheby's)   **$4,844**

var Aalto, manufactured by Oy.
onekalu-Ja Rakennustyötehdas AB,
nland, 'Paimio' armchair model No.41,
signed 1931-32 originally for the Paimio
anatorium, laminated birch seat, painted
ninated plywood frame, black overpainted
th white, underside of rear seat support
th 'Finmar' metal label.
otheby's)   **$12,512**

Claude Siclis, an enameled tubular steel
lounge chair, designed 1935-36,
manufactured by Thonet Frères, Paris, for
use in the Val D'Isère resorts, the padded
seat and back with red leathercloth
upholstery, within gold painted tubular steel
frame, with ebonized beech armrests, 32in.
high. *(Christie's)*   **$4,400**

A oak reclining library armchair, late 19th century, with *Foots Patent* label, the reclining wingback and sweeping arms with attached reading slope above a sliding foot rest, raised on castors.
(Bonhams) .   **$1,920**

An unusual pair of branch-form laur 'Centennial' armchairs, signed by W.¡ Carter, Marietta, Pennsylvania, circa 187¡ (Sotheby's)   **$7,70**

A magnificent pair of asymmetrical throne chairs, circa 1900, in various woods and vellur each with circular back with asymmetrical uprights, one terminating in flat circular shelf, th other with tall turned column, 'U' shaped seat raised on four stepped columnar feet, th whole with beaten copper banding, elaborately inlaid throughout with bone and yellow ar gray metal and hung with knotted silk fringes, each 154cm. high x 77cm. wide.
(Sotheby's)   **$35,00**

An oak open arm chair designed by MacLaren, with shaped trestle supporting deep upholstered black hi zebra skin seat backrest.
(Christie's) **$4,**

An important and unusual carved and painted pine armchair, Jonas Bergren, Bishop Hill, Illinois 1915-1920, the chair back elaborately carved in high relief with a scrolling phoenix above a scrolling dragon, each with inset glass eyes, the arms carved with eagle-serpent beasts with scaly torsos, each clutching a gilt ball in its beak, the seat inlaid in bone with a strapwork band, the apron carved with laurel branches above scrolls centering a pinwheel, the front legs headed by satyr's masks continuing to paw feet, the whole painted in yellow, green, gold, silver, blue and peach, 45½in. high.
(Sotheby's) **$6,000**

Attributed to Gerrit Rietveld, an oak and leather armchair, executed circa 1920, executed by Cees Uiterwaal with rectangular panel back and armrests supported on linear open framework of lap-jointed rectangular members, each with black-painted terminals, tan leather seat supported on ebonized dowels, 30in. high.

This design illustrates constructional aspects of Rietveld's Red Blue Chair of 1918. The geometry of rectangular members forming the frame relate to the structure of this former chair, features which are further assessed in Rietveld's High Back armchair design for the Schroder House in 1924. Similar rectangular panel backs are evidenced in a number of chairs executed during this period, while the use of dowels to support a leather sling seat can also be seen in Rietveld's circa 1919 high chair and his 1923 designs for piano chairs.
(Christie's) **$18,400**

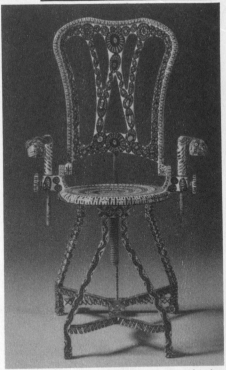

Ron Arad, Israel, 'Rolling Volume', designed 1989, hand made by Ron Arad, number 2 of an edition of twenty limited examples produced at One Off, London. An important early hand welded and beaten mild steel single volume rocking armchair weighted with lead to balance the sitter, the chair tilting upwards when not in use.
(Bonhams) **$18,875**

A whimsical paint-decorated wrought iron adjustable chair, 20th century, the armrests painted in the form of red and green serpents, the back painted with red and green pinwheels on a white ground.
(Sotheby's) **$1,610**

An unusual carved and stained wood chair, late 19th or early 20th century, modelled as a bird, with padded seat, 31in. high.
(Christie's) **$3,520**

An unusual antler mounted armchair, last quarter 20th century, 34in. high.
(Christie's) **$2,000**

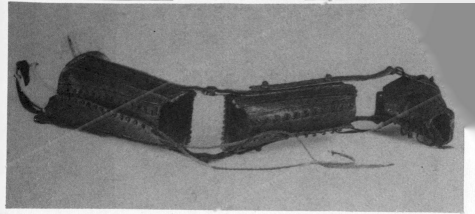

A late 19th century iron, leather and canvas artificial leg, unsigned, the iron bracings copper-riveted to the leather, with thigh section, calf and foot, the latter with half boot, some laces remaining, and tie rivets on the leather, with waist strap, 38in. long. overall. (Christie's)   **$368**

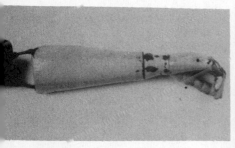

A painted steel and wood artificial arm, with articulated hand and leather upper gaiter, 23in. long. (Christie's)   **$184**

carved wood articulated hand, with brass mounting for implements, with leather hinged forearm and tieholes, 11¾in. long. (Christie's)   **$736**

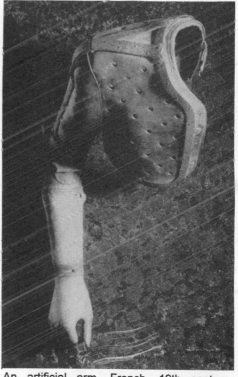

An artificial arm, French, 19th century, signed *Con H.M. BORDEAUX*, with leather and steel shoulder, wooden arm and hand, 74cm. shoulder to waist. (Bonhams)   **$640**

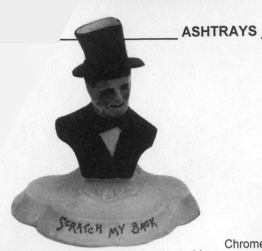

'Scratch my Back' late 19th century china match striker and ashtray.
(Lyle) **$280**

Chrome yacht ash tray, 7in. high, 1930s. *(Muir Hewitt)* **$65**

Chrome ashtray with female figure, 1930s *(Muir Hewitt)* **$75**

A Brandt wrought iron ashtray, modelled as a stylized pelican with wide open mouth supporting circular bowl, on rectangular base, stamped *E. Brandt*, 13.5cm. high. *(Christie's)* **$640**

An Art Deco Royal Dux figural ashtray, reputedly modelled on Greta Garbo. *(Academy)* **$272**

Royal Doulton John Barleycorn ashtray designed by Charles Noke, issued 1936-1960, 2¾in. high. *(Lyle)* **$128**

A coin-operated musical carousel automaton, in hexagonal glazed case with turned ebonized frame on inlaid burr-walnut base, the carousel with painted metal figures on horses and composition dolls in chair-boats, two dancing dolls, mirrored center column and bead fringes and hangings, 26in. high, circa 1890.
(Christie's) **$14,720**

A clockwork driven mechanical workshop by J. I. Austen Co., Chicago, the Art Nouveau house with a metalworking workshop on the ground floor. Two men stand in the center and hammer a flat piece of steel against the rear wall is a forge with bellows, where an apprentice is occupied. One man is working at the pillar drill winch and another has a horseshoe in a vice and is shaping it with a file, 1900.
(Auction Team Köln) **$9,379**

A large Monkey Band automaton, with velvet jacketed monkey musicians with turning heads and eyes, arms, and legs, and the mouth of the leading bass player all moving. With papier mâché limbs. Lacking musical works but with room for loudspeaker in the stage. Undocumented, made in Germany, exported without works, circa 1930, 90 x 50 x 115cm.
(Auction Team Köln) **$800**

Thirty-two different examples of 1870 and 1880 barbed wire. Some examples include necktie, greenbriar, buckhorn, lazy plate, single track, small plate, small barb, applied barb, flat ribbon, Y barb, diamond point, medium holdfast, corsicana clip, large ribbon sawtooth, hammer, twist, flat, brink flat, clines rail and reissue 6914. Each example mounted with a plaque on a wooden display case, 32 x 43in. *(Christie's)* **$1,840**

BEADWORK

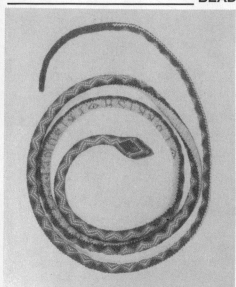

A beadwork snake, worked in black with a blue and yellow zigzagged back, the belly worked with the inscription in beadwork *Turkish Prisoners of War, Cyprus, 1919,* 265cm. long. *(Christie's)* **$475**

Eskimo woman's beaded cap, the domed hat consisting of rows of beads in alternate colors, separated by thin hide spacers 7in. high. *(Butterfield & Butterfield)* **$1,380**

A pearlware Napoleon bear jug and cover, modelled with the chained bear holding the bust of Napoleon in its arms, enriched in blue and ocher glazes, circa 1800, 25cm. high. *(Christie's)* **$920**

A Staffordshire pearlware coffee pot and cover modelled as a muzzled bear seated on his haunches, the spout formed by a dog held between his forepaws, impressed *J. Morris Store*, circa 1820, 12½in. high. *(Christie's)* **$12,512**

A Staffordshire saltglaze bear jug and cover, circa 1740, 24cm. high. *(Christie's)* **$9,982**

A Staffordshire saltglaze white stoneware bear baiting jar and cover, typically formed, with a ring through its nose, holding a stylized dog in its forepaws, applied all over with chipped clay, decorated in brown slip, circa 1760, 26cm. high. *(Christie's)* **$4,785**

A Staffordshire saltglaze bear jug and cover, circa 1740. *(Phillips)* **$3,840**

A Bavarian carved bear revolving piano stool. *(Phillips)* **$3,500**

A Black Forest carved oak hall stand, circa 1890, naturalistically carved as a tree surmounted by a bear-cub, above a shield-shaped beveled glass mirror and coat hooks, an adult bear standing at the base supporting an umbrella stand, 79in. high. *(Christie's)* **$8,625**

A Black Forest carved and stained wood bear tobacco jar, late 19th or early 20th century, shown seated, with a tree trunk fitted with a recess, the head hinged, 12½in. high. *(Christie's)* **$3,496**

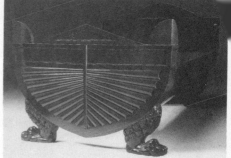

Early 19th century Russian mahogany, fruitwood and ebonized bed, of navette shape, the headboard with arched pediment panelled with stiff leaf moldings and shaped ears, with plain sides and the foot board with fanned gadroons surmounted by a rectangular panel and a further pediment with conforming stiff leaf motifs, flanked by shaped angles, above hairy paw feet, possibly German, 83in. wide. *(Christie's)* **$24,000**

A Regency mahogany metamorphic chair bed, by Morgan & Saunders, with folding arched canapé with brass finials, on ring-turned baluster columns and eight sides with hinged slatted seat to form a bed on detachable turned legs with cushions, bearing a brass label inscribed *Patent Morgan & Saunders, Manufacturers 16 & 17 Catherine Street, Strand, London*, also bearing label of *Phillips of Hitchin*. *(Christie's)* **$13,800**

A George III oak metamorphic bureau-bed, the rectangular top above a hinged slope and four simulated long drawers enclosing a folding bed, 43½in. wide. *(Christie's)* **$12,825**

A turned walnut and pine campaign field bed, American or English, circa 1800, with turned flaring head- and footposts hinged just above the rails, the headposts centering a horizontal headboard, the footposts with urn-form supports, all on turned tapering legs and turned spade feet, height to top of tester 6ft. 8in. *(Sotheby's)* **$2,875**

A bell push in Fabergé style, the white guilloché enamel body with gold and silver gilt mounts and set with a sapphire and demantoid garnets, apparently unmarked, 5cm. *(Lawrences)* **$3,388**

A Meissen Augsburg decorated table bell, circa 1725-30, probably decorated in the Seuter Workshop, the bell gilded with a continuous garden with chinoiserie figures beneath a gilded bobbin handle with ball knop, the interior with wooden clapper, 4¼in. *(Bonhams)* **$16,000**

A Chinese export painted metal bell in the form of a kneeling bearded man wearing a hat and holding a hammer, the head articulated, 4¼in. high, 19th century. *(Christie's)* **$960**

A gemset bell-push in the form of a rabbit, marked *K.Fabergé* with Imperial Warrant, Moscow, 1896-1908, with partially illegible scratched inventory number 9009[?], realistically cast, chased and engraved in crouched position, with its head slightly raised and ears up, its red cabochon eyes as pushpieces, marked on right ear, 6in. long, 536gr. gross.
(Christie's) **$160,487**

A late Victorian novelty reception bell cast in the form of a tortoise or terrapin with red glass eyes, by J.B. Carrington, 1896, 16cm long. *(Christie's)* **$4,609**

A good Dursley-Pedersen pedal bicycle with three speed gearing, circa 1905. *(Lyle)* **$2,560**

An English B.S.A. safety bicycle with brass fittings, circa 1885. *(Lyle)* **$6,400**

An early American boneshaker bicycle of New York manufacture. *(Auction Team Köln)* **$7,670**

An early gentleman's tricycle, having steel tubed frame with large radial spoked wheels, large-pitch chain drive angled to rear sprocket; direct steering via curved double handlebars with spoon-brake to front wheel; steel rims; French manufacture, circa 1890, diameter of driving wheels 44in. *(Christie's)* **$5,900**

An early Pedestrian Hobby Horse with wooden frame. *(Lyle)* **$4,800**

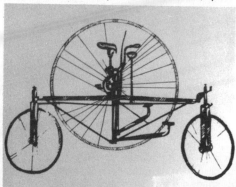

An unusual James Starley Coventry lever tricycle built by Haynes & Jeffy's, circa 1877. *(Lyle)* **$5,600**

'The Royal Bidet', a Victorian and gilt rectangular bidet, the stand on Grecian style saber legs with acanthus leaf cappings, 24 x 15 x 19in. high. Bears inventory brand mark for Windsor Castle, with Royal cipher and date *1866, Room 243*, and letter from The Lord Chamberlain's Office, St. James's Palace, London confirming that the Windsor Castle Inventory shows this description and was originally covered in crimson satin damask. *(Canterbury)* **$1,120**

An antique French Provincial carved walnut bidet in the Louis XV taste, with raised padded end with hinged compartment. *(Phillips)* **$2,400**

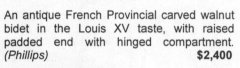

A Regency mahogany cased bidet, the rectangular mahogany lid lifting to reveal a Spode 'Tower Pattern' liner, circa 1812-15, of shaped form, depicting a view of the bridge of Salero, with underglaze blue mark, 50cm. wide, the base set on four ring turned legs, 56cm. wide. *(Bonhams)* **$1,600**

A Chinese Export red and gilt-japanned bidet, mid 18th century, the porcelain Yong Zheng, circa 1730, the cartouche-shaped caned back within a floral frame, and with hinged toprail enclosing compartments and with paper label inscribed *gat2376 / tes,* above a horse-hair hinged padded felt seat covered in red and gold painted leather enclosing a porcelain bowl and caned seat back, the underside inscribed *a DJ*, the sides with raised leaf decoration with a central floral spray, on channelled legs, claw and ball feet, the decoration distressed 36¼in. high. *(Christie's)* **$6,400**

A North Italian blackamoor side table, late 19th century, the shaped top supported by an acrobatic figure on cushion base, 18½in. high. *(Christie's)* **$4,542**

A polychrome and giltwood blackamoor figure, late 19th or early 20th century, the crouching figure seated on a draped plinth and supporting a shell above his shoulders, his gilt painted cloak decorated overall with flowers and foliage, 39in. high. *(Christie's)* **$9,688**

A pair of polychrome decorated blackamoors, 20th century, each modelled as a turbanned boy dressed in a scarlet jacket with a monkey on his knee with chained collar supporting a tray, each boy sitting on a tree stump raised on associated floral modelled metal stands, each 73in. high. *(Christie's)* **$3,200**

A pair of reproduction carved wood kneeling blackamoor stands, gilded and painted, the square tops and bases with cream marbling, 34in. high. *(Woolley & Wallis)* **$1,851**

A 19th century 'Blackamoor' half length figure of a man wearing a wide brimmed straw hat and dressed in an open necked striped shirt and holding an oval basket, 2ft.4½in. high.
(Greenslade Hunt)   **$1,672**

A pair of late 19th century Venetian blackamoors, the richly decorated carved wood and gesso figures of two negro boys holding detachable scallop trays, on circular simulated marble bases, 175cm. high. (Bristol)   **$8,160**

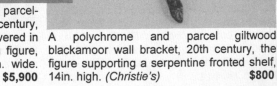

A pair of ebonized, red-painted and parcel-gilt blackamoor stools, 19th or 20th century, each with rectangular padded top covered in red cord, supported on a crouching figure, on canted rectangular base, 18¼in. wide. (Christie's)   **$5,900**

A polychrome and parcel giltwood blackamoor wall bracket, 20th century, the figure supporting a serpentine fronted shelf, 14in. high. (Christie's)   **$800**

A Black Forest carved wood book slide, early 20th century, the ends carved as owls with glass eyes hinged to sliding panels, the overall rectangular shaped base incised with leaf motifs, 17in. long.
(Christie's) **$640**

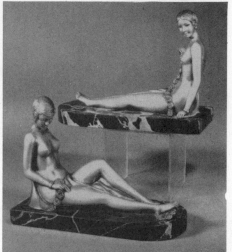

A pair of silvered and cold-painted bronze bookends, cast from a model by Scribe, each of a seated naked girl, holding length of cloth and rose garland to her chest, on an oval striated black and brown onyx base, 15.5cm. high. *(Christie's)* **$1,440**

Marcel Bouraine, pair of maribou stork bookends, 1920s, patinated bronze and ivory, modelled as two birds in perched pose with their heads hunched into their wings, stepped green veined black marble base, each base marked *Bouraine*, one bird numbered *287*, the other *288*, each 25cm. *(Sotheby's)* **$4,000**

A pair of gilt and cold-painted bronze and ivory bookends, cast and carved from a model by Roland Paris, one of a seated jester wearing gilt and red costume, smiling at an owl perched on his knees, other of a stylized man wearing black top hat and cape, seated with small bird on knees, each on striated brown and black onyx bases, 17.5cm. high. *(Christie's)* **$3,200**

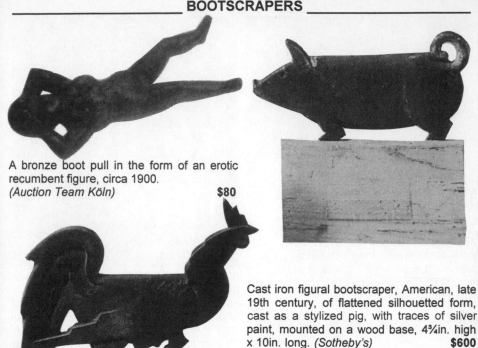

A bronze boot pull in the form of an erotic recumbent figure, circa 1900.
(Auction Team Köln) **$80**

Cast iron figural bootscraper, American, late 19th century, of flattened silhouetted form, cast as a stylized pig, with traces of silver paint, mounted on a wood base, 4¾in. high x 10in. long. *(Sotheby's)* **$600**

Cast iron figural bootscraper, American, late 19th century, of flattened silhouetted form, cast as a stylized rooster, 9in. high x 13½in. long. *(Sotheby's)* **$800**

A pair of 19th century cast iron bootscrapers in the form of gryphons with canon barrel bases.
(Russell, Baldwin & Bright) **$1,333**
▼

'Suffolk Bitters' – 'Philbrook and Tucker' figural pig bitters bottles, medium golden amber, flattened collared lip, 10in. high, America, 1870-80. *(Skinner)* **$450**

Early pattern molded dog bottle, patterned in ribs, diamond and daisy designs, applied feet and head, colorless, 4¼in. high. Germany or France, early/mid 18th century. *(Skinner)* **$286**

Martins Patent bottle 1902. The bottle stands as shown, the U bend is believed to act as a trap to prevent spilling the contents. Various sizes and embossings exist with the rare types having *Poison, Not To Be Taken* embossed on side, with others just *Poison*, also embossed *The Martin Poison Bottle* can be found in aqua and ice blue glass and are thought to exist in amber and cobalt blue. *(Lyle)* **$400**

A Harden Star fire grenade in blue glass. *(Lyle)* **$80**

Anna-type pottery railroad guide pig, large railroad map around body, mint condition, 4in. high, probably Anna Pottery, Anna, Illinois, 1890. *(Skinner)* **$3,700**

Mid 19th century 'Bonaparte' ink bottle, the hollow body forming the reservoir while the front hole acts as a quill holder. *(Lyle)* **$320**

Beiser and Fisher pig figural whiskey bottle, amber, double collared lip, smooth base, 9½in. America, 1865-1875.
(Skinner) **$200**

'Mr. Punch', one of the most sought after salt-glaze ink bottles, incised on the back *Gardeners Ink Works, Lower White Cross St., London*, together with the U.K. Registration Diamond mark for 1851, 4½in. high. *(Lyle)* **$240**

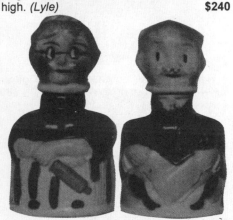

Unusual skull-form cobalt blue glass poison bottle, U.S. Patent Office design patent number 23,399 granted to Carlton H. Lee of Boston, Mass., June 26, 1894, 4½in. high. *(Eldred's)* **$935**

American red and blue ceramic bottles known as 'MA' and 'PA' with removable heads forming the cork stoppers. The 'Mr. & Mrs. Carter's Ink' were patented by C. H. Henkels of Philadelphia for Carter's Ink Co. of Boston and were made in Germany prior to World War I and later in the U.S.A. From 1914-16 they were offered in a National magazine for 25 cents together with a coupon from the magazine and as a result over 50,000 coupons were received. *(Lyle)* **$320**

Martin poison bottle with shaped neck, 4½in long. *(Lyle)* **$120**

An extremely rare circular cottage inkwell in aqua glass embossed on the base for August 1868, 6cm. high.
(Lyle) **$320**

'E.G. Booz's', figural Whiskey bottle, cabin shape, bevelled roof edge variety, Whitney Glassworks, Glassboro, New Jersey, 1870-80, 7¾in. high. *(Skinner)* **$950**

Ceramic pig whiskey bottle, inscribed *Whiskey 1875* and *put your mouth to my* on the opposite side, 9in. long, America, 1860-80. *(Skinner)* **$1,600**

O'Reilly's Patent, known as Binoculars Poison. Bottle is ice blue, has *Poison* across shoulder and embossed on cylinder bottom sections, and is also embossed on the base *O'Reillys Patent 1905*. Only two of these bottles are known, the other bottle is in an American collection.
(Lyle) **$1,600**

An unusual glass 'Cottage' inkwell.
(Lyle) **$80**

A pair of miniature display cases, in the form of sedan chairs, fabric covered, bevelled glass panels, the hinged doors revealing shelves, 10½in. high.
(Woolley & Wallis) **$512**

A silvered and gilt bronze figural box and cover, cast from a model by A. Grevin, of a naked 'mouse' girl kneeling on a pile of banknotes which she furtively eats, the hinged cover above open grille, 14.5cm. high. *(Christie's)* **$3,200**

A pair of carved wood chicken boxes, Pennsylvania, late 19th-early 20th century, each with stylized crown and eyes above a swelled body opening to a hinged and latched compartment on two legs, on a rectangular plinth, 9½in. high.
(Christie's) **$30,000**

A French bronze bust of a native Indian, circa 1870, formed as a box with hinged scalp and left shoulder, 13in. high. *(Christie's)* **$1,840**

A Chinese hardwood butterfly shaped box and cover inset and carved in relief with mother of pearl, tortoiseshell, boxwood and horn, 9.8cm. wide, 19th century. *(Christie's)* **$737**

A painted and decorated shopkeeper's bag sorter, American, late 19th century, 16in. high. *(Christie's)* **$863**

A massive black painted cast-iron offertory box, with riveted gilt bronze floral decoration and sheet steel coin chute, three hard-to-open puzzle locks and one key, circa 1900. *(Auction Team Köln)* **$254**

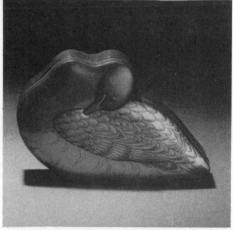

A fundame ground kogo, Edo Period, 19th century, modelled as a duck, decorated in gold, silver and iroe hiramakie, realistically rendered, its head turned towards its wing, the rims in silvered metal, the interior in hirame, minor old wear, 5¼in. wide. *(Christie's)* **$3,187**

A rare black lacquered casket, Japanese, 1630-50, the pagoda shaped hinged top with a sliding panel revealing a well, the sides with a further sliding panel enclosing a secret drawer and revealing the original lacquer decoration, the corners with turned half moldings on later gilt-metal lion couchant feet, 17in. wide. *(Sotheby's)* **$12,483**

A painted and decorated peacock box, probably Pennsylvania, 19th century, in the form of a standing peacock with yellow, red, and black-paint embellishment on an olive-painted ground, the body swinging open to a compartmented interior, all on a stepped rectangular plinth in red and black, 6⁵/₈in. high. *(Christie's)* **$3,000**

A rare 'erotic subject' rectangular box and cover, Kangxi, the interior divided into three compartments representing a two-storeyed interior with applied enamelled figures and furniture, the ground floor with two couples conversing in separate rooms, the top floor with a couple engaged in amorous pursuits, 4³/₄ x 3¼in. *(Christie's)* **$4,800**

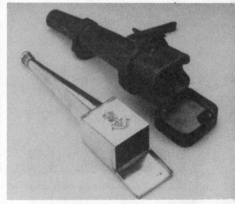

Carved wood book-form slide top box, signed and dated *Michel Thomas 1759*, chip carved borders centering high relief carved male and female figures, 3⁵/₈in. high. *(Skinner)* **$1,610**

A combined travelling flask and snack/sandwich box, the conical flask section with a screw-cover, the other plain oblong section with hinged flap and cover and gilt interior engraved with a crest and monogram, maker's mark, *N.T.*, 1851, 26.5cm. long. *(Christie's)* **$1,650**

n English brass-mounted fruitwood box, 9th century, in the form of a lady's purse, ½in. high. *(Christie's)* **$4,830**

iron bound oak alms box with aperture to cover, with lockplate and key, parts 17th ntury and later adapted, 8½in. high. *hristie's)* **$640**

Victorian brass and velvet 'perambulator' wing box, possibly America, circa 1880, in. long. *(Skinner)* **$640**

A Northern Northwest Coast bent corner storage box, probably Tlingit, with corner oriented design painted in black and red formlines, ovoids, circles, U forms and eye forms on all four sides with two bilaterally symmetrical designs, one showing a frontal face at the top with joint designs at the bottom, the other showing two confronting animal faces in profile, 14¼ x 11in. *(Christie's)* **$10,925**

A Ninsei-style incense box, fitted box signed *Ninsei O Saku*, Edo or Meiji Period, 19th century, modelled as a kingfisher in Oribe palette, fitted box inscribed *Kawasemi Kogo* [Kingfisher incense box] and with a long inscription inside the lid praising both the workmanship and the glaze and ascribing the piece to [Nonomiya] Ninsei, 2in. high. *(Christie's)* **$2,166**

A brass pen tray in the form of a roarin hippopotamus with hinged back, 12½i wide. *(Christie's)* $5,80

An 18th century gilt brass curfew of typical form, repoussé decorated with portraits, animal and figure subjects, 17in. wide. *(Christie's)* $1,165

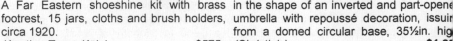

'Boa' Constrictor', a large brass motor hor snake's head pattern with flexible bras hose, complete with bulb. *(Christie's)* $1,43

An 18th century lodestone, with brass mounts and suspension ring, in fishskin case, 2in. high. *(Christie's)* $2,311

A Far Eastern shoeshine kit with brass footrest, 15 jars, cloths and brush holders, circa 1920.
(Auction Team Köln) $575

A brass umbrella stand, early 20th centur in the shape of an inverted and part-opene umbrella with repoussé decoration, issuir from a domed circular base, 35½in. hig *(Christie's)* $1,28

54

A Japanese bronze tiger seated with head turned looking left, its tail curled across its thigh, 7½in. wide, 19th century.
(Christie's) **$348**

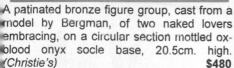

A patinated bronze figure group, cast from a model by Bergman, of two naked lovers embracing, on a circular section mottled ox-blood onyx socle base, 20.5cm. high.
(Christie's) **$480**

A gilt and patinated bronze model, realistically cast as a leather jacket hanging on a clothes peg, approximately 93cm. high.
(Christie's) **$1,840**

A rare bronze bird-form water-dropper and attached cover, Western Zhou Dynasty, shown in a crouching position with its long scaly legs folded under a plump body covered overall with feathers defined by semi-circular dotted segments, the underside with two confronted chi dragon heads, its linear wings tucked into the sides and decorated with bird heads, the head, supported on a long neck, with pronounced sharp beak, beady eyes, low crest and small 'horns', above the short spout at the breast, the hinged cover of rectangular shape cast with a small bird of conforming design adjacent to an animal-form loop arching onto the fan-shaped tail, the bronze of an olive tone, 12.4cm. high.
(Christie's) **$32,200**

A small French bronze model of a mouse, cast from a model by C. Masson, late 19th century, cast as a mouse on its haunches eating a slab of cheese on a naturalistic base, raised on a marble plinth, signed *C. Masson*, 3¾in. *(Bonhams)* **$800**

An Art Deco bronze group, inscribed *Flischer*, of naked girl astride a leaping goat, on green marble base, 25cm. long x 30.5cm. high. *(Phillips)* **$1,920**

A bronze model of Daruma with pendulous earlobes, standing, stretching and yawning with head back, on a domed base, the eyes gilt, 5in. high, 19th century, incised signature. *(Christie's)* **$1,014**

A large bronze vase, cast from the model by P. F. Berthous, circa 1900, the massive body with twin loop handles, cast in high relief with the smiling face of a woman emerging from behind feathered wings, 25in. maximum height. *(Christie's)* **$15,835**

An unusual Viennese painted bronze group of three carousing foxes, each dressed in similar 19th century style costume, 3½in. high. *(Phillips)* **$765**

A bronze group by R. Schnauder (1856-1923), of a naked girl on a horse, on a rocky base and marble plinth, signed and incised *Guss v. Pirner & Franz, Dresden*, with brown patination, 75.5cm.
(Sotheby's) **$7,402**

Austrian cold painted bronze figure, depicting a gorilla holding a Lapierre Carrée style lantern, 4½in. high, 1890s.
(Christie's) **$330**

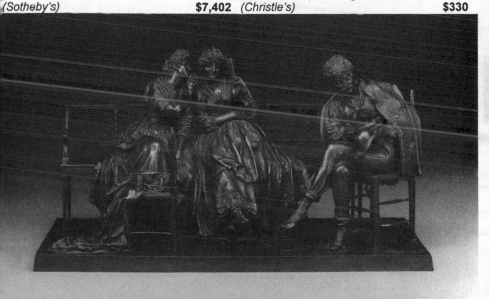

An Italian bronze group, dated *1889*, after a model by Constantino Pandiani, modelled with two ladies in conversation seated on a bench looking at a gentleman in the foreground, the rectangular base inscribed *Proprieta Riservata, C. Pandiani, Milano 1889*, 24in. wide.
(Christie's) **$6,992**

A 20th century bronze model of a turtle, after Giovanni Antoniati, piped to emit water through mouth, 89 x 61cm. *(Christie's)* **$3,102**

A Viennese erotic bronze, the model of an Egyptian Queen opening to reveal a nude woman, 17cm. high. *(Phillips)* **$1,450**

Franz Bergman, Austrian cold painted and gilt bronze figure of an Arabian Dancer, with skirt lifting to reveal naked body, on circular base covered with a tasselled carpet, 7¾in. high. *(Canterbury)* **$644**

A Viennese cold painted bronze turkey, cast by the Bergman foundry, early 20th century, the displaying bird stamped with Bergman seal, *Geschutzt, 5301*, 17cm. high. *(Bonhams)* **$2,400**

An Austrian cold painted bronze letter clip, late 19th or early 20th century, in the form of two horse's heads issuing from a saddle, 6¾in. long. *(Christie's)* **$1,090**

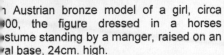

n Austrian bronze model of a girl, circa 00, the figure dressed in a horses stume standing by a manger, raised on an al base, 24cm. high.
hillips) **$640**

bronze model of a hippopotamus, first half th century, mounted on a marmo giallo nth, the bronze 16cm. long.
Christie's) **$2,795**

'Celuy quy fut pris', a silvered and gilt bronze figure group, cast from a model by Clemencin, modelled as a knight in full armor carrying a female nude on a large platter, she reaches under his helmet to embrace him, on a circular base with inscription, signed in the bronze, stamped foundry mark, 38cm. high.
(Christie's) **$5,760**

A patinated bronze dish, cast from a model by M. Bouval, of oval section, cast in low relief with the head of an Art Nouveau maiden emerging from pond with reeds and lily pads, signed in the bronze, 40cm diameter. *(Christie's,* **$4,000**

◄

A Chinese bronze model of a standing infant Buddha with one finger pointing upwards and the other down, wearing a bib with floral designs, 7¾in. high. *(Christie's)* **$640**

Joseph Descamps, French 19th/2 century, The Naughty Dutch Girl, bron with light brown patination, stamped *Su Freres,* the base molded with a process of ducks, 13in. high.
(Skinner) **$1,4**

'Belle Recolte', a patinated and gilt bronze figure group, cast from a model by K. Curts, modelled as a young peasant boy holding a rake before a haystack which lifts to reveal reclining naked female, on shaped integral base with title, signed in the bronze *K. Curts* ec. with stamped foundry seal and *Made in Austria,* 16cm. high.*(Christie's)* **$5,152**

gilt-bronze mythical dragon, Han Dynasty, the striding beast cast with a sinuous body nd simplified details to head, gilding worn and some malachite encrustation, the tail cast eparately, 15.5cm. long. *(Christie's)* **$8,000**

Bruno Zach (Austrian, active 1918-1935), Erotic nymph, dark brown patinated bronze, signed, 6¾in. high. *(Skinner)* **$1,495**

An Austrian cold painted and gilt bronze figure of an Arabian dancer by Franz Bergman with hinged skirt, 10¾in. high *(Canterbury)* **$2,237**

E*** Sanglon, French, early 20th century, a pair of cod and a squid candlesticks, signed: *Sanglan*, both inscribed *Thiebaut frères Pars Pumiere & Gavignot S^rs* and one with *I Eprev…* gilt-bronze, on pale green amethystine quartz bases, 34cm. *(Sotheby's)* **$4,800**

Franz Bergman Viennese patinated and gilded bronze novelty figure of a long-eared owl, figure opening to reveal a further gilded bronze figure of a nude female, signed, 7¾in. high. *(Lawrences)* **$4,185**

Pair of figural bronze bat sconces, 20th century, full-bodied flying bats with a brass foliate light fixture suspended from rings at mouths, dark brown patina, wingspan 21½in. *(Skinner)* **$5,175**

A German bronze aquamanile, Nuremberg, circa 1400, in the form of a standing lion with chest thrust forward with zoomorphic spout, teeth bared with tongue protruding, the mane and forelock extensively chiselled, hinged cover between the ears, the tail curling upwards over the back terminating in a dragon's head, 10in.
(Sotheby's) **$72,800**

Patinated-bronze figure: Batwoman, after a model by Agathon Leonard, the seminude maiden attired in head-dress and flowing skirt, her arms outstretched before her large bat wings, raised on an irregular rocky base, signed *LEONARD, 3CA, AB.* 13½in. high. *(William Doyle)* **$15,000**

A French bronze study of a bucking mule, entitled 'La Ruade', cast from a model by Jacques-Charles Froment-Meurice, early 20th century, on a rectangular naturalistically-cast base inscribed *J. Froment-Meurice* and with foundry stamp *CIRE/PERDUE/A.A. HEBRARD*, on rectangular veined marble plinth, 11¾in. high. *(Christie's)* **$8,280**

'Space Cards', 1959, A.&B.C. Chewing Gum Ltd. *(Lyle)* **$55**

'Hocus Pocus', 1955, Wow Productions Ltd. *(Lyle)* **$80**

Star Trek, Topps Chewing Gum, 1979. *(Lyle)* **$10**

'My Chum' (Popeye), 1945, Klene's Holland, imported. *(Lyle)* **$80**

'Mars Attacks', 1962, Bubble Inc. *(Lyle)* **$240**

'Roy Rogers', 1955, Times Confectioner Co. Ltd. *(Lyle)* **$55**

Three French papier mâché buckets, 20th century, the tapering bodies later decorated, with black painted iron loop handles, 10¼in. high. *(Christie's)* **$1,280**

George III brass-mounted mahogany ate-bucket, of cylindrical form with pierced ertical sides and lion-mask carrying andles, on paw feet, the opening in the de now filled by a removable stained metal ate, 14½in. high.
Christie's) **$4,100**

mid 18th century mahogany peat bucket simple cylindrical form and with brass ving handle, 41.5cm. high.
earnes) **$800**

A large Irish brass-bound mahogany bucket, late 19th/early 20th century, of cylindrical tapering form with spirally-reeded sides and a pair of carrying-handles, 26½in. high. *(Christie's)* **$29,500**

Victorian enamel slop bucket complete with lid. *(Lyle)* **$50**

A Georgian mahogany caned plate bucke with brass liner and loop handle, 14in *(Worsfolds)* **$3,520**

1st World War water carrier of kidney section, painted red and bearing crest, rope carrying handles, 21in. high. *(Wilson)* **$105**

First World War canvas nosebag with U. insignia. *(Lyle)* **$2**

A brass bound mahogany bucket, with gadrooned rim, the sides with lion mask and ring handles, 13¾in. high. *(Christie's)* **$2,093**

An 18th century wrought iron bound sa bucket with swing handle, 7¼in. diamete *(Lyle)* **$32(**

CADDY SPOONS

A rare George III cast caddy spoon, decorated in relief with a Chinese Mandarin holding a tea plant, by Edward Farrell, 1816. *(Phillips)* **$2,400**

A rare William IV die-stamped eagle's wing caddy spoon, the bowl chased with overlapping feathers, by Joseph Willmore, Birmingham, 1832. *(Phillips)* **$1,600**

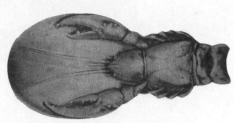

A caddy spoon with lobster design handle, import marks for Bernard Muller, Chester 1900. *(Christie's)* **$640**

A rare George IV caddy spoon, Birmingham 1825, maker's mark of R. Mitchell, shovel form, embossed with two scenes of Brighton Pavilion, ropework border, foliate handle, 5.8cm. long. *(Bonhams)* **$640**

CAGES

An unusual treen animal cage, early 19th century, of rectangular form with shaped pediment inlaid overall with boxwood lozenge and ebony stringing, the double cages beside a wheel treadmill above a small drawer, 19in. wide. *(Bonhams)* **$800**

A Victorian architectural birdcage, probably American, circa 1900, composed of painted fret-work elements in the shape of a Victorian mansion with Gothic arch, working doors and feed-holders, 36in. high. *(Sotheby's)* **$3,000**

A painted wood and iron wire bird house, American, late 19th/early 20th century, the rectangular form with central peaked roof issuing four projecting gables with chimneys flanked by four iron wire turrets above a conforming framework set with cylindrical and corkscrew-twisted iron wire alternating with ring and baluster-turned columns, with one long end centering an arched door, the short ends fitted with glazed windows and doors all enclosing an interior set with perches, on a conforming base, 21in. high. (Christie's)

$2,990

Painted tin riverboat birdcage, America, 19th century, three-tiered vessel with twin smoke stacks, filigree doors and panels, the figure of the captain standing at the wheel on the foredeck, red, white, blue and gold paint, 20½in. high. (Skinner) $6,900

A glazed redware birdcage, possibly Pennsylvania, 19th century, in the form of a building with pierced rectangular and circular openings all over and applied faces in the front, 9½in. high. (Christie's) $3,000

1930s novelty calendar 'Folks hevn't changed much since the good old days'. *(Lyle)* **$32**

Calendar for 1900 by E.P. Dutton & Co. with moving paddle steamer, 15in. wide. *(Lyle)* **$80**

An easel back circular desk calendar, the foliage engraved and initialled silver colored metal mount with printed ivory dials, on pierced feet, 5in. diameter. Maker Shreve, Crump & Low Co. *(Woolley & Wallis)* **$350**

Varga Calendar, 1948, with verses by Earl Wilson. *(Lyle)* **$95**

The Pirelli Pin-up Calendar, 1973. *(Lyle)* **$320**

Matchbox camera, Eastman Kodak Co., Rochester, NY; metal-body with United States War Department identity card with photograph credited *SIGNAL CORPS U.S. ARMY*, fingerprints and subject name *Demetre Vignovich, 1st Lt. Cav. o-1011247* dated *Feb. 5, 1943*, identity bracelet engraved *D. Vienovich*.
(Christie's) **$4,784**

A very rare decoratively engraved spy camera in the form of a finger ring, reputedly used by the Russian KGB.
(Christie's) **$20,812**

A. Lehmann, Berlin, a metal-body Ben Akiba walking stick camera no. 772 with decoratively engraved exterior, winding key and engraved exposure counter 1-20.
(Christie's) **$21,912**

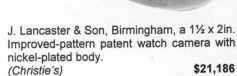

Eastman Kodak Co., Rochester, New York, a 120-rollfilm cardboard-body George Washington Kodak camera with blue star-patterned body covering, nickel fittings, the body with red window.
(Christie's) **$30,000**

J. Lancaster & Son, Birmingham, a 1½ x 2in. Improved-pattern patent watch camera with nickel-plated body.
(Christie's) **$21,186**

Septon Camera Works, Japan, a 16mm. Septon pen camera with a Septon f/2.8mm. lens No. 14114. *(Christie's)* **$3,703**

Ertee camera no. 199, Romain Talbot, Germany, 25mm. diameter ferrotype plates, with a Laack Schnellarbeiter f/3.5 60mm. lens. *(Christie's)* **$1,195**

Photo-Cravate camera, L. Bloch, Paris, 25 x 25mm., metal body, with internal six-plate changing mechanism, lens, metal plate on reverse *PHOTO-CRAVATE. BLOCH, BTEÉE EN FRANCE ET À L'ETRANGER*, original blue and white-piped cloth cravat with fastening clip and metal horseshoe retaining clip.

Bloch's Photo-Cravate camera was first shown to the Sociéte Française de Photographie on 5 December 1890. It was also the subject of British patent 12,766 of 14 August 1890.
(Christie's) **$19,200**

Ticka camera, Houghtons Ltd., London; nickel-metal body, with lens cover, in maker's box. *(Christie's)* **$299**

Pair of Chinese Export polychrome pewter figural pricket candlesticks, early 19th century, each a kneeling gentleman, 12½in. high.
(Skinner) **$7,150**

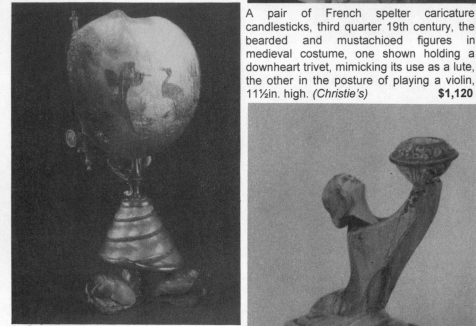

A pair of French spelter caricature candlesticks, third quarter 19th century, the bearded and mustachioed figures in medieval costume, one shown holding a downheart trivet, mimicking its use as a lute, the other in the posture of playing a violin, 11½in. high. *(Christie's)* **$1,120**

A Continental mother of pearl and silver plated candlestick with screen, last quarter 19th century, the foliate clasped nozzle above a conical base supported by three models of snails, the adjustable screen carved in relief with a cherub and a bird by a river bank, 13¼in. high.
(Christie's) **$1,817**

Clarice Cliff Bizarre candlestick in the form of a water nymph holding aloft a bowl, printed marks, 17.5cm. high.
(Wintertons) **$627**

A rare carved carousel frog, Herschell-Spillman Co., North Tonawanda, New York, circa 1914, 42in. long. *(Sotheby's)* **$19,800**

A carved wood Uncle Sam chariot, with a deeply carved image of Uncle Sam and an American eagle above an American flag. *(Christie's)* **$7,150**

A carved and painted wood carousel figure of a jumper horse, stamped #37, C.W. Parker, Leavenworth, Kansas, circa 1917, the galloping figure of a horse carved in racing pose with head lunging forward, forelegs up and hind legs back, with windswept mane and cropped tail, having a jewelled bridle and saddle painted in shades of green, yellow and red, height 37in. x length 69in. *(Sotheby's)* **$15,000**

A carved and painted carousel goat jumper, probably New York, late 19th century, the leaping full-bodied figure with tucked head, bent forelegs and extended rear legs with articulated facial features and fur, brown glass eyes, ribbed curled horns and wearing a scroll-carved saddle with coin-carved girth, 19in. high, 56in. deep. *(Christie's)* **$8,625**

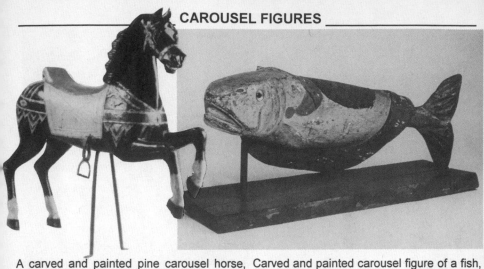

A carved and painted pine carousel horse, American, late 19th century, the black-painted horse with red and yellow bridle, saddle blanket and eagle-carved saddle, retains original horsehair tail, height 59in. x length 61in. *(Sotheby's)* **$10,000**

Carved and painted carousel figure of a fish, late 19th century, the green-gray and turquoise painted carved fish with glass eyes and carpeted seat, 48in. long. *(Skinner)* **$1,725**

Carved carousel horse, attributed to C.W. Parker Co., Abilene, Kansas, late 19th/early 20th century, the running horse with raised head and bridle with a carved animal saddle pad, 53in. high. *(Skinner)* **$3,737**

An unusual carved and painted pine giraffe carousel figure, American, late 19th century, the stationary figure of a giraffe with glass eyes, height 69in. x 42in. long. *(Sotheby's)* **$15,000**

Figural hooked rug, New England, 19th century, depicting a hen and rooster with seven eggs between, worked in cream, indigo, red and black, 23¾ x 40¾in. *(Skinner)* **$9,200**

Pictorial hooked rug, American, early 20th century, bearing the inscription *Old Shep,* 27 x 34in. *(Skinner)* **$1,600**

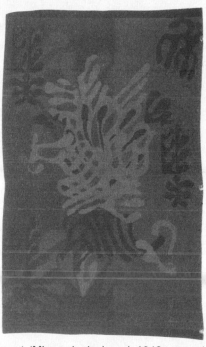

A wool hooked rug, American, early 19th century, rectangular, worked in various plums, yellows, blacks, red, green and white depicting a large standing black dog with tail up, tongue out and wearing a red collar, all on a yellow ground enclosed in a conforming mottled plum border, 31 x 40in. *(Christie's)* **$3,000**

A fine and rare American pictorial hooked rug, late 19th century, worked in beige, red, slate blue and black fabric, 37in. x 44in. *(Sotheby's)* **$13,225**

Carpet 'Mimosa', designed 1949, executed 1951, machine-woven wool, Axminster construction, monogrammed in the weave *HM,* the reverse with printed label *This rug designed by H. Matisse and named Mimosa by him, has been woven by Alexander Smith in a limited edition of 500 of which this is number 212,* 150 x 92cm., 59 x 36¼in.

This is the only carpet design by Matisse. It is produced in a limited edition of 500 by Alexander Smith & Sons. *(Sotheby's)* **$12,184**

A Norwegian polychrome and chip carved birch skala, late 18th century, the twin handles modelled as stylized horse's heads, a faded inscription to the rim, the interior painted with foliage, the underside gouged with the initials and date *M.G.D.H. ANO 1790,* 14in. wide. *(Christie's)*   **$4,050**

A Japanese boxwood model of a standing female fox, dressed in robes carved with leaves, carrying a box in one hand and holding her robes with the other, horn inlaid eyes, 6¾in. high, signed.
(Christie's)   **$640**

A Scottish George III burr wood specimen tobacco coaster, circa 1800, of natural gnarled outline, applied with a copper plate to the base, on three brass castors, 16in. wide. *(Christie's)*   **$4,050**

A Rajasthan gessoed wood model of the child Krishna, seated with both arms raised, wearing a necklace and dhoti, the details gilt and lacquered, 11¾in. high, 18th century. *(Christie's)*   **$3,200**

A fine carved and painted pine foal, Lexington, Kentucky, late 19th/early 20th century, of slatted construction with hollow head and body and solid carved legs, ears, mane and tail, 35in. high.
(Sotheby's) **$9,200**

A Black Forest carved wood model of a hare, late 19th or early 20th century, shown standing on its haunches amongst foliage, the body hinged at the shoulders, 17½in. high. *(Christie's)* **$10,120**

A carved wooden sculpture of a pig slaughter, American 20th century, depicting a man holding a knife beside a tree, with an overhanging branch from which a pig is suspended on a knotted string, 9⅝in. high. *(Christie's)* **$1,200**

A Spanish polychrome wood head of St. John the Baptist, mid 17th century, the decapitated head finely carved with fine detail to the hair which falls off the gilt dish onto the integrally carved square incurved base, ivory teeth, 14in., one tooth missing. *(Sotheby's)* **$23,000**

A carved giltwood figure of a sheep, early 19th century, modelled in relief, suspended with a band about its middle, in representation of a Nativity gift, inscribed to the reverse, *24 Aout 1821*, 9½in. long. *(Christie's)* **$640**

A Chinese wood model of an emaciated lohan, with smiling expression, resting both hands on one knee, on a rockwork base, 10¾in. high. *(Christie's)* **$640**

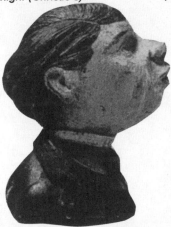

A double-sided painted pine circus lion, Cole Brothers, mid-Western, circa 1930, in the form of a lion with full mane seated atop a red and black base, 60in. x 34in. *(Sotheby's)* **$1,610**

A carved and painted pine profile plaque of a young man, American, late 19th century, the brown-haired man facing right with nose in the air, wearing a white shirt, a black tie, a brown waistcoat and a black jacket, 7in. high. *(Sotheby's)* **$800**

carved and painted figure of a turtle, American, 19th century, the full-bodied form with ostracted head and arched neck joined to a black-painted hollow-carved shell decorated ith white-painted dot-decoration and leather tail, on chamfered legs, 4¼in. high, 9in. long. Christie's) **$6,000**

set of twenty seven specimen-wood dummy books, late 18th / early 19th century, each th one or two printed leather labels, *Greenheart / Demerara; Satinwood / East Indies, 'm Pollard / English, Butternut / America, Fustic South America; Lacewood / Levant, range Tree; Laburnum / English, Walnut / English; Hemlock / Brunswick; Palmetto / India; oromandel; Locust Tree / North America; Hackmatack / Canada; Red Cedar / New South 'ales; Sycamore / English, Lime Tree / English; Box / Europe, Birch / English; Harewood, amphor Wood / Brazil; Satinwood / Porto Rico; Larch / Scotch; Red Pine / America; ahogany / Africa; Teak / Moulmein; Mahogany / Panama; Teak / Africa; White Cedar / ew Brunswick; Rock Elm / America; Red Fir / Baltic; Mahogany / Cuba; Pencil Cedar / orth America; and another burr-ash and satinwood with no label. Variations in height, ost approximately 10¾in. high; and three 9½in. (Christie's)* **$44,160**

An articulated artist's lay figure, 19
century, 23in. high.
(Christie's) **$2,75**

Two stained pine cherub wall carvings, possibly Neapolitan, with a cherub seated in a tasselled swing supported by another cherub above, 43in. high; the second as a winged cherub suspended from a tasselled drape, 34in. high. *(Christie's)* **$1,920**

A Black Forest carved stained fruitwo string barrel, late 19th century, of cylindri form, the cover carved with naturalistic vi leaves and fruit, the finial as a carved seat setter dog, the body with lion masks issu from acanthus leaves, each mask holding ivory stopper, supported on three scrolli feet, with a horn stopper to the base, 11½ high. *(Christie's)* **$1,1**

A carved and white-painted figure of a polar bear, American, 20th century, the abstracted figure with rounded head, articulated ears, facial features and blue bead eyes on an arched body and seated, on an oval notched plinth, 3in. high. *(Christie's)* **$2,000**

An 18th century wood figure of a Northumbrian Piper, carved in a seated pose, wearing a red coat with white collar and cuffs, his feet resting on a three step spiral stair case, 32.5cm. high.
(Tennants) **$9,749**

A rare carved and painted pine theatrical carving of a goddess, American, probably Maine, third quarter 19th century, the seated figure of a red-haired goddess wearing a diadem and a blue gown, seated on a scrolled socle device carved in the form of the masks of tragedy and comedy, 41in. high. *(Sotheby's)* **$5,462**

A carved and painted animal figure, American, probably Pennsylvania, 19th century, red-painted with black spots and carved in the form of a mythical savage kangaroo about to pounce, with long undulating tail, long back feet, raised front feet, long curving neck and grinning mouth with carved teeth and tongue, the head with carved beaded eyes and applied pointed ears, 28in. high.*(Christie's)* **$18,000**

A Continental painted and gilded limewood torso, 19th century, the male figure in ecclesiastical robes with tassel overthrows, 22in. high. *(Christie's)* **$1,379**

A rare and important burr-maple silver mounted loving cup or mazer bowl, early 17th century, the deep bowl of slightly tapering form, on a spreading circular foot, 7in. diameter, overall, the foot 4¼in. diameter. *(Christie's)* **$18,400**

A pair of polychrome carved wood and antler mounted models of recumbent deer, late 19th century, each with a coronet about their necks, on D end platforms, 59in. long, overall. *(Christie's)* **$4,800**

A carved and gilded pine mermaid, 19th century, the buxom female figure wearing a diadem, with tail curled mounted on a rod on a shaped painted wood base, 15 x 16½in. (Sotheby's) **$1,495**

▶

A rare and important Classic New Mexican polychromed wood female bulto of Nuestra Señora de la Rosario, Rafaél Aragón, circa 850, of unusually large scale, carved in an typical manner from a single block of wood, the female saint standing in an elegant pose, with exaggerated flaring skirt merging from a small rectangular base, and decorated with a foliate design on her apron in green and red against a yellowed ivory ground, her gesturing arms sculpted away from her torso and held in a classic pose, the thick, almost columnar neck supporting a classical ovoid head, with face set in a pensive yet serene expression. (Sotheby's) **$31,050**

A carved and painted stockade scene, probably Delaware, late 19th century, on two levels joined by a ladder, the upper depicting two prisoners in a stockade above a third prisoner attached to a whipping post and flanked by two guards, inscribed below *Delaware Justice*, 16½in. high. (Christie's) **$7,000**

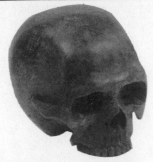

A carved wood skull, 7½in. high.
(Christie's) **$676**

An Eskimo wood head, of round form wit
open down turned mouth, bird bone inlays a
eyes, a groove running around face
elongated curved neck, 4in. high. This hea
could have been held as a small danc
wand by a shaman.
(Christie's) **$4,60**

A pair of George III mulberry and silver gilt
salts, early 19th century, the silver gilt liners
with gadrooned borders above treen bowls
with silver gilt bands engraved, *Let him be
(Shakespeare) and he will I care not, give
me faith, say I*, and monogrammed *E.S*,
above gilt metal stepped circular bases, the
mounts by Samuel Hennell and John Terry,
1815, 2¼in. high.

This pair of salts is reputedly made
from the wood of the mulberry tree planted
by William Shakespeare himself in the
garden of his house in Stratford-upon-Avon.
David Garrick was amongst those who were
entertained beneath its branches in 1742.
Following the sale of the house to the Rev.
Gastrel in 1765, the tree was felled but
rescued by a local silversmith named Sharp
who manufactured Shakespeare
memorabilia from the wood.
(Bonhams) **$2,400**

A carved and painted pine mannequin
head, late 19th century, the stylized hea
with almond-shaped eyes, straight nose ar
incised ears, on a stepped rectangular bas
stamped on the side *Louter Grand Mar*
and numbered *58*, painted light brow
10¼in. high. *(Sotheby's)* **$1,15**

Meissen model of a cat seated on its aunches with a rat in its mouth, his front aw raised, naturalistically colored with ray stripes, on shaped oval base, blue ossed swords and incised numerals, late 9th century, 8cm. high. Christie's) **$1,285**

A pair of Continental faience models of seated cats, circa 1900, possibly French, both with script *E* marks to bases, modelled seated, with applied glass eyes and wearing fierce expressions, with their tails curled about their haunches and painted in iron-red, yellow, blue and green with bouquets of flowers, their fur picked out in manganese, 10½in. high. *(Christie's)* **$1,380**

patinated terracotta figure from a model by artel, of a stylized seated cat, on a ctangular base, impressed signature, .8cm. high. *(Christie's)* **$6,400**

A Gallé-style pottery cat, circa 1900, with applied glass eyes and a cheerful expression, modelled seated and wearing a gilt-tasselled Union flag on the back and a similarly-colored bow-tie, the features picked out in naturalistic colors, 34.5cm. high. *(Christie's)* **$920**

A three legged low chair, Scottish Lowlands or English, second half 19th century, the narrow back and shaped seat covered in canvas, the base constructed of hawthorn branches, the front legs carved as stockings and boots, the left leg with a projecting point carved as a dog's head, 18½in. wide.

A carved painted chair in the form of lobster, early 20th century, the hinged ba and seat incorporating upholstered padd panels. *(Christie's)* **$34,9(**

This unusual chair is visually striking and is a fine example of one individual's imaginative craftsmanship. The style of boot depicted was fashionable during the second half of the 19th century. It is tempting to surmise that the chair may be Manx or Scottish, for certainly there are traditions in which hawthorn and blackthorn branches were used for chairmaking in the Scottish highlands and islands. The canvas seat appears to be the original covering for the chair and contains various grasses amongst its stuffing. An analysis of these gives us one or two limited pointers as to the chair's origin. Amongst several common grasses whose distribution is throughout the British Isles, Marsh Fern has been identified, which is not recorded on the Isle of Man and is very rare in Scotland. Of the six recordings for Scotland, not one is in the Highlands. *(Christie's)* **$5,851**

Willy Guhl, a fibrated concrete lounge ch designed 1954, for Eternit A.G., continuous form, intended for outdoor us *(Christie's)* **$1,2**

An oak and horn side chair carved in the form of cow-skin, the back in the form of a cow's head, 19th century.
(Christie's) **$21,528**

A George III brass mounted black-painted leather sedan chair, bordered overall with foliage wrapped reeding with a hinged rectangular domed roof above a hinged door and lined with ivory colored material, the sides each with an opening for a sliding window and iron brackets for the later carrying poles, 37½in. wide.
(Christie's) **$2,400**

n Edwardian walnut patent combined edroom chair and trouser press, with a olid panelled back, drop-in rush seat and rned tapering legs, the reverse with two nged wings forming the trouser press, earing a label *V C Bond & Sons, 61 ackney Grove, London, E8* and printed structions for use.
(Christie's) **$400**

A mahogany carved chair in the form of a hand. (Christie's) **$626**

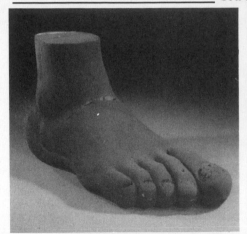

Gaetano Pesce, an up-7, Il Piede seat, this example believed to be a prototype, designed 1969, produced by B&B Italia, polyurethane form designed to resemble an oversized foot, 63in. long.
(Christie's) **$5,427**

A walnut and gilt-wood chair, Italian, circa 1870, in the form of a shell, with hinged top, the interior with upholstered back and seat, on a rocaille base, 57cm. high.
(Sotheby's) **$12,880**

A pair of William IV grained-oak heraldic hall chairs, each with turned lance uprights with metal spear finials flanking a shield with the arms of Alexander Maconochie-Welwood, Lord Meadowbank, with helmet crest, above a bowed seat with reeded edge on turned waisted legs, the lances shortened, refreshments to the decoration, 87in. high.

In 1824, Sir Thomas Dick Lauder wrote to Sir Walter Scott from Reluga describing with great enthusiasm a pair of hall chairs he had designed. *I have had two of them executed here for my vestibule, and the arms emblazoned on them in the true tinctures and metals and their effect really exceeds my most sanguine expectations. The idea occurred to me of giving the chair somewhat the appearance of the shield and helmet as erected in the chapel previous a tilting match;... The front feet of my chair are made to represent the butts of two tilting lances.... (Christie's)* **$40,00**

Gerrit Rietveld, an unstained elm Zig-Zag chair, designed 1934, for G.A.v.d. Groenikan, the geometric form of butt-ointed construction, secured by brass bolts and nuts, with chromed metal studs to the underside, stamped *H.G.M. G.A.v.d. Groenikan De Bilt Nederland.*
(Christie's) **$3,200**

An oak side chair, designed by Carlo Mollino for the 'Casa del Sole', Cervinia 1947, and the Ristorante Pavia, Cervinia 1954, twin vertical back slats, brass nuts, 36¾in. high.
(Christie's) **$15,835**

Gaetano Pesce made by Bracciodiffero for Cassina, 'Golgotha' chair, 1972-3, molded fiberglass, cloth and polyester resin, 39½in. high. This chair was produced in an edition of approximately 50.
Sotheby's) **$12,880**

An orange painted bentwood side chair, the design attributed to Josef Hoffmann and Oswald Haerdtl, probably manufactured by Thonet-Mundus, Vienna, 1929, gently curved back pierced with three rows of circles, pressed bentwood seat, 29¼in. high, stencilled mark *Thonet.*
(Christie's) **$6,520**

A mahogany and leather side chair, designed by Adolf Loos, manufactured by F.O. Schmidt, circa 1900, tan leather upholstered seat and back with square space nailing, copper plated inset handle, sabots and curved inset panels at base of backrest, 35½in. high.

The inspiration for this design came in part from chairs supplied by the London firm of Maple's (1890s) for the dining room at Queen Victoria's country residence at Sandringham.

Loos was particularly struck by the practicality of the grip inset into the chair back and in translating this to his own design became permanently associated with it; from this time on any chair exhibiting such a feature was à la Loos.

(Christie's) **$20,500**

A yellow painted simulated bamboo child' correction chair, 19th century, decorate with lines, with a panelled back, bearing paper label printed *B.S. Davies*.
(Christie's) **$80**

▶

Carlo Bugatti, chair, circa 1900, square seat, almost triangular back with central stem, arched towards the seat, 35½in. high.
(Sotheby's) **$9,149**

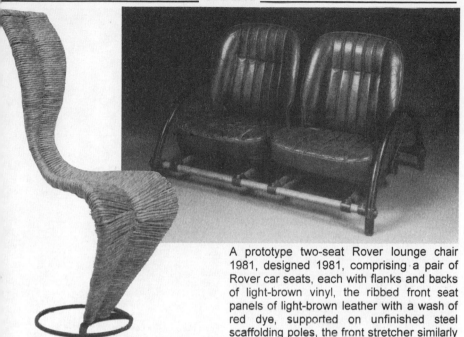

om Dixon, 'S' chair, Made by Space, U.K., 988, bent mild steel frame ending on rcular foot, with rush woven 'S' shape seat. 3onhams) **$2,202**

A prototype two-seat Rover lounge chair 1981, designed 1981, comprising a pair of Rover car seats, each with flanks and backs of light-brown vinyl, the ribbed front seat panels of light-brown leather with a wash of red dye, supported on unfinished steel scaffolding poles, the front stretcher similarly unfinished, the rear stretcher painted red, the key-clamps with original black, red or yellow finish, with black-painted side arches.

The Rover lounge chairs later manufactured and retailed by One-Off were generally either a black, or less frequently a red seat, supported on highly finished black-enamelled or chromed metal scaffolding frames that implied a primitive juxtaposition of industrial materials.
(Christie's) **$9,200**

A gray painted Zig-Zag chair, designed by Gerrit Rietveld, 1932, upright back with Z-form seat and base, 29¼in. high.
This was the first of Rietveld's designs to be mass-produced, first by Van de Groenekan and then Metz & Co. He elaborated this basic form in many ways, reducing the size, including perforations, adding arms and employing different materials. The later editions were strengthened by larger support wedges and metal bolts.

The greater number of dovetail joints at the base of the backrest denote this chair as an early example.
(Christie's) **$10,245**

91

A chalkware figure of kissing doves, Pennsylvania, 19th century, the hollow molded figure of kissing doves mounted on circular pedestal with red, green and mustard paint-decoration, 11¾in. high. *(Christie's)* **$1,000**

A chalkware figure of a cat, Pennsylvan 19th century, the hollow molded figure of seated cat with black spots and articulat ears, facial features, collar and tail in blac red and yellow paint-decoration, 15¾ high. *(Christie's)* **$5,0**

A chalkware figure of a rabbit, Pennsylvania, 19th century, the hollow molded figure of a seated rabbit decorated red, green, black, and gold paint, on a green and red rectangular plinth, 5¼in. high. *(Christie's)* **$800**

A chalkware figure of a cat, Pennsylvan 19th century, the hollow molded figure o seated cat resting on a yellow ball with r and black ears and facial features, bla spots on hind leg, and yellow and black t wearing a red, pink, and gold collar, 3¾ high. *(Christie's)* **$5**

An eight light deer antler hanging light, 20th century, of open circular form, 35in. wide approximately. *(Christie's)* **$1,089**

n antler mounted carved wood four-light ural candelabra, 20th century, in the form f a polychrome painted mermaid wearing a eaked cap, with an arm outstretched from er foliate clasped torso with writhen fishy il, a pair of antlers issuing mounted on her ack, each with two iron socles, chain uspension, 116cm. wide.
Christie's) **$1,280**

A garniture of five silver painted metal and enamel glass ceiling lights, circa 1940, comprising a large center light of octagonal tapering form, the sides applied with models of butterflies, the molded and frosted glass bodies forming outset shades, the wings heightened in blue and yellow enamels, below a central rod support, with square stepped corona, and the set of four matching pendant lights, each modelled as a conforming butterfly, the center light 39in. high overall, the matching pendant lights 30½in. high. *(Christie's)* **$7,720**

n Edwardian antler hanging light, of ntwined conjoined antlers, the suspension ains with antler bosses below the nforming corona, 28in. diameter. *Christie's)* **$6,990**

A 19th century Staffordshire porcelain character jug of female snuff taker and companion male figure, 22 and 18cm. respectively. *(Locke & England)* **$175**

An unusual majolica character jug, modelled as a balding figure with a long brown overcoat, his lilac collar forming the spout, one hand holding a scroll behind his back, wearing green breeches and blue stockings, circa 1880, 27cm. high. *(Tennants)* **$700**

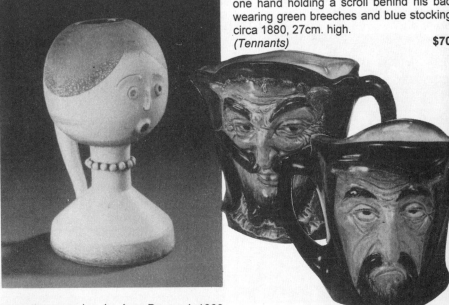

An earthenware jug, by Jean Besnard, 1930, modelled as a stylized female head with beaded choker at the neck, in shades of mushroom and stone gray, 12in. high. *(Christie's)* **$8,383**

Royal Doulton character jug depicting Mephistopheles D5757, designed by H. Fenton, issued 1937-1948. *(Lyle)* **$1,36**

A Rajasthan polychrome ivory chess set, late 18th century, in yellow and red, heightened with gilt decoration, the king seated under a temple shaped canopy with two attendant figures, the queen also under a temple canopy, the bishops on camels, the knights on horseback, the rooks as elephants with riders, the pawns as foot soldiers armed either with a rifle or shield and dagger, king 3½in. *(Christie's)* **$8,832**

A Doulton 'Mouse' chess set, designed by George Tinworth, the pawns holding axes or shields, the Kings holding orb and scepter, the Queens Bibles, the Bishops with their crooks, the Knights holding swords, painted with red or black highlights, kings 11cm. pawns 5½cm., impressed *DOULTON.* *(Bonhams)* **$24,000**

An Indian ivory John Company chess set, 19th century, gilt heightened, natural and green stained, the royal pieces as elephants with howdahs, bishops as camels, knights as horses, rooks as turrets, pawns as foot soldiers, king 3½in. high. *(Christie's)* **$3,200**

A pair of Chinese porcelain models of hens, circa 1900, later gilt bronze mounted and adapted as table lamps, the white glazed bodies with brown tails and red crestings, standing on blue rockwork bases, 15in.
(Christie's) **$2,208**

A fine and rare pair of ormolu-mounted famille rose cockerels, the porcelain 18th century, the mounts Louis XV, each modelled standing with raised chest and outstretched wings, the head looking straight ahead with prominent comb and wattles, the plumage covering the body and head colorfully enamelled in pale pink, yellow blue and green, the legs in vivid orange-red with bright yellow claws firmly grasping the rockwork base, the cockerels 14¼in. high.
(Christie's) **$80,000**

An Alcora vinegar-bottle, circa 1765, manganese *A* mark, manganese *C* over *V*, in the form of a hen, modelled with her head slightly to the right and with orange, manganese, red, blue and green plumage and manganese tail-feathers, each with a manganese *V*., seated on an oval green mound base, with a raised circular opening through the center of the back and a pierced beak, 11.1cm. high.
(Christie's) **$9,600**

A Continental cold-painted bronze model a cockerel, late 19th century, mounted on wooden branch, 22½in. high.
(Christie's) **$5,99**

Gebrüder Heubach all-bisque 'handstand
?y' German, 1910-20, impressed
?pyrighted with Heubach sunburst mark,
?m the 'Children at Play' series, the figure
?anding on his hands with legs bent over
?s head, in pale blue shirt and purple
?users, painted face with blue intaglio
?es, on an oval base with simulated foliage
?hind, 10in. high. *(Sotheby's)* **$800**

A pair of porcelain figures, designed by
Josef Wackerle, manufactured by
Nymphenburg, 1920s, 18th century fops,
one holding a pipe with a hound beside him,
the other with a tobacco jar at his feet, each
approximately 21¾in. high.
(Christie's) **$6,400**

?large Palissy type model of a snake,
?turalistically modelled curled, impressed
?th scales and enriched in a typical palette,
?e 19th century, 62cm. wide.
?hristie's) **$2,025**

A creamware arbor group of Whieldon
type, modelled as a garden shelter of semi-
circular form, a woman in a crinoline sitting
on either side of the curved seat, 14.5cm.
high. *(Bearne's)* **$64.704**

A cheese dish in the form of a bull's hea
(Worsfolds) **$32**

An English delft puzzle jug, probably Liverpool circa 1750, painted in pale blue with verse in four lines, floral sprays and dotted loop handle, the neck pierced with flowers and petals, 18.5cm.
(Bristol) **$810**

A Tiffany porcelain coffee service on bridge theme, comprising; twenty four cup twenty four saucers; and twelve side plate each with a gilt border and mottled grour painted with playing cards, the underside inscribed *Tiffany & Co. made in Franc*
(Christie's) **$7,35**

A pair of English majolica blackamoor figures, modelled as a male and companion, wearing hat, red yellow-lined coat and blue trousers and red head scarf, green dress and beaded yellow necklace, each standing before a stack of parcels, holding a shaped oval basket which rests on their knee, on shaped mound base, circa 1895, 52cm. and 53cm. high. *(Christie's)* **$1,745**

Royal Doulton figure entitled 'Dreamla designed by L. Harradine, issued 1931-3 4¾in. high.
(Lyle) **$1,7**

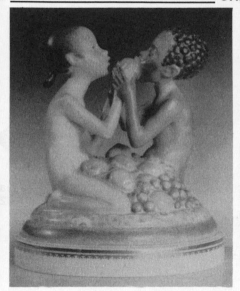

A Royal Copenhagen model of Adam and Eve, both are kneeling amidst a heap of fruit while the fair skinned Eve offers black Adam an apple, raised upon a circular base, encircled by a snake, various factory marks, 5½in. (Woolley & Wallis) **$496**

A pearlware figure of a man seated on a goat, possibly Scottish, the man wearing black hat, green jacket and crimson breeches, holding an umbrella in his right hand, the goat standing on rocky mound base applied with a plaque titled I, hope, I, dont, Intrude, circa 1830, 25cm. high. (Christie's) **$3,300**

A pearlware bull baiting group, typically modelled with the tethered bull being attacked by a terrier, a man standing at the other end with outstretched arms and a hat in his right hand, the bull with iron-red patches, enriched in ocher, iron-red, brown and green, on rectangular base, first quarter 19th century, 37cm. wide: (Christie's) **$6,450**

Rosenthal white glazed figure group, modelled as a nude female riding the back of an ostrich, 18in. high. (Skinner) **$920**

A faience ewer, modelled as an oriental man astride a cockerel, painted in bright colors, 22.5cm. orange painted mark. *(Bonhams)* **$480**

A Palissy-style jug modelled as a lizard in monk's robes, its head forming the spout, the tail the handle, the base molded with vine leaves and fruit, impressed mark, circa 1900, 33cm. high. *(Christie's)* **$800**

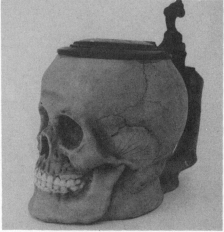

A vase from the Swan service, circa 1737-41, blue crossed swords mark, modelled by J.J. Kändler and J.F. Eberlein as a spirally-molded oviform vase supported on the backs of two swans, their necks curved about the shoulder, on an oval rockwork mound applied with flowers and foliage, the swan's feet enriched in black and with touches of black to their wings, the top rim gilt, 15cm. high.*(Christie's)* **$16,000**

Unusual bisque tankard with pewter mount and thumb catch and lid, modelled as a skull, decorated in white and beige, 5½in. *(G.A. Key)* **$200**

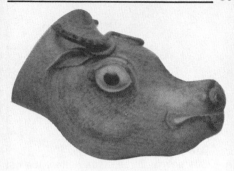

One of a pair of water-buffalo-head rhytons, 4½in. long. *(Christie's)* (Two)   **$3,262**

A Bristol Delft Adam and Eve blue-dash charger, circa 1720, painted in blue, green, yellow and iron-red with the Tree of Knowledge at the center, the serpent curled in its branches with an apple in its mouth, flanked by the ill-fated couple, holding leaves to cover themselves, Eve with an apple in one hand, between sponged trees, 13in. diameter. *(Christie's)*   **$4,801**

German bisque novelty figure of a young boy, circa 1910, 3½in. high. *(Thirault's)*   **$240**

A Victorian earthenware christening egg, printed in black with a couple and a dog watching goldfish in a bowl, the verso printed with a boy bird nesting, inscribed *A Present for A Good Boy*, 6.5cm. *(Tennants)*   **$426**

A William Goebel pottery wall plaque, in the form of a young woman's face with light green curly hair, 29cm. high, inscribed, specially designed by Agnes Richardson. *(Bearnes)*   **$480**

A 1930s novelty three piece pottery tea set. *(Greenslade Hunt)* **$160**

A fine painted chalkware cat, probably Pennsylvania, mid 19th century, the hollow figure of a seated cat, painted with black, red and yellow markings on a white ground, 15¾in. high. *(Sotheby's)* **$6,325**

A pair of Clarice Cliff teddy bear book ends decorated in the 'Red Flower' pattern, painted in colors, 6in. high. *(Christie's)* **$7,900**

Capo di Monte glazed pottery centerpiece, 20th century, depicting a line of fancifully clad young musicians, 30in. long. *(Skinner)* **$1,380**

Early 19th century slipware two handled cylindrical loving cup, inscribed *Happiness Lies in Imagination Not in Possession*, decorated with treacle and green foliage on ocher ground and dated 1800, 5½in. high. *(G.A. Key)* **$315**

Beswick Beatrix Potter figure Duchess, style one (holding flowers), printed mark in gilt, 9.5cm. *(Tennants)* **$3,475**

A Goldscheider (USA) glazed pottery head of young woman, her features picked out in muted tones, wearing a 'manganese' ground lace shawl over her hair, printed marks, 29.5cm. *(Phillips)* **$400**

A Kornilov Manufactory figure of a pugilist, circa 1850, wearing black boxing gloves and a green waistcoat, oval marbled base, 15.8cm. *(Sotheby's)* **$1,280**

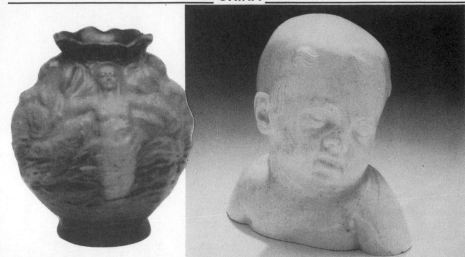

Vance faience vase with molded mermaid decoration, Ohio, circa 1905, with repeating figures and fish (some chips and roughness), 12½in. high. *(Skinner)* **$400**

Böttger porcelain white head of a child, circa 1715, turned to the right, his face surrounded with incised curls of hair, 9.2cm. high. *(Christie's)* **$8,000**

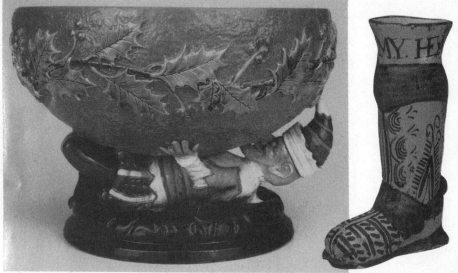

A George Jones 'Punch' bowl, the bowl formed as an orange half, molded with a continuous branch of holly leaves and berries, supported by Mr. Punch, recumbent on his back, on a dark-blue mound, the interior in lilac the underside with tortoiseshell glazes, circa 1873, 35cm. diameter. *(Christie's)* **$12,800**

An English delft blue and white drinking-vessel modelled as a spurred boot, inscribed beneath the flared rim *OH. MY HEAD* above a wide blue band and painted with scroll, triangular and semi-circular ornament, Southwark, circa 1650, 17.5cm. high. *(Christie's)* **$19,360**

Delphin Massier Art Pottery pitcher, French, early 20th century, tapered oviform in fiery metallic luster glaze in shades of green, rose, and gold decorated with a modelled portrait of a satyr and a draped nude figural handle, signed *DM, Vallauris, AM* on base, 10in. high. *(Skinner)* **$1,495**

A pair of Derby Mansion House Dwarfs after engravings by Callot, painted in colors and gilt, incised *Nos.227*, iron-red crossed batons and crown marks, circa 1830, Robt. Bloor & Co, 17cm. and 18cm. high. *(Christie's)* **$2,760**

Three bisque bathing beauties, German, early 19th century, one lady reclining resting on her elbow the other lady crouching holding the other lady's ankles, with painted features and blue and pink ballet shoes, 8½in. high. *(Bonhams)* **$480**

A Staffordshire earthenware Vicar and Moses group, the brown painted double pulpit with angel mask mount and with the two characters seated before open Bibles, early 19th century, 23.5cm. *(Tennants)* **$480**

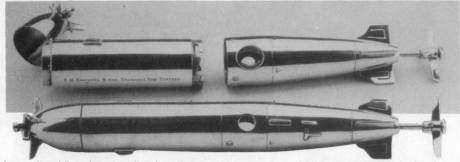

A rare late Victorian novelty cigar cutter cum vesta case, Birmingham 1897, maker's mark of George Unite and Sons, modelled as a Whitehead Torpedo, the hinged front opens to reveal a vesta holder and striker, the propeller pushes in to activate the cigar cutter, the body opens to reveal a section for the cut ends, inscribed *H.M Emanuel & Son, Ordnance Row, Portsea*, 19.5cm. long.*(Bonhams)* **$4,000**

Silver plated cigar cutter in horse-head form, 5¾in. long. *(Eldred's)* **$143**

Cigar and cutter, bronze patinated silver, formed as a cigar, one end with vesta case, the other fitted with a cigar cutter, lacking maker's mark, London 1892, 11cm. long. *(Christie's)* **$960**

A Fabergé circular cigar cutter in silver gilt and blue basse taille, enamel painted with trailing leafage frieze in white, 1.6in. diameter. *(Russell Baldwin & Bright)* **$11,520**

CIGARETTE DISPENSERS

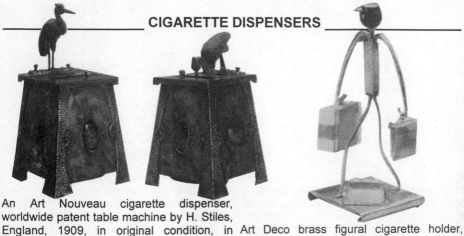

An Art Nouveau cigarette dispenser, worldwide patent table machine by H. Stiles, England, 1909, in original condition, in working order. *(Auction Team Köln)* **$803**

Art Deco brass figural cigarette holder, circa 1935, unsigned, 9¾in. high. *(Skinner)* **$240**

A Penguin typewriter petrol lighter, Japanese. *(Auction Team Köln)* **$122**

Cast aluminum Jeep/Land Rover lighter, Germany, circa 1960, with incised windows and doors, pop-up lighter and ashtray, stamped *Baier Ges Gesch*, 3in. high. *(Skinner)* **$700**

A gas-fuelled lighter in the form of a camera. *(Auction Team Köln)* **$81**

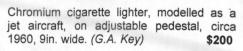

Chromium cigarette lighter, modelled as a jet aircraft, on adjustable pedestal, circa 1960, 9in. wide. *(G.A. Key)* **$200**

A Ronson 'Bar Tender' Touch Tip lighter, comprising a combined lighter and cigarette box in a chrome plated and brown enamelled 'bar' behind which stands a black, enamelled barman perkily agitating a cocktail shaker, American, 1930s. *(Bonhams)* **$560**

German smoker's companion, 1930s, nickel plated metal in the form of an aeroplane, the body forming the cigar compartments, the cockpit doubling as match holder and striker, 9½in. long. *(Sotheby's)* **$2,815**

Dunhill, an 18ct. white gold, diamond and emerald-set petrol burning lighter with watch inset to the hinged front cover, 43 x 38mm. *(Christie's)* **$4,500**

Brass cigar lighter in the form of Puck, 7½in. high. *(Eldred's)* **$231**

A Dunhill tinder pistol petrol lighter, British, 1962. *(Auction Team Köln)* **$149**

A rare Dunhill 'Eight' silver compendium, London, 1935, with eight functions, double wheel petrol lighter, watch with jewelled lever movement, stamp box, ruler with Imperial and metric scales, pencil holder, pocket knife, cigarette box and ivory note tablet in the lid, with engine turned decoration and silver gilt interior, 12.4cm. wide. *(Bonhams)* **$2,400**

A white metal table lighter in the shape of a monkey, marked *Fabergé*, realistically modelled, the upright monkey turning to look at its tail, 4¼in. high, 13.5oz. *(Christie's)* **$21,994**

The 'Don' cigarettes by J.J. Holland, London, pack of five, 1900-20. *(Lyle)* **$40**

Dandy Dan Cigarettes, by A.H. Franks & Sons, pack of five, 1900-20. *(Lyle)* **$55**

Circus Girl Cigarettes by Cohen, Weenen & Co., pack of 5, 1900-20.*(Lyle)* **$55**

Rich Uncle Cigarettes, by S.J. Gore & Co., London, pack of 5, 1900-20. *(Lyle)* **$40**

Star of the World Cigarettes by the J.L.S. Tobacco Co., pack of 5, 1900-20. *(Lyle)* **$65**

The New Alliance Best Virginia Cigarettes by David Corre & Co., pack of 5, 1900-20. *(Lyle)* **$32**

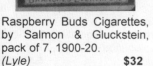

Raspberry Buds Cigarettes, by Salmon & Gluckstein, pack of 7, 1900-20. *(Lyle)* **$32**

Pear Blossom Compressed Cigarettes, by A. Baker & Co., London, pack of 5, 1900-20. *(Lyle)* **$40**

All Gay Cigarettes by Harris of London, with 'handsome colored photo', pack of 5, 1900-20. *(Lyle)* **$50**

A Victorian mounted clear glass spirit jug, in the form of a cockatoo or cockatiel, with hinged head, red glass eyes, textured plumage and feet, by Sampson Mordan, 1881, 13.5cm. *(Christie's)* **$2,400**

A Victorian silver mounted novelty claret jug, London 1882, maker's mark of Alexander Crichton, also marked with a registration mark, modelled as a sitting duck, hinged head, central carrying handle, the glass body etched with feathers, 28cm. long. *(Bonhams)* **$4,000**

A Victorian claret jug formed as a seal, the central loop carrying handle linking front and back flippers, with detailed cast head and black glass eyes, London 1881 by Alexander Crichton, 16.5cm. *(Bristol)* **$16,320**

A white metal novelty claret jug, modelled as a duck, hinged cover, the wings modelled as scroll handles. *(Bonhams)* **$320**

A Continental silver plated and cranberry glass claret jug, late 19th century, in the form of a long eared owl, the head hinged, standing on splayed claw feet, 12½in. high. *(Christie's)* **$4,600**

A pale-turquoise and white-metal-mounted parrot claret jug and stopper, with hinged white-metal head and legs, applied with an amber loop handle, circa 1900, 25cm. high. *(Christie's)* **$735**

A Victorian silver-mounted glass claret jug, maker's mark of Alexander Crichton, London, 1881, in the form of a duck, the head and tail realistically chased, with hinged cover, the glass body cut with a monogram beneath a coronet, marked on mounts and with registration mark, 25.5cm. long. *(Christie's)* **$17,370**

A Victorian carved walnut shelf-clock b Seth Thomas Company, Thomastor Connecticut, circa 1890, 29in. high *(Christie's)* **$3,92**

A German giltwood and porcelain mounted longcase clock, circa 1880, the panels by J. Hoss, surmounted by a square stepped pediment, the front with a circular porcelain dial depicting putti, the twin-train movement stamped to the reverse *Medaille d'Or/ Gustav Becker.../,* the sides each with a panel depicting three graces bathing, signed supported by a pair of cylindrical porcelain columns depicting graces and putti, 76¾in. high. *(Christie's)* **$47,435**

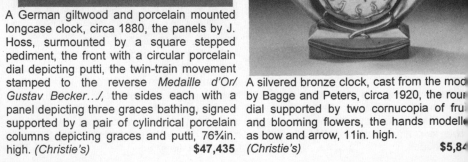

A silvered bronze clock, cast from the mod by Bagge and Peters, circa 1920, the rour dial supported by two cornucopia of fru and blooming flowers, the hands modelle as bow and arrow, 11in. high. *(Christie's)* **$5,84**

An onyx and marble clock, French, circa 1920, butterfly form, panels of mixed marble, applied with gilt edging, 13in. high. *(Christie's)* **$4,175**

Fabergé silver violin-form desk clock, late 19th century, the front hinged to reveal a covered well and watch, manufactured by Ellis Samuel Yates & Co., Liverpool, etched with faux graining, with Fabergé marks, mark for Erik Kollin, Workmaster, and 84 standard. *(Skinner)* **$4,000**

A Black Forest carved and painted wood cuckoo and quail wall clock, early 20th century, the case of chalet form, with cresting of crossed rifles, centered by a calf's head with inset glass eyes, with rabbit and gamebird trophies to the sides and hunting pouch below, the three train movement with cuckoo and quail emerging beneath the roof on the quarters, each with twin bellows, and countwheel hour strike on gong, 36in. high. *(Christie's)* **$2,236**

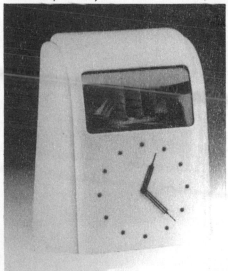

A bakelite Vitascope clock, 1930s, pale blue bakelite case with rocking ship in view, 12½in. *(Bonhams)* **$640**

A Restauration negro clock in patinated and chased gilt bronze, the dial set in the stomach of a smoking negro in embroidered dress, his moveable head linked to the movement, lacking pipe, 19½in. high. This representation is inspired by Toussaint l'Ouverture (1746-1803), the liberator of Haïti. There is similar clock in the Spanish Royal collections, Madrid. *(Christie's)* **$33,120**

A Victorian walnut celestial clock, Theodore R. Timby, New York State, circa 1860, the swan's-neck pediment surmounted by a shaped finial above acorn pendants centering a revolving globe and calendar aperture, 27in. high. Generally referred to as the Timby Solar Clock, Theodore R. Timby, of Baldwinsville, New York, received a patent for this timepiece in 1863. The clocks were made by L. E. Whiting of Saratoga Springs. Many clocks had paper labels and numbers. Timby only made 600 of the form. *(Sotheby's)* **$5,175**

An amusing moving-eye dog timepiece, German, circa 1950, the open spring movement with pin pallet and balance escapement connection to the eyes and indicating minutes by the right eye and hours by the left, 6in. *(Bonhams)* **$800**

A carved and painted longcase clock in the form of a woman standing with arms akimbo, with glazed convex painted dial signed *Joh Ylie Konnig Tlmola*, late 19th century, 7ft. high. *(Christie's)* **$7,623**

17th century Augsburg polychrome painted and giltwood astronomical quarter striking and quarter repeating monstrance clock, the backplate signed *Ciprianus eütter Augsburg*, and later engraved *1626*, the movement with five gilt baluster pillars with crenellated rings, foliate pierced and engraved set-up work to the going train barrel, chain fusee, foliate engraved gilt ring barrels for the hour and quarter strike two bells. *(Christie's)* **$40,000**

A novelty games clock, French, circa 1890, 9in. checker board with applied Arabic numeral cartouches, playing card spandrels and billiard motifs, Japy Frères gong striking movement with Brocourt escapement, in a molded square case the chess piece arcade across the pediment, 24in. *(Bonhams)* **$960**

A fine and large pair of cloisonné enamel Qilin censers and covers, 18th century, each sturdy beast standing four-square on powerful legs with sharpened claws, the rounded body enamelled with blue scales reserved with burgundy flames and a pale mauve chest, applied with a gilt-bronze band suspending a bell and tassels, the detachable tail in multi-colored stripes 21in. high. *(Christie's)*

$16,000

A very fine pair of cloisonné enamel seated qilin, Wanli, the striking beasts with gilt-bronze horns, manes and hooves, the scaly bodies enamelled in midnight-blue with green and red flares and an imposing green bushy tail, the mouth opened to a fierce snarl, 9½in. high.
(Christie's) **$40,000**

A pair of Chinese cloisonné enamel bronze models of elephants, 19th century, the caparisoned elephants carrying detachable faceted and baluster shaped towers with a pricket to the petal finial, standing on rectangular shaped bases with bracket feet, decorated overall with blue and green enamels on a white ground 34in. high. *(Christie's)*

$6,99?

A rare, George III clothes whisk, of faceted conical form, chased with foliate scrolls and terminating in a ring finial, the square bristle pad with straight bristles, 1760, 11.75cm. high. *(Christie's)* **$640**

George I silver-glit mounted clothes brush, nmarked, circa 1720, oval and with shaped n and molded borders, the center inset ith an oval plaque depicting a putto and a rd within a rocky landscape with a unflower, within husk and scrolling foliage order, 4½in. long.
Christie's) **$1,600**

A George I silver-gilt clothes whisk, maker's mark of Anthony Nelme struck four times only, London, circa 1720, of tapering square section and with cut corners and baluster finial, the sides chased with putti holding foliate scrolls on a matted ground and stylized foliage, 5in. long.
(Christie's) **$2,025**

COAL

late 19th century parrot oal figure of a seated lion, arved in a naïve manner ith textured body and ane, and with polished ars and features, inset mber eyes, 24cm. high.

The Fife mason Thomas /illiamson, renowned for s parrot coal furniture, is nown to have made nimals such as this.
Phillips) **$960**

A chromium plated cocktail shaker in the form of an airship with spirit measures contained in the base, German, 1920s 30.5cm. high. *(Christie's)* **$1,280**

German aeroplane cocktail set, 1930s nickel-plated metal, the wings formed from two screw-top flasks with mixing spoon and fork attached to the undercarriage, the body functioning as the shaker with the detachable nose revealing strainer and containing four small tumblers, a small canister, mixer flask, measure and cork screw, the strainer marked *D.R.G.M. Made in Germany*, 9½in. long.
(Sotheby's) **$3,200**

Unusual silver plated novelty cocktail shaker in the form of a penguin, the base stamped *Napier*, 12in. high, 20th century. *(G.A. Key)* **$1,024**

A large American chrome and glass cocktail shaker, designed by Norman del Geddes, made by Revere, modelled as a large ferris wheel, supporting twelve frosted glass tumblers and two cylindrical cocktail shakers, 59.5cm. high.
(Christie's) **$8,000**

A Modernist cocktail shaker, designed Sylvia Stave, manufactured by Hallberg Sweden, spherical with loop handle, 7¼in. high. *(Christie's)* **$10,624**

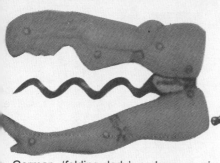

German 'folding lady' corkscrew, circa 1900, height closed 2⁵/₈in.
(Lyle) **$640**

Victorian engine-turned silver gilt travelling set comprising sandwich box and pair of beundlets with corkscrew and railway carriage key, London 1869. (Graves Son & ilcher Fine Arts) **$2,325**

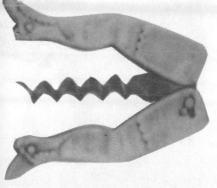

ate 19th century silver 'lady's legs' folding rkscrew, probably American, marked erling, height closed 2in. high. hristie's) **$418**

19th century Merritt brass and wood bar corkscrew with steel clamp, 1880. (Lyle) **$440**

A rare wooden 'Gentleman' corkscrew by Syroco Wood, Syracuse, NY/USA, said to be in the image of Senator Volstead, who through the 18th Amendment in 1919 introduced 'Prohibition' in the USA. This ban on alcohol was not lifted until the passing of the 21st Amendment in 1933. This model, with its large cylinder, is much rarer than the 'Waiter', circa 1930, 21cm. high. (Auction Team Köln) **$267**

A Staffordshire pearlware cow creamer an stopper with a pink lustered border, milkmaid seated to one side, 14cm. *(Phillips)* **$89**

An English creamware cow creamer and cover enriched in brown glazes, typically modelled with a calf suckling, and a bird finial, supported by a stepped rectangular base, enriched in brown glaze, circa 1770, 16cm. long. *(Christie's)* **$640**

A late 19th century Continental cast co creamer with textured hair, horns and harness around its neck, with English impc marks for Berthold Muller, Chester, 189 14cm. long. 7.75oz.*(Christie's)* **$1,6**

A late 18th century creamware cow, creamer with milk maid, the beast standing four square on a shaped rectangular green washed base, her body mottled in brown, a seated maid at work by her side, circa 1780, 14.5cm. high. *(Cheffins)* **$602**

A George II cow creamer, textured simulate hair, the hinged cover chased w a border of flowers and applied with a fly, John Schuppe, 1757, 14.5cm. long, 5 *(Christie's)* **$9,9**

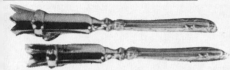

Pair of silver-handled frog legs servers, American, late 19th century, reeded handles with leaf and vine decoration. *(Skinner)* **$172**

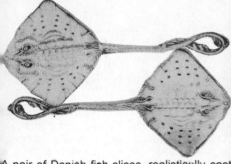

A pair of Danish fish slices, realistically cast and chased as flat fish, maker's mark *M. Aase. (Christie's)* **$620**

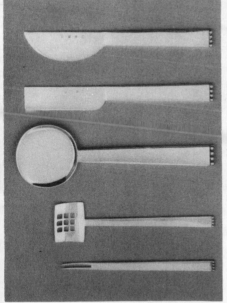

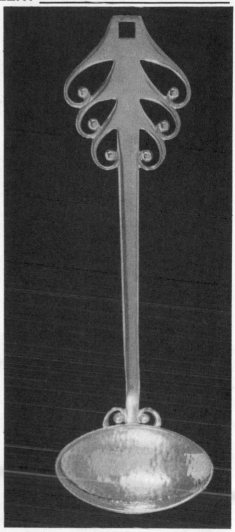

Josef Hoffmann for the Wiener Werkstätte, executed by Alfred Mayer, scroll motif spoon, 1905, silver-colored metal, the bowl with martelé finish, the reverse with designer's and maker's monograms, *WW* monogram and trademark, 15.8cm. long.

This spoon is documented in the Wiener Werkstätte archive at the Austrian Museum of Decorative Art, in Vienna. These records confirm that only two examples of this spoon were made. The production day is stated as 10 October 1905. The price then was 70 Kronen.

A five piece serving set, designed by Josef Hoffmann, manufactured by the Wiener Werkstätte, 1904, each with tapering handle and four-ball finial, length of serving spoon 8¾in., each piece stamped with maker's mark and *WW. (Christie's)* **$40,572**

(Sotheby's) **$12,975**

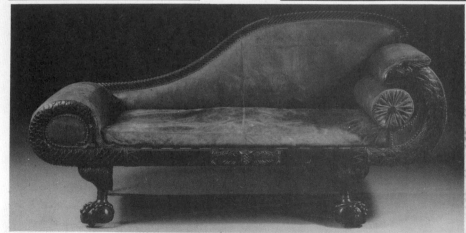

An Irish Regency mahogany daybed, the shaped rising padded back, scrolled ends, bolster and seat-cushion covered in brown leather, the back with a gadrooned border, the front outlined by an eagle's head and neck to one end and a fish tail to the other, the center of the seat-rail with foliage, on eagle legs and claw feet, with remains of a paper label to the seat for *..BUTLER LTD., /..TOR AND RESTORER OF/ 'Chippendale' 'Adams' and 'Sheraton' / Furniture/ 127 & 128 UPPER ABBEY STREET, DUBLIN.*
(Christie's) $38,180

A Regency green-painted and parcel-gilt couch, of scrolled scallop-shell form, the head end arched, the foot-end scrolled, with a caned seat and two buttoned squab cushions covered in lime-green velvet, on crocodile legs and rectangular plinths with sunk brass castors, stamped to the underside *WH*, redecorated, 38in. high, 67in. wide
(Christie's) $24,000

A red painted ebonized and parcel-gilt boat shaped daybed of antique Egyptian style, the dished seat covered in black horsehair, 76in. wide. *(Christie's)* **$3,218**

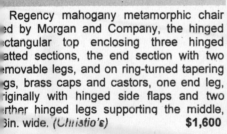

Regency mahogany metamorphic chair ed by Morgan and Company, the hinged ctangular top enclosing three hinged atted sections, the end section with two movable legs, and on ring-turned tapering gs, brass caps and castors, one end leg, riginally with hinged side flaps and two rther hinged legs supporting the middle, 3in. wide. *(Christie's)* **$1,600**

Chippendale style mahogany daybed, in e Philadelphia tradition, 20th century, the haped crest above a pierced strapwork olat and leather-upholstered slip seat on quare molded legs joined by stretchers, ft. 4in. long. *(Sotheby's)* **$1,035**

A Dutch mahogany metamorphic wing armchair, mid 18th century, the channelled toprail centered by a rockwork cartouche, with padded back, cushion and two seat cushions covered in cream cotton, each side with a latch to let the back down and the back with a hinged stand, above a hinged seat-rail opening to reveal two padded panelled sections and a hinged head board, on cabriole legs and pad feet, restorations to the back, formerly with a further strengthening strut to the back. *(Christie's)* **$13,363**

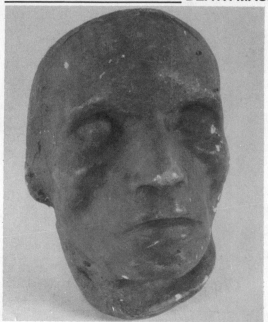

Grant, Ulysses S. (1822-1885) plaster Death Mask of Grant with pencil inscription on the interior *Mt. McGregor, July 24 1885*, with flesh colored paint 9in. long.
(Skinner) $4,800

DECALOMANIA

The Victorians were prone to go somewhat over the top when it came to fuss and clutter in their decorations. They were also not above having a go themselves. It was after all perfectly acceptable for genteel ladies with a bit of time on their hands to give expression to any artistic pretensions they might have in the innocent embellishment of household items such as screens, china, or glass.

One of the materials they had to hand for this purpose were scraps, brightly colored pieces of paper with pictures or scenes on them, which were a fashionable collectable of the time, and were usually pasted into albums.

Someone had the bright idea of sticking them instead on to screens and vases, and applying a coat of lacquer over the top to afford them some protection. In no time at all this became all the rage, and the art of decalomania (from *decal*, a transfer or design) was born. It proved immensely popular as a parlor craft in the late 19th century, and such items regularly appear at auction today.

A pair of early Victorian green and parcel-g decalomania vases, each with a facet scalloped rim above a faceted bod decorated with various fancy figures ar flower bouquets, on a faceted, panelle circular base, 13in. high.
(Christie's) $1,19

ne grain painted shipping clerk's desk, ew England, first half 19th century, the ctangular top with canted sides above two ort drawers and two long drawers and lift p, centering a gallery with block turned sts, all set into a frame of square legs ned by straight skirt and box stretchers, l grain painted brown to resemble ahogany on dark green painted base, in. wide. *(Christie's)* **$1,200**

George IV ormolu-mounted and brass-aid ebony davenport, the rectangular top th three-quarter pierced baluster gallery ove a black leather-lined writing slope closing a satinwood-lined fitted interior li four small drawers, the writing surface :h a removable stop, with a fitted ink awer to the right hand side, on Corinthian lumn supports headed by lappeted panels nked by scrolling foliage, on scrolled paw :t, brass and leather castors, 35in. high x in. wide.

This elegant Grecian-black, brass-aid and ormolu-enriched desk is nceived in the French/antique manner moted in France by La Mesangère's urnal et Objects de Gout, 1802-1835 and England by the connoisseur Thomas pe (d. 1842). The palm-flowered trusses its laurel-wreathed composite pillars, as l as its Roman-lamp 'claws' or lion-nopodia, derive from patterns in Hope's usehold Furniture and Interior Decoration, idon, 1807. *ristie's)* **$9,430**

A Victorian walnut veneered chair-desk, stamp of Stephen Hedges, New York City, circa 1854, 33in. wide. This unusual combination chair and desk closely resembles drawings accompanying Stephen Hedges' patent no. 10, 740 for a "convertible chair." Patented in April 1854, the invention was described by Hedges as "A new and useful Piece of Furniture, Intended to Serve as a Table Alone or as Chair and Table combined." What he claimed as unique was the manner of hingeing "a table of ordinary construction" with a chair to form a small stand, writing desk, and chair in one. *(Christie's)* **$8,050**

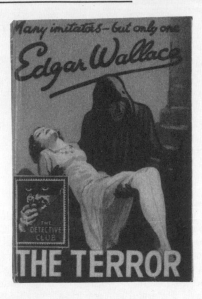

The Terror by Edgar Wallace, the first talkie horror film, Warner, 1928.
(Lyle) **$130**

Sizzling Detective Mysteries, August 193
(Lyle) **$.**

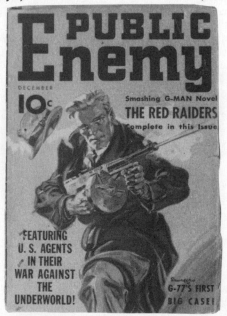

Public Enemy featuring U.S. Agents in their War against the Underworld, December 1935, Number One Issue.
(Lyle) **$130**

Complete Detective, May 1938, featur Rhapsody in Death by Wayne Roge Number One Issue.
(Lyle) **$1**

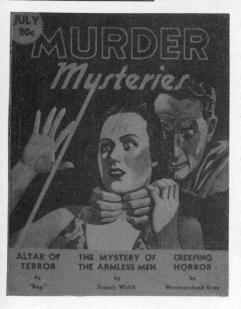

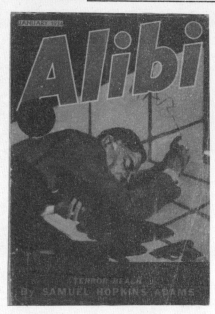

Murder Mysteries featuring The Mystery of the Armless Men by Francis Welch, July 1935. *(Lyle)* **$25**

Alibi, January 1934 featuring Written in Blood by H. I. Gates, Number One Issue. *(Lyle)* **$130**

All Aces Magazine, April 1936, featuring Under Sealed Orders by Hugh Pendexter, Number One Issue. *(Lyle)* **$95**

Prison, Life Stories featuring Federal Agents by J. Edgar Hoover, September 1935, Number One Issue. *(Lyle)* **$65**

Part of the attraction of things odd and unusual has always been their value as conversation pieces and very few can have greater cachet in the corner of the living room than a genuine dinosaur egg.

These have started to appear from time to time at auctions of antiquities and objects of scientific interest, and are eagerly sought after. Given their age and the fascinating mystery of why the dinosaur population disappeared, it is hardly surprising that these lumps of rock fetch tens of thousands of pounds At least in their fossilized state they are still readily recognisable for what they are, which is more than can be said for the fossilized dino droppings which sometimes also come up for auction.

A spherical dinosaur egg, Saltasaurus Cretaceous, from Patagonia, Argentina, 7¼in. diameter. *(Christie's)*   **$11,265**

A rare nest of ten Sauropod eggs, embedded, egg size 5½in. diamete
(Bonhams)   **$77,92**

Popeye Pipe Toss Game, 1935.
(Lyle) **$160**

A carved and painted wood figure in the form of Mickey Mouse, 1930s/40s, 92cm. high. *(Bearnes)* **$445**

Paragon child's mug decorated with an amusing picture of Mickey Mouse and signed *WALTER E. DISNEY*, the base of the mug bearing the legend *Wishing you a happy Christmas from H.R.H. Duchess of York, Dec 25th 1932*. This mug was given to a young boy in the T. B. ward at Mearnskirk Hospital, Newton Mearns, Glasgow. *(Academy)* **$816**

A set of Chad Valley Snow White and The Seven Dwarfs, English late 1930s, with pressed felt faces with painted features on cloth bodies, the dwarfs wearing brightly colored clothes and hats, Snow White wearing a white dress, Snow White 16in. tall. *(Bonhams)* **$800**

An 18ct. gold and diamond-set 'Mickey Mouse' octagonal wristwatch with bracelet signed *Gerald Genta, Geneve*, recent 32mm. diameter. *(Christie's)* **$9,650**

Rare 1947 Mickey Mouse Ingersoll watch in-store display, the only one known to exist, together with a 1947 Ingersoll Mickey Mouse watch.
(Butterfield & Butterfield) **$23,000**

A rare Donald Duck bisque toothbrush holder, marked *copyright Walt Disney*, 1930s, Donald standing next to a green post with hand on hip wearing his famous sailor outfit, on orange base, 4¾in. tall.
(Bonhams) **$1,280**

Mickey and Minnie Mouse soft toys, probably American, 1930s, with bodies, limbs and heads of black, ribbed fabric, with white faces with stitched smiling mouths, noses and 'piecrust' eyes of black ribbed fabric, stuffed glove-type white hands with four fingers, long black tails, Mickey in green shorts with red belt and red shoes, Minnie in red and white striped skirt with bloomers beneath and dark green boots with heels, Mickey, 16in., Minnie 15in.
(Sotheby's) **$1,600**

Snow White And The Seven Dwarfs, six hand-painted porcelain toothbrush holders, modelled as Snow White, Grumpy, Bashful, Happy, Dopey and Sneezy, all printed *Genuine Walt Disney Copyright Foreign* distributed by S. Maw & Son, London, Snow White 6in. high. *(Christie's)* **$640**

A Mickey Mouse mechanical display clock with moving legs, right hand and eyes, 1955. (Auction Team Köln) **$655**

A Mickey Mouse alarm clock, Ingersoll, 1920s, the square clock with paper printed Mickey and friends round sides, the white enamel face showing Mickey running with outstretched arms with pointing hands, circular seconds movement with two running Mickeys, 4in. high. (Bonhams) **$545**

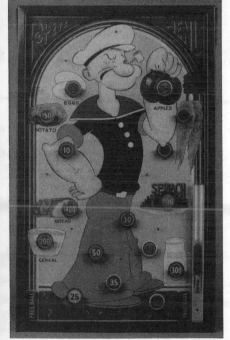

A Popeye bagatelle board, American, 1935, the brightly colored tinplate board showing Popeye surrounded by food, with pins and scoring circles with tinplate half circles for catching the balls, made by the Durable Toy and Novelty Corp New York, 23 x 14in. (Bonhams) **$960**

An original Knickerbocker Mickey Mouse, a very rare stuffed cloth toy with composition feet for balance. Produced under official Walt Disney licence by the Knickerbocker Toy Co. Inc., New York, with very rare folded cardboard label, also in the form of Mickey Mouse, circa 1932, 38cm. high. (Auction Team Köln) **$870**

A late 19th century large electro-plated dog collar with a leather lining, a ring for attaching a leather lining, a ring for attaching a lead and two rows of pyramidal studs, flanking a row of domed circular studs, decorated with wriggle work engraving, 16.5cm. diameter.
(Christie's) **$480**

A George III brass dog's collar, late 18th century, engraved *William King White Holme, 1772* within dog's tooth bands. *(Bonhams)* **$960**

A brass mounted leather dog collar, late 18th/early 19th century, with padlock clasp, applied with initials *JN HR* flanked by shaped symbols, 4¼in. diameter.
(Christie's) **$2,377**

A white metal dog's collar, early 19th century, engraved, *Stewarton Coursing Club, 1825. (Bonhams)* **$560**

A late Victorian brass and morocco leather dog's collar, late 19th century, stamped, *Massey. (Bonhams)* **$250**

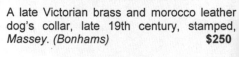

A brass dog's collar, with pierced circle and diamond medallion decoration.
(Bonhams) **$290**

An 18th century brass dog collar, of plain adjustable strap form, with later padlock and key, inscribed *Mr John Bordwisell of Booth Ferry owner in Yorkshire 1721*, 14cm. diameter. *(Tennants)* **$1,360**

A rare pair of black and green-glazed Chinese porcelain hounds, first half 18th century, seated upright with heads cocked to the left and right, each slender body lightly molded with ribs and a long tail looped around the hindquarters to the front, all under unusual blackish-brown glazes fired paler in irregular patches, the neck with a green collar suspending a bell, both about 7¾in., high. (Christie's) **$19,200**

A pair of carved and painted seated Dalmatians, Lancaster County, Pennsylvania, dated 1880, the full-bodied figures of seated Dalmatians painted white with black spots, each with gilt collar inscribed 1880 in red, 25in. high. (Christie's) **$50,000**

A carved and painted figure of a dog attributed to Wilhelm Schimmel, 1817-1890, Carlisle, Cumberland County, Pennsylvania, 1865-1890, in the form of a standing dog, the body painted in yellow with black spots, on a green rectangular base, 2¾in. high. (Christie's) **$5,000**

A carved and painted figure of a dog, American, probably 19th century, the full-bodied brown-painted form depicted crouching, with raised and turned head and smiling face, the body with all over incised fur and toes, black-painted collar, 11in. high, 25in. long. (Christie's) **$5,000**

A Japanese white glazed pottery model of a Pekinese, seated with its right paw raised, wearing a patterned collar, 5½in. high.
(Christie's) **$358**

A rare Meissen model of a scruffy dog, sitting on the top of his kennel, his head turned to the side and with a chain from his collar to the roof, painted with brown / black patches, his mouth detailed in red, the roof tiles black, the sides of the kennel as grained wood, crossed swords mark to the base, circa 1740.
(Woolley & Wallis) **$1,272**

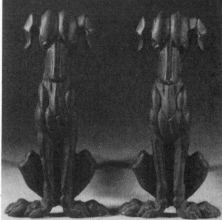

A carved and stained wood model of a hound, 19th century, shown seated on its haunches, 16½in. high.
(Christie's) **$1,280**

A pair of cast iron hound andirons, 20th century, cast in the half round, 14in. high.
(Sotheby's) **$6,900**

late 19th/early 29th century cast model of ▶
hound or hunting dog, standing with tail
ised and head erect in a snarling pose,
xtured to simulate hair and wearing a
llar around his neck, import marks for
ertholt Muller, 1902, 33cm. long, 41oz.
:hristie's) **$900**

pair of giltwood and silvered grayhounds,
ch in the form of sitting grayhound with a
llar, on a shaped rectangular plinth with a
peted border, 29¾in. high.
hristie's) **$3,818**

Rare papier-mâché mechanical bulldog pull-
toy, circa 1900, tan with brown and black
spots, brown glass eyes, squeezing a wire
leader to neck activates mouth to open with
a growl, 27in. long.
(Eldred's) **$1,980**

white glazed terracotta figure of a
:umbent hound, Continental, 20th century,
delled life-sized with head turned to one
e, 89.2cm. wide.
hristie's) **$880**

An Australian pottery model of a pug dog,
late 19th century, modelled standing,
naturalistically colored, set with glass eyes,
12½in. (Sotheby's) **$1,280**

Max and Moritz, a rare pair of Kammer & Reinhart comic character dolls, with widely grinning watermelon mouths, sleeping and flirting eyes, molded brows, original black and auburn stiffened wigs and jointed fixed-wrist bodies with molded boots, dressed in contemporary outfits, 15½in. high, circa 1913. *(Christie's)* **$24,000**

▶

A fine J.D. Kestner bisque head 'Googly' eyed character doll, with brown hair wig, weighted blue eyes and closed 'watermelon' mouth. *(Bonhams)* **$6,080**

Hertel, Schwab & Co., a bisque china hea 'Googly' eye doll with closed mouth impressed *165.5* having silver blonde wi and blue paperweight glass eyes, o composition bent limb body with knitte clothing, 35cm. high.
(Bearnes) **$3,888**

Late 1970, American limited edition 'glamour' doll complete with sequinned top and roller skates, 28in. high. *(Lyle)* **$400**

, fine J.D. Kestner googly-eyed doll, German, circa 1913, impressed *J.D.K. 221*, with large round, startled eyes, delicately painted lashes, upward pointing brows, curved watermelon smile, dense light brown wig, on jointed wood and composition toddler body, in original smocked ivory silk gown, leather shoes and cotton socks, 23¾in. *(Sotheby's)* **$4,800**

, 1964 set of four Beatles dolls, wearing black suits with trademark bowl-style haircuts, with facsimile signatures in gold, in. *(Christie's)* **$1,150**

A J.D. Kestner bisque googly-eyed doll, German, circa 1913, impressed *J.D.K. 221* with weighted brown sidewards glancing round eyes, watermelon smile, upwardly pointing brows, remains of short brown wig, on jointed wood and composition toddler body, 17in. *(Sotheby's)* **$4,000**

Lenci boy and girl Art dolls, Italian, 1930s, both with painted brown eyes and Lenci trademarks to feet, the boy in original orange and blue knitted cardigan with matching socks, beige felt shorts and brown leather shoes, 16¼in., the girl with long fair plaits in green wool V-neck jumper, white felt shirt with collar, beige felt skirt and brown leather shoes, 17in.
(Sotheby's) **$1,920**

▶

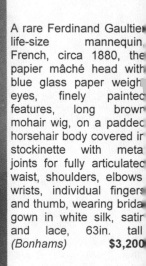

A rare Ferdinand Gaultier life-size mannequin, French, circa 1880, the papier mâché head with blue glass paper weight eyes, finely painted features, long brown mohair wig, on a padded horsehair body covered in stockinette with metal joints for fully articulated waist, shoulders, elbows, wrists, individual fingers and thumb, wearing bridal gown in white silk, satin and lace, 63in. tall
(Bonhams) **$3,200**

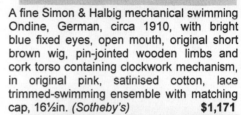

A fine Simon & Halbig mechanical swimming Ondine, German, circa 1910, with bright blue fixed eyes, open mouth, original short brown wig, pin-jointed wooden limbs and cork torso containing clockwork mechanism, in original pink, satinised cotton, lace trimmed-swimming ensemble with matching cap, 16½in. *(Sotheby's)* **$1,171**

A composition 'Kitchener' doll, English, circa 1915, with painted eyes, molded hair and mustache, on a cloth body with composition lower arms, wearing army uniform, 19in. tall.
(Bonhams) **$240**

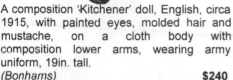

Two large Norah Wellings dolls, depicting the evil witch and Snow White, English, mid 1930s, Snow White made of felt with painted brown eyes, and painted mouth, black mohair with blue ribbon, stitched ears, label to left arm, wearing white cotton dress with blue felt trimmings, the witch with oil painted face over felt, having haggard features and black mohair wig, stitched ears with gold earrings, label to left arm, wearing red felt dress with gold buttons, black felt shawl with red lining, both 34in. *(Bonhams)* **$1,920**

A pair of Deans rag dolls, English, 1920s, the brightly printed dolls of a young boy and girl holding a doll, both 16in. tall. *(Bonhams)* **$130**

Set of four articulated paper dolls, circa 1890, each 9in. high. **$160**

A George III wooden doll dressed as a nun, English, late 18th/early 19th century, the carved wood and gesso covered face with unusual close-set pale blue enamelled eyes, the eyebrows formed from almost linked fine arcs with tiny dots above, the eyes similarly outlined, painted gesso covered lower arms and hands with carved finger nails, 19in. high.
(Sotheby's) **$6,400**

A Shirley Temple composition doll, with sleeping eyes, smiling mouth and curly blonde wig, 21in. high, marked *Shirley Temple Ideal. (Christie's)* **$597**

A rare three face doll by Carl Bergner, the laughing, sleeping and crying faces colored brown, pink and black under a card hood with jointed cloth, wood and composition body, 13in. high.
(Christie's) **$4,000**

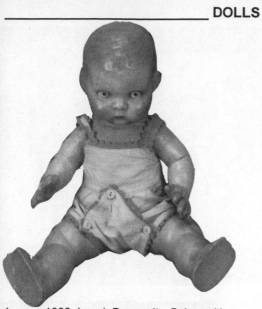

A rare 1933 Lenci Prosperity Baby, with painted cellulose head, pale blue eyes, blonde hair, closed mouth, stuffed cotton torso and stuffed, painted washable legs and arms, wearing original white cotton underwear with blue felt trim, 14½in. high. *(Christie's)* **$480**

An early Grodnerthal doll, with painted blue eyes, pink lips and black hair, carved bodice and joints at shoulders, elbows, hip, knee and waist, left leg and bottom section of right leg missing, on plexiglass stand, 18in. head to knee, circa 1810. *(Christie's)* **$880**

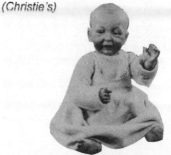

An all-bisque Kestner googlie-eyed doll, tha painted eyes glancing to the left, with closed watermelon mouth and joints at shoulder and hip, the legs with painted blue socks and black shoes, wearing contemporary cream dress, 4½in. high. *(Christie's)* **$589**

A Kämmer & Reinhardt bisque character 'Baby Kaiser', German, circa 1909, with molded blonde hair, five piece composition body in white knitted jumper and white pinafore, 15in. *(Sotheby's)* **$960**

A set of A.M. 351 'Quintuplets' Dream Baby dolls, German circa 1930, the five composition dream babies in their original cardboard box, with weighted blue glass eyes, painted hair, open mouths with two lower teeth, on bent limb composition bodies, wearing identical embroidered pink and white cotton baby gowns, each with extra pink romper suit, all 6in. tall. *(Bonhams)*   **$560**

A pair of bisque-headed baby dolls, with open/closed mouths, gray painted eyes and baby's bodies, 15in. high, impressed *36 K ✱ R 100. (Christie's)*   **$1,599**

Lenci 300 Series pressed felt boy and girl dolls, circa 1930, the molded faces with painted brown side glancing eyes, painted mouths and eyebrows, the boy wearing felt brown shorts and beige shirt, the girl felt beige pleated skirt and knitted mustard jumper, both with socks and leather shoes, both 17in. high. *(Bonhams)*   **$1,600**

A pair of all-bisque Kewpie dolls, with jointed arms, 5½in. high, impressed *O'Neil* on the feet, in original boxes.
(Christie's) **$1,317**

Series 1500 Bride and Groom Lenci dolls, Italian, circa 1930, the bride having painted brown eyes glancing to the left, painted mouth with shaded lips, blushed cheeks, blonde hair, on a stiffened body, jointed arms, legs and neck, wearing a layered white organza wedding dress with train and pink underclothes, yellow felt gloves, holding felt bouquet of flowers, veil decorated with more flowers, shoes and socks. The groom with brown painted eyes glancing to the right, painted mouth with shading, brown hair, on a stiffened body with jointed arms, legs and neck, wearing traditional top hat and tails made of felt and holding white gloves in right hand, white felt flower to left button hole, leatherette shoes and socks, both 17½in. tall. *(Bonhams)* **$4,000**

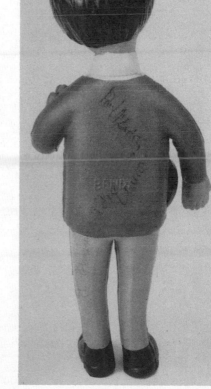

▶

The Beatles, a foam Bendy doll circa 1964, modelled as a Beatle, signed on the back in black ballpoint pen by Paul McCartney and John Lennon, on the back of the left leg in blue ballpoint pen by George Harrison and on the side of the right leg by Ringo Starr, 10½in. high. *(Christie's)* **$1,745**

Victorian turned wood crumpet pricker with steel spikes. *(Lyle)* **$16**

Peter Behrens for the Allgemeine Berliner Elektrizitäts Gesellschaft AEG, Fan 'GB 1', circa 1912, dark green painted iron, brass original metal label marked *Type GB 1* and other technical details, 29cm.
(Sotheby's) **$2,162**

Decorative painted cast iron tobacco cutter, one of the famous Long Nose style with a elf thumbing his nose.
(Auction Team Köln) **$120**

A pair of tinned sheet metal cookie cutters, Pennsylvania, 19th century, comprising a man wearing a hat and a woman in a dress, 5½in. high. *(Christie's)* **$400**

A Victorian japanned metal footbath modelled as a boot, the ocher ground decorated with brown chequer banding 16¼in. high. *(Christie's)* **$64**

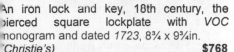

An iron lock and key, 18th century, the pierced square lockplate with *VOC* monogram and dated *1723*, 8¾ x 9¾in.

(Christie's) **$768**

An oak drizzling machine, late 18th century, the rectangular box fitted with three spikes and a pierced board to the interior, the cover with turned finial, 10½in. wide.

Drizzling machines were used in France in the 18th century and, later in England during the early 19th century to recover gold and silver used in elaborate lace work. The procedure shredded the embellished material, with the heavier particles of precious metals falling into a collecting tray below.

(Christie's) **$1,120**

Peter Behrens for the Allgemeine Berliner Elektrizitäts Gesellschaft AEG, electric tea kettle and cover, designed 1908, manufactured circa 1908, nickel-plated brass, of octagonal section, decorated with beading, on round base, wicker-covered handle, black painted wooden finial the underside marked *AEG*, numbered *42412* and *20*, 20cm.

(Sotheby's) **$901**

Unusual mechanical pin catcher, 19th century, turning a knurled knob activates a yellow bird to fetch a pin out of a red velvet covered box, 6in. wide.

(Eldred's) **$220**

A very unusual and early set of personal scales, undocumented, cast iron spring balance with enamel dial, for weights up to 280 lbs., with patent details in the cast base, in full working order, circa 1860. *(Auction Team Köln)* **$173**

A large Victorian green japanned cast ar sheet iron coffee grinder, by Bartlett Bristol, with ornate pierced and scrollin base, 26in. high. *(Christie's)* **$80**

An American Reading Apple Parer, cast iron, with table clamp, 21 x 30 x 18cm., 1878. *(Auction Team Köln)* **$234**

A brass tinder box, 18th century, th cylindrical case with domed ends, with chai suspension loop, 4in. long. *(Christie's)* **$54**

British made alloy juice extractor 'Instant No. 1'. *(Lyle)* **$16**

Plated tin tongue press, circa 1900. *(Lyle)* **$40**

Set of four large dolly pegs. *(Lyle)* **$16**

'Alberto's Kettle', an aluminum, steel and blue painted kettle, by Ron Arad, the cut and angled form with curved spout and arched strap handle, 21cm. high. *(Christie's)* **$1,024**

Late 19th century plated tin milk can, ½ gallon. *(Lyle)* **$32**

secret dual key, the bow unscrewing from the shank to reveal an inner shank with folding bit of different pattern, 6in. long, probably early 19th century. *(Christie's)* **$470**

Juice-O-Mat, tilt-top juicer by Rival Mfg. Co., Kansas City, Mo, cast aluminum and chrome plate, with an advanced tilt mechanism. *(Bonhams)* **$201**

Arne Jacobsen; Denmark, a pair of nickel plated metal door handles, designed 1957, each handle of tapering elliptical form. *(Christie's)* **$82**

A gilt bronze door knocker, an Art Nouveau gilt bronze appliqué, cast from a model by Max Blondat, in the form of a naked young woman seated on a door handle, peering through the keyhole, the lock plate in the form of a woman's head with flowing tresses, signed in the bronze, stamped foundry mark *Siot-Paris*, 33.2cm. *(Christie's)* **$6,400**

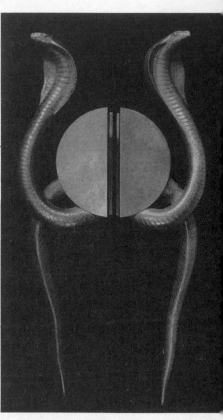

A bronze door handle and lock plate, designed by Henry Van De Velde, 1904, the handles of sculptural organic form, 8¾in. high. *(Christie's)* **$2,318**

Edgar Brandt pair of massive serpent door handles, circa 1925, brown patinated bronze, the bodies decorated with a pattern of scales and twisted into a loop, mounted on semi-circular holders, 36¼in. wide, each stamped *E. Brandt*, the mounts faintly marked *Pull* on either side. *(Sotheby's)* **$16,000**

var Aalto, a birch plywood door, designed
ca 1929-32, specifically for use in a
tient's room of the Paimio Sanatorium, the
ctangular frame with birch-faced plywood
nels, the reverse white painted, with metal
ndle to both sides, and chromed metal
tient's identity bracket to front, 81in. high.
hristie's) **$1,083**

A pair of Moorish polychrome decorated
doors, 19th century, each decorated with
floral tendril design, the lower panels fitted
with an ogee arched panelled door between
decorated uprights with a multi-panel
decorated to the reverse, each 130¼in. high
x 27½in. wide. *(Christie's)* **$2,370**

◄

Two pairs of cast steel doors, designed by
Raymond Subes, circa 1955, decorated with
formalized cartouches each enclosing the
monogram *SF*, each door approximately
33½in. wide x 81¼in. high. These doors
originally opened on to the Salle du Conseil
of the Chambre Syndicale de la Sidérurgie
Française. They form part of the
commission by Subes and André Arbus,
amongst others, to redecorate 5, rue de
Madrid in the early 1950s.
(Christie's) **$6,400**

A pair of Italianate carved oak and ▶
polychrome decorated doors, 19th century,
each with geometric molded upper and
lower panels centered by a cherub mask
and with a central panel depicting a
seahorse and acanthus leaves, with iron
handles and locks, 81½in. high.
(Christie's) **$2,900**

A jailhouse cell door, the rectangular panel
with a central iron bordered aperture, carved
with script *1638 HT I was compleat in length
and height the 22th of December here was I
set I well remember Tho..s C Rimer a place
of care,* 59 x 26in.
(Christie's) **$1,600**

▶

The front doors of the English gun-maker
Thomas Bland and Sons, probably 1890
through 1920. The large walnut panel doors
bear the large double glass panels with the
gilt lettering of *T. Bland/and/Sons,* each door
noting to *H.M. War/Department* and to *H.M.
Indian Government* in turn.
(Christie's) **$3,450**

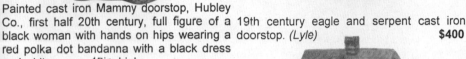

Painted cast iron Mammy doorstop, Hubley Co., first half 20th century, full figure of a black woman with hands on hips wearing a red polka dot bandanna with a black dress and white apron, 12in. high.
(Skinner) **$1,265**

19th century eagle and serpent cast iron doorstop. *(Lyle)* **$400**

Farmhouse doorstop cast in the half round and colored, 20 x 14cm.
(Auction Team Köln) **$160**

A polychrome cast iron door stop, late 19th/early 20th century, the splayed base cast as twin dolphins below the part fluted and foliate upright, 29in. high.
(Christie's) **$960**

Late 19th century cast iron Mr Punch doorstop. *(Lyle)* **$160**

A painted eagle tricycle, American, 20th century, the tricycle-form with eagle's-head above a single front wheel and extended wings as steering arms joining a plank seat over two rear wheels, 19in. high, 39in. deep. *(Christie's)* **$3,500**

A pair of polychrome carved wood models of eagles, 20th century, each shown standing on a naturalistic plinth holding down a serpent with a claw, 49in. high. *(Christie's)* **$6,400**

A carved and painted wooden eagle, Pennsylvania, late 19th century, the full-bodied figure with carved and articulated head, breast, wings, tail and feet standing on a demi-orb, 14in. high, 17in. wide.
(Christie's) **$4,000**

A carved painted pine and gesso American eagle, Wilhelm Schimmel, Cumberland Valley, Pennsylvania, circa 1880, the standing figure of a spread-winged American eagle with outstretched lappet-carved wings dovetailed into the body, painted with yellow and black markings on a dark brown ground, 6½in. high.
(Sotheby's) **$17,250**

A carved and painted pine American eagle wall plaque, American, third quarter 19th century, carved in the half round, the figure of an American eagle with talons grasping thirteen arrows and an olive branch, a shield-shaped breast plate and a banner inscribed *E Pluribus Unum* in its beak, 36½ x 31½in. *(Sotheby's)* **$21,850**

A carved and painted figure of an eagle, attributed to Wilhelm Schimmel (1817-1890), the maroon and black painted spread-winged perched eagle with yellow-painted claws, the body carved with cross hatches and articulated feathered wings, 16in. high. *(Christie's)* **$30,000**

A carved and painted pine American eagle, probably New England, 19th century, the stylized rotund figure of an eagle with upraised wings painted with speckled feathers in green and black, red and brown on a cream ground, the figure mounted on a wood stand, 10¼in. high.
(Sotheby's) **$5,175**

A fine carved and painted pine American eagle, late 19th/early 20th century, finely carved, the full-bodied life-size eagle with raised wings on a rockwork base mounted with gold and silver metal medals one inscribed *US Customs Treasury Department Past President,* overall height 56in.
(Sotheby's) **$10,925**

◄

A large and impressive carved oak eagle lectern, English, 18th century, the slope supported by the figure of an eagle with displayed wings and detailed plumage shown perched upon an orb with cylindrical column support, on a molded domed base with cruciform base, 83in. high
(Christie's) **$24,000**

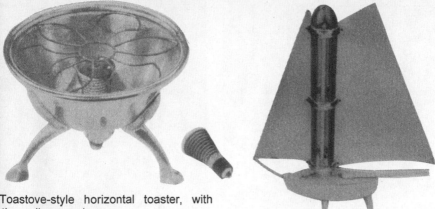

Toastove-style horizontal toaster, with
ating coil, unused.
uction Team Köln) **$78**

A Punning designer heating lamp, electric
heater in the form of a yacht, the two
chromed tin sails serving as heat reflectors,
circa 1930.
(Auction Team Köln) **$295**

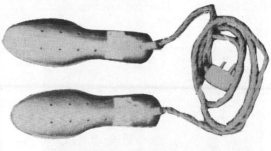

Pair of 1950s electric shoe warmers with
original wire. *(Lyle)* **$16**

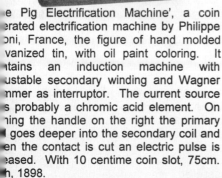

e Pig Electrification Machine', a coin
erated electrification machine by Philippe
oni, France, the figure of hand molded
vanized tin, with oil paint coloring. It
itains an induction machine with
ustable secondary winding and Wagner
nmer as interruptor. The current source
s probably a chromic acid element. On
ling the handle on the right the primary
goes deeper into the secondary coil and
en the contact is cut an electric pulse is
ased. With 10 centime coin slot, 75cm.
h, 1898.
ıction Team Köln) **$10,034**

Aluminium and metal butterfly electric fire,
1930s. *(Muir Hewitt* **$320**

Antoine-Louis Barye, French, 1795-1875, Eléphant du Sénégal Chargeant, (A running elephant), signed *Barye*, inscribed *F.Barbedienne* and incised underneath *42*, bronze, dark brown patina, 7 x 9.5cm. *(Sotheby's)* **$6,198**

An important silver-plate mounted, etche and cut-glass tantalus, circa 1880, Baccarat, the frosted glass elepha surmounted by a draped cupola with hinged compartment fitted with four etche glass stoppered bottles in a removab stand and cast with pierced foliate scroll and applied with cartouches with reli depicting a seated Indian god ov enamelled panels, the elephant in f headdress, the saddle hung with ropes wi cordial cup hooks over a chamfere 'diamond' cut plinth on a stylized gadroone molded base on bracket feet, 24¾in. hig This whimsical elephant liquor cabinet wa first exhibited in the Glass Pavilion at th 1878 Exposition Universelle in Par *(Christie's)* **$68,5(**

◄

A late Ming blue and white elephant ken Wanli, the elephant-head spout applied w two small tusks and a trunk, the ba supporting a long narrow spout, painted w rockwork issuing flowering branches, t body painted with a saddlecloth a tasselled harness, 8¾in. high. *(Christie's)* **$2,2(**

156

A German group of three warriors and a blackamoor on an elephant, Meissen, late 19th century, blue crossed swords mark, impressed *163* and incised *15*, the animal wearing a 'jewelled' and tasselled purple saddle-cloth and a howdah in the form of a turret, the warriors defending their position with weapons and a rock, the blackamoor holding a bow and arrow, 15¼in. high. *(Christie's)* **$6,000**

Shibayama-style box and cover modelled a bijin seated on a caparisoned elephant, eiji Period, 19th century, the elephant jewelled in ivory and various colored ays on a rich kinji ground with the head- ess and strapwork in silver, the ddlecloth decorated with ho-o birds facing ch other in gold hiramakie, nashiji, gyobu d kirikane on a red ground with an outline aogai, the cover modelled as a seated in similarly decorated, gently holding an ory and silver fan in front of her chest, her ht knee raised while her leg hangs along e saddlecloth, 22cm. long.

The elephant and rider, sometimes stakenly identified as the bodhisattva gen but in reality more often a female ure inspired by the designs of Utamaro d other ukiyoe artists, is a common bject in later Shibayama work. *hristie's)* **$46,368**

▶

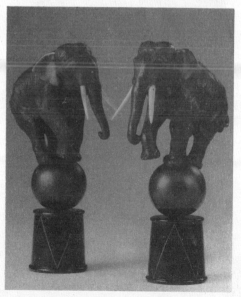

pair of Japanese Meiji bronze models of cus elephants, late 19th or early 20th ntury, each with ivory tusks, shown nding on a sphere above a colored ering plinth, 28.2cm. high. *hristie's)* **$3,540**

A cast iron silhouette of an elephant, signed *King Amusement Company*, American 20th century, the silhouetted figure of an elephant with details in bas relief, painted silver gray, 16¼in. high. x 23in. long.
(Sotheby's) **$690**

An Indian gold-painted compositio elephant, decorated overall with glass bead and brocade carrying a raised howdah wit fabric cushion and with feather head-dress 41in. high. *(Christie's)* **$3,50**

A Chinese cloisonné censer and cove modelled as a recumbent elephan decorated with archaic style animals ar foliage on a turquoise ground, 9½i long, 19th century. *(Christie's)* **$50**

Royal Doulton figure group Princess Badoura, HN3921, designed by H. Tittensor, H. Stanton and F Van Allen Phillips, 20in. high. *(Lyle)* **$21,200**

Large late 19th century Japanese bronze jardinière, modelled in the form of a group of elephants, 16in. high with signature panel to base. *(Lawrences)* **$1,920** ▶

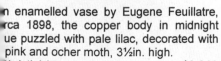

n enamelled vase by Eugene Feuillatre,
rca 1898, the copper body in midnight
ue puzzled with pale lilac, decorated with
pink and ocher moth, 3½in. high.
Christie's) **$3,312**

An ormolu-mounted enamel rectangular
casket, the cover painted with a
Watteauesque view of ladies singing and
playing the lute, signed *L. Cattentz*, 12½in.
wide. *(Christie's)* **$2,700**

pair of cloisonné enamel ducks, each
:anding on bronze legs with webbed feet
cised with naturalistic detail, Jiaqing,
1cm. high. *(Christie's)* **$7,084**
►

silver gilt and enamel three masted ship, decorated with pearls and semi precious
ones, gifted to Admiral Horty, German administrator in Hungary, 44cm. high, 1920s,
ight 3500gm. *(Kunsthaus am Museum)* **$12,800**

Europa and the Bull, 1925, porcelain, modelled as a semi-naked woman in a turban stretched along the back of a bull reaching down to pat its neck, on an oval base scattered with stylized gilt flowers, heightened with gilding, base marked *Nacke*, the underside with factory mark *Fraureuth Kunstabteilung*, 13in. high. x 19¼in. *(Sotheby's)*   **$4,80⬤**

A Goldscheider patinated terracotta figure group modelled as Europa and the Bull, stamped factory marks, 71.5cm. high. *(Christie's)*   **$2,208**

Europa and the Bull, 1920s, brown and black patinated bronze, cast as a large standing bull with a naked female figure seated side-saddle on a drape on his back on a rectangular base set on a rectangular section mottled red marble slab, the base marked *Ant. Grath* and *Europa*, 19in. high. *(Sotheby's)*   **$5,00⬤**

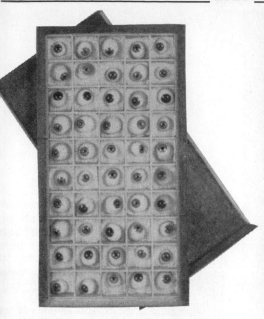

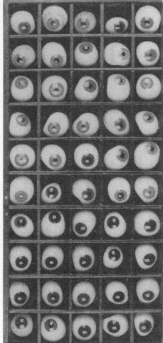

A collection of nInety finely modelled glass eyes, of various colors including blue-gray, brown, green and other tints, contained in two cases with compartments and padding to protect each eye, the cases 36.5cm. wide, with sliding covers.
(Christie's)   **$1,375**

A case of fifty artificial eyes, English, late 19th century, the naturalistic glass eyes in various shades of blue and brown contained in a leather case divided into fifty compartments, 32.5cm. wide.
(Bonhams)   **$480**

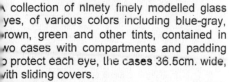

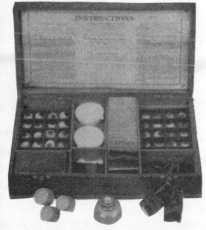

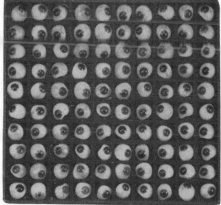

A fine optician's set of ceramic and glass artificial eyes, by Bruneau & Dr. Charpentier 28 rue Vignon Paris, comprising four trays of twenty artificial eyes, in fitted teak case, 16½in. (Christie's)   **$3,280**

A comprehensive collection of glass eyes, of various colors, contained in one square and four rectangular fitted cases with leatherette covers, each 13¼in. wide.
(Christie's)   **$2,950**

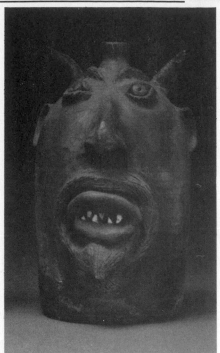

A green-glazed grotesque jug, American, 20th century, the bulbous form with applied strap-handles above applied articulated ears flanking a human face, 16in. high. *(Christie's)* **$1,150**

A large Redware figural devil jug, probably Robert Brown, Arden, Buncombe County, North Carolina, 1960-1970, baluster form, with a strap handle, the body decorated with a devil's face with protruding horns, 13½in. high. *(Christie's)* **$3,000**

A glazed redware grotesque jug, H.F. Rhinhardt, Vale, North Carolina, late 19th/early 20th century, squat form with applied facial features, 7¼in. high. *(Skinner)* **$1,400**

A glazed earthenware votive figure, Easter Alabama, 19th century, molded in the form of a man with brimmed hat and hollow eye above a body with clasped hands, all glaze with iron oxide, 16½in. high. *(Christie's)* **$18,00**

A glazed stoneware face mug, Edgefield, South Carolina, 1862-1865, tapering cylindrical with applied and molded facial features, all covered in olive glaze, the eyes and teeth covered with kaolin, 4¼in. high. *(Christie's)* **$4,000**

A small glazed earthenware figural vessel, Edgefield, South Carolina, 19th century, the everted rim above the top spout over a swelled head with applied facial features above a swelled body, all covered in olive glaze, 5½in. high. *(Christie's)* **$5,000**

A glazed Redware face vessel, Southern States, probably 19th century, baluster form, with applied top strap handle and rear facing spout above a body embellished with applied ears, nose, and mouth, 8¾in. high. *Christie's)* **$1,200**

A glazed earthenware figural jug, possibly Alabama, 19th century, the olive-glazed form with domed wide brimmed hat centering a spout above a human laughing face set over a cylindrical body with applied arms terminating in clasped hands, on a conforming base, 12in. high. *(Christie's)* **$15,000**

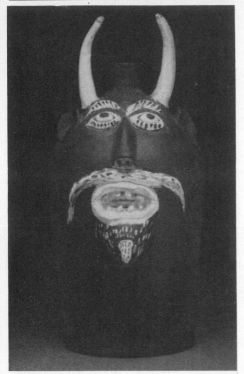

Brown salt glazed stoneware sculptured jug, probably Missouri or Ohio, circa 1860-70, the jug with a lizard or salamander applied handle above the sculptured face of a man, his features in high relief with coleslaw eyebrows, moustache and beard, the jug with pouring mouth and air intake, 9¾in. *(Skinner)* **$26,450**

A large polychrome-decorated devil jug possibly Javan Brown, Arden, Bunscombe County, North Carolina, circa 1930, the cylindrical black form with conforming neck and sloping shoulders mounted by white horns above black ears and centring on one side stylized facial features including white eyes, eyebrows and moustache with black line detail, red-decorated nostrils, white lips and teeth and a black beard in relief with white line details, 23¼in. high.
(Christie's) **$3,000**

▶

A salt-glazed and cobalt-decorated stoneware double-faced jug, attributed to Richard Clinton Remmey (working 1859-1880), Philadelphia, late 19th century, baluster form with applied handle flanked by two spouts above two devil faces with applied ears, and facial features, broken and repaired, 7in. high.*(Christie's)* **$7,000**

If you had gone to a travelling fair in the 1860s and had proved your prowess on the hoopla stall, chances are that you would have returned home the proud owner of a small china figure bearing a humorous and probably slightly risqué legend on the base. These are referred to nowadays as 'Fairings'.

Most are about 4in. high and stand on rectangular bases measuring 2in. by 3in. Subjects include themes like courtship, marriage, politics, war, childhood and animals behaving as people.

With something so typically English as fairings, it comes as a surprise to learn that most were made in Germany, the main manufacturer being Conte and Boehme of Possneck.

A fairing entitled 'An awkward Interruption'.
(Bonhams) **$192**

A very rare fairing, 'Two Different Views', audaciously bordering on the unseemly.
(Lyle) **$1,200**

Rare German porcelain fairing 'Cancan'.
(Lyle) **$800**

A rare German porcelain fairing 'Hit Him Hard', a standing figure of a gentleman in top hat about to beat a boy, 4½in. high.
(Canterbury) **$864**

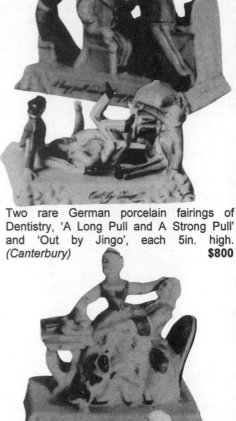

German porcelain fairing 'Let us do business together'. *(Lyle)* **$120**

Two rare German porcelain fairings of Dentistry, 'A Long Pull and A Strong Pull' and 'Out by Jingo', each 5in. high. *(Canterbury)* **$800**

A fairing entitled *That's funny, very funny! very, very funny*, no 340. *(Bonhams)* **$145**

Rare German porcelain fairing 'Taking Dessert'. *(Lyle)* **$800**

A rare pair of German porcelain fairings 'Before' and 'After'. *(Lyle)* **$960** eltwork was another drawing room ccomplishment for Victorian ladies with ne on their hands. It involved taking small eces of felt and cutting them up to make etals, leaves or whatever. These would en be stuck onto a background to form an tractive relief picture.

Childrens' Fuzzy Felt toys are to me degree the descendants of this adition, but the art is by no means dead, nd kits are still available in craft shops.

An early Victorian feltwork picture, depicting a basket of strawberries, in a giltwood and glazed shadow box, 13¾ x 11¼in. overall. *(Christie's)* **$800**

rare felt-covered Flip the Frog with ean's Rag Book Co. Ltd., logo on one ot, *Made in England* on the other, 8in. gh. *(Christie's)* **$669**

Victorian feltwork panel, modelled with a ral basket, in an oval glazed giltwood me, 16¼in. high. *hristie's)* **$640**

A two dimensional display, 19th century, modelled as a floral basket, in a later associated glazed and painted wood shadow box, 16¼ x 12in. overall. *(Christie's)* **$640**

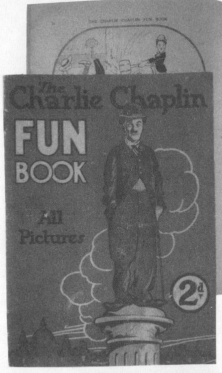

The Charlie Chaplin Fun Book, 1915, firs
Chaplin book. *(Lyle)* **$24**

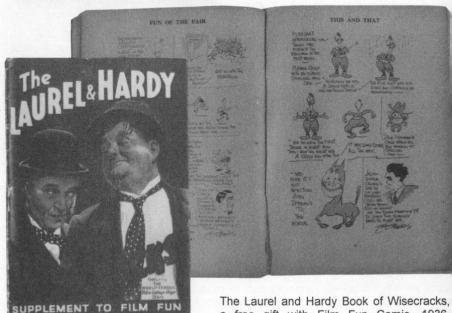

The Laurel and Hardy Book of Wisecracks,
a free gift with Film Fun Comic, 1936.
(Lyle) **$480**

Girls' Cinema No. 212, November 1, 1924. *(Lyle)* **$55**

Film Fiction, from the month's best pictures, August 1921, No.1. *(Lyle)* **$120**

Picture Plays, featuring Miss Alma Taylor, November 15th 1919, No.1. *(Lyle)* **$120**

Film Pictorial, with free Star Portrait Album, February 27th 1932, No.1. *(Lyle)* **$120**

Picturegoer Weekly, featuring Marlene Dietrich, May 30th 1931, No.1
(Lyle) $9

The Picture Show, For people who go to the pictures, with free art plate of Mary Pickford, May 3rd 1919, No.1.
(Lyle) $9

A Dutch brass coal scuttle, late 19th century, of barrel shape, the hinged cover to the end embossed with flowers, raised on lion paw feet, below the baluster turned handle to the top, 16½in. high. *(Christie's)* **$528**

'Les Roses', a wrought iron firescreen, designed by Edgar Brandt, circa 1927, rectangular form, circular central panel decorated with roses and leaves, within scrolls, leaves and berries and bordered with stylized foliate motifs, 33½ x 44in. *(Christie's)* **$31,280**

A pair of Charles X ebonized wood and ormolu mounted fire bellows, the mounts pierced and cast with Gothic tracery, with a stained wood stand, of tapering fluted form, on a rectangular molded plinth, 14½in. long. *(Christie's)* **$827**

A late Regency or William IV japanned metal and cast iron purdonium, circa 1830, of rectangular form, with rounded underside, the black ground heightened in gilt with foliate border to the hinged cover, ring handles to the sides, the X frame supports to the ends cast with stylized panther head terminals on stylized paw feet, 18½in. wide. *(Christie's)* **$1,472**

19th century American carved wood and metal fishing decoy in the form of a brown painted tadpole with small sheet metal fins, 6in. long. *(Christie's)* **$500**

Early 20th century American carved and painted decoy in the form of a dragonfly, 7½in. wide. *(Christie's)* **$500**

A very rare Gregory brass flexible jointed 'Cleopatra' bait, circa 1890, stamped *Gregory* to fin, 3¾in.
(Bonhams) **$3,586**

Late 19th century American painted wood and metal decoy in the form of a turtle with a black painted head and tail, a red painted and articulated shell, on black painted legs, 3in. wide. *(Christie's)* **$1,000**

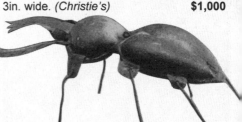

American 20th century carved and painted decoy in the form of a beetle, 11½in. long. *(Christie's)* **$700**

An American blue painted mouse fishing decoy with small sheet metal fins and a leather tail, 20th century, 7in. long. *(Christie's)* **$600**

American late 19th century painted wood and metal figural decoy in the form of a full bodied jumping frog with green painted body decorated with beige, yellow and black spots, its legs extended and body flanked by similarly painted tin fins, 9in. long. *(Christie's)* **$700**

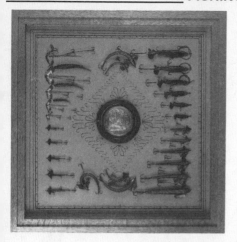

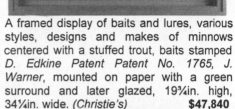

A framed display of baits and lures, various styles, designs and makes of minnows centered with a stuffed trout, baits stamped *D. Edkine Patent Patent No. 1765, J. Warner*, mounted on paper with a green surround and later glazed, 19¾in. high, 34¼in. wide. *(Christie's)* **$47,840**

A framed display of artificial baits, centered with a gilt medal inscribed *Dissociata Logis Concordi Pace Ligavit, Leonard G. Wyon, Des & Sc* and *Royal Mint, London*, surrounded by fishing line, an arrangement of graduated hooks and various baits, some stamped *W.B. & S., Patent Sepentanic ine* others *Archer, Patent*, paper mount and later glazed, 21½in. high, 22in. wide. *(Christie's)* **$11,040**

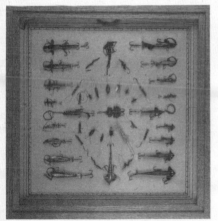

19th century blue brown and yellow painted and faux scaled fish decoy with tripartite metal lure and glass eyes, 9in. long. *(Christie's)* **$400**

A framed display of artificial baits, centered with a frog lure and surrounded by an arrangement of bugs and minnows of differing styles and designs, some with *Patent* stamped and one inscribed *Geens Patent 2102*, mounted on paper and later glazed, 21¼in.high, 22in. wide. *(Christie's)* **$36,800**

A framed display of baits and lures, represented as insects, frogs, prawns etc., arranged around a central stuffed fish, mounted on paper with a green surround and later glazed, 19¾in. high, 33¼in. wide. *(Christie's)* **$29,440**

A galvanised live-bait can, with removable perforated interior container, perforated lid and folding handle, circa 1900, 10 x 7in. *(Lyle)* **$65**

A 'Hardy Zane Grey' sea spinning reel, 4¼in. in a fitted leather case with implements. *(Bearne's)* **$3,245**

A treen pocket line winder and tackle container, the central cylindrical section with four compartments and six winding arms around, 6in. high. *(Christie's)* **$342**

An American U-shaped halibut hook, with a bone bard, tied and bound with rush and a gut line, 6½in. long. *(Christie's)* **$643**

A pair of Victorian embossed card pictures displaying a day's catch of game fish o one; and coarse fish on the other, both tie to hooks with grasses. *(Christie's)* **$3,50**

A Dutch brass carriage or foot warmer, possibly late 17th or early 18th century, of octagonal form, with pierced cover and embossed sides, the doors with rolled rivets, with loop handle, 8¼in. wide. *(Christie's)* **$638**

Antique American foot warmer, in poplar, pierced heart motif on obverse with *1834* inside, reverse with pierced heart motif and initials *CA Z*, pierced ends with star motif, original tin burner, 6½in. high x 10in. long. *(Eldred's)* **$440**

Glazed Redware ram-form footwarmer, 19th century, 6¾in. high x 13½in. long. *(Skinner)* **$517**

A rare green and yellow-glazed handwarmer, early Tang Dynasty, 1st half 7th century, of domed shape, incised bands to the sides and three equally-spaced groups of three vertical slits below the shallow domed top with circular aperture, 2¾in. high. This shape is among the rarest of Tang dynasty vessels. *(Christie's)* **$7,475**

A brass handwarmer of circular form, pierced and incised with foliate decoration, the internal reservoir on gimbal support, late 18th/early 19th century, 6in. diameter. *(Hy. Duke & Son)* **$494**

175

A large stone figure of a frog, 20th century, 21in. high. *(Sotheby's)* **$3,162**

18ct. yellow gold, emerald and diamond frog pin, pavé-set emeralds and diamonds with cabochon-cut ruby eyes, signed *Fride Virgilio. (Skinner)* **$5,500**

Papier-mâché frog, circa 1900, painted green with wide open mouth, cigar in right hand and left hand on belly. *(Eldred's)* **$330**

Continental Siberian jade, silver, and enamel frog and pedestal ornament, with engine-turned enamel decoration and foliate cast mounts, 6¾in. high. *(Skinner)* **$1,380**

A late-nineteenth century wooden novelty snuff box, unmarked, modelled as a frog, textured body, glass eyes, hinged base *(Bonhams)* **$76**

A South East Asian red-lacquered howdah, the rectangular seat with flowerhead carved and bobbin supported gallery with turned finials, on spreading supports with a caned sub structure, 63in. wide.
(Christie's) **$800**

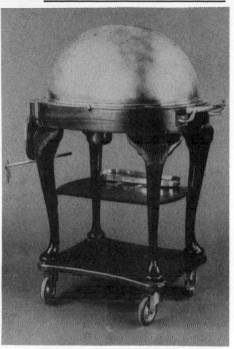

An electroplated meat wagon, oval form, the revolving hinged cover opens to reveal a lift out warming section, above two spirit burners, also with a pulling/pushing handle, a plate holder, and a tray, supported by four cabriole legs, the whole on four wheels.
(Bonhams) **$3,200**

A birch dentist cabinet, early 20th century, the raised top with a pair of cupboard doors above an open section with three banks of six graduated short drawers above two further deep drawers and a further panelled cupboard door modelled as a pair of drawers, with a shaped apron, on block feet, Waring & Gillow Ltd. London.
(Christie's) **$480**

An Art Deco sycamore cocktail cabinet, with a pair of carved cupboard doors, of stylized shell form, enclosing mirrored interior, 54in. wide. (Christie's) **$3,152**

Phipps & Wynne custom-made dry sink, with painted shorebird decoration, 32in. high. *(Eldred's)* **$385**

A large mahogany cheval linen airer, George IV, circa 1825, the two turned and graduated tiers with tapered rectangular supports joined by a turned stretcher on a pair of plinths with lotus lappets and bun feet, 183cm. wide. *(Sotheby's)* **$3,673**

A carved bamboo, oak, and bronze revolving bookcase, Japanese, circa 1900 with a central rectangular pilaster supporting six shelves surmounted by a carved eagle finial, each shelf divided by circular dowel and carved and dyed rectangular panel with bamboo frames variously decorated with landscapes, cranes, courtly figures and demons, flanked by four bamboo pole variously carved with a dragon, and with birds and monkeys in trees, attached to the shelves by fierce bronze dragons, raised on four scrolled acanthus-carved legs ending dragon's heads and feet, on four further square feet, 252.5cm. high. *(Sotheby's)* **$46,00**

A chromed tubular steel and painted wood cradle, Dutch, circa 1930, the blue painted, wood cradle with arched panel to one end, in chromed tubular steel frame, the top-rail composed of three slender metal tubes to allow draping of veil, 40in. wide. (Christie's) **$992**

An amusing Scandinavian cabinet on stand, designed by Osten Kristiannson, in oak, modelled as an army officer, his flies opening to reveal a mechanical curiosity, 169cm. high. (Phillips) **$6,548**

non, Austrian, dining room table and eight chairs, circa 1910, the chairs veneered with ebonized and honey colored wood in a zebra pattern, the table similarly veneered in checker pattern, the chairs re-upholstered with black leather, the table with glass top. (Sotheby's) **$17,940**

A set of twenty 19th-century carpet bowls comprising four large and five smaller with cross hatch decoration and four large and six smaller with sponge ware decoration and a large jack.
(Phillips) **$2,320**

Cast iron painted arcade shooting gallery, America, early 20th century, the four horizontal rails each with eight bird targets, painted black, green, yellow, orange, and red, 51½in. high. Purportedly from Coney Island, New York. *(Skinner)* **$2,530**

The game of 'Toupe Royale', a French style table-top game of Skittles with a spinning top, the gilt brass gallery with leaf finials enclosing playing surface with five figures of a jester and four other attendants, each astride two columns, within outer gallery and on turned legs, 67 x 32 x 35in. high. *(Canterbury)* **$2,970**

A rare 'Toad in the hole' pubgame, English, probably 1920s, of pine construction, the playing field with cast iron molded toad, two arches, spinner, and eleven scoring holes, 32in. high. *(Bonhams)* **$960**

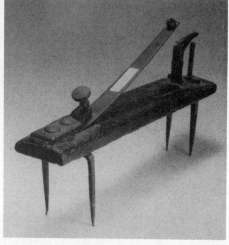

ate Victorian mahogany roulette table, 19th century, by Shoolbred & Co., the ed leather top with patented hinged chanism and concertina legs, with brass es inscribed *THE IDEAL, PATENTED IN EAT BRITAIN, IN OTHER COUNTRIES, ANDS PATENT NO.5316,* the baize lined ior with inset roulette wheel, with frieze wer, on tapering square section legs with ss castors, 31¼in. high.

ristie's) **$5,600**

usical game by Ann Young, early 19th tury, the mahogany and satinwood ssbanded oooo opening to reveal the two s of the playing board overlaid with er printed with staves, keyboards, key atures etc., pierced with numerous es, the base with central lidded partition taining space for dice shakers and ring printed label: *By His Majesty's Royal ers Patent/The Newly Invented/Musical ne/Dedicated by Permission to Her al Highness/Princess Charlotte of 'es,* the sides with two small drawers taining ebony and ivory discs, pegs, dice turned wood cylindrical boxes taining ivory counters, length 1ft.5¼in.

Princess Charlotte was the cousin of abeth Fitzclarence, the natural daughter William IV, who married William-George, Earl of Erroll in 1820.

heby's) **$3,073**

A knurr and spell ball launcher, English, nineteenth century, the oak rectangular launcher supported by four tapering iron feet, mounted by a spring loaded iron mechanism with release catch for launching a ball, 26in. long.

The ancient game of Knurr and Spell has been played in Northumberland, Yorkshire and other northern counties from as early as the twelfth century. It is a game of distance, with each competitor attempting to strike the knurr, the hard ball used in the game, as far as possible by means of a wooden spell.

The spring loaded launchers were of superior quality and cost to many similar devices used in the game at this period. Others relied on a simple see-saw motion to launch the ball.

(Sotheby's) **$861**

A Victorian cast iron bench with 'dragon' ends. *(G.E. Sworder & Sons)* **$2,888**

Pair of painted cast iron figural gard posts, the two-part casting forms bro painted tree trunks with bark and limb sc entwined with red grapes, green foliage a vines, cut-outs and holes for cross piec 41in. high. *(Skinner)* **$1,0**

An 'Egyptian slave girl' garden seat, probably Brown-Westhead, Moore & Co., modelled as a young woman wearing a yellow striped robe and blue sash, seated with her knees tucked up supporting her elbows, the quatrefoil seat pierced with a handle and molded with fans of leaves above an owl, its wings spread between palm leaves, perched in stylized flowers on a ground simulating snake's skin above two cobra, circa 1875, 54cm. high. *(Christie's)* **$12,800**

Late 19th century pottery garden s probably France, whimsically depicting cushion resting on a basket, 20in. h *(Skinner)* **$7**

A gilt-metal figural fountain in the form of a dolphin, the mouth plumbed for water, 18in. high. *(Sotheby's)* **$2,587**

A glazed terracotta garden seat, the low shaped back centered by a lion's mask continuing to nude female supports with paw feet. *(Sotheby's)* **$2,587**

A pair of stoneware 'rustic' garden seats, late 19th century, each as a tree stump, with branches as a back support, 44in. and 46in. high. *(Christie's)* **$2,815**

A composition bust of Pan, 20th century modelled with grotesque bearded face and horned head draped with bunches of grapes, both hands clutching a set of pipes beneath his chin, 22½in. high. *(Christie's)* **$480**

One of a pair of garden seats modelled as crouching monkeys holding coconuts and supporting cushions on their heads, 46.5cm. high. *(Christie's)* (Two) **$15,950**

A silver trompe-l'oeil vodka set, marked with unrecorded workmaster's initials *P.L,* St. Petersburg, 1895, tapering shaped rectangular, the body and twelve charki with square bases and circular rims chased and engraved to simulate bast-weave, the body with twisted rope with hooks, the frosted glass bottle with shaped cover imitating tied cloth, 8¼in. high. *(Christie's)* **$6,146**

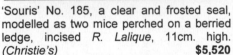

'Souris' No. 185, a clear and frosted seal, modelled as two mice perched on a berried ledge, incised *R. Lalique,* 11cm. high. *(Christie's)* **$5,520**

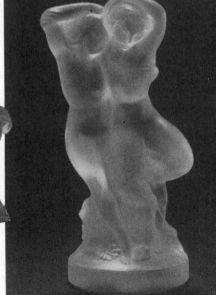

A pair of Barovier & Toso glass figures of jazz musicians, circa 1930, each seated figure in blue powders cased in clear bullicante glass, the applied heads, hands and feet in clear glass with foil inclusions, 6½in. high. *(Sotheby's)* **$2,875**

A clear and frosted figure group, modelled as naked female embracing a satyr, against floral mound, stencil *mark R. Laliqu France,* 13.5cm. high. *(Christie's)* **$48**

The Beatles, a rare set of four blown glass Christmas tree decorations, modelled as the Beatles with handpainted faces, shirts, ties, hands and feet, 6¼in. high. in original box stamped *Made in Italy*, circa 1960s.
(Christie's) **$1,486**

Rare Frederick Carder Cire Perdue sculpture head of 'Ophelia', delicate form in opaque pink-beige glass with a sculpted marble quality, three quarter view of a woman with closed eyes, signed at base *F. Carder*, 4in. high.
(Skinner) **$6,900**

A Murano glass figure of a drum major, attributed to Barovier Seguso Ferro, circa 1930s, in clear glass with applied hat, epaulets, buttons and tooled leaf in striated cobalt blue glass, 8¾in. high.
(Sotheby's) **$517**

Josef Hoffmann for J. & L. Lobmeyer, drinking glass, 1912, clear glass, 18.8cm., this glass belongs to a series of 12 which were designed in 1912 and exhibited at the Werkbund exhibition in 1914.
(Sotheby's) **$5,766**

A pair of glass horse heads, designed by Archimede Seguso, the dark blue glass covered with white fragments, Murano, Made in Italy, 16.5cm. high.
(Christie's) **$1,566**

'Calypso' No. 413 a clear and frosted bowl, molded on the underside in low relief with sea sprites, incised *Lalique France*, 35cm. diameter. *(Christie's)* **$3,200**

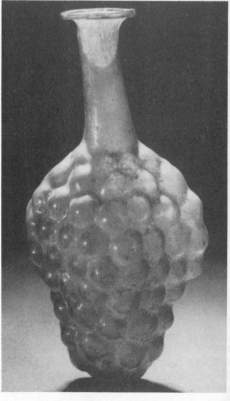

'Sauterelles' No. 888, an emerald green and white stained vase, of spherical form, molded in low relief with a design of grasshoppers amongst blades of grass, incised mark *R. Lalique France*, 27cm. high.
(Christie's) **$6,400**

▶

An amber mold-blown glass grape flask, realistically molded in the form of an asymmetrical bunch of grapes, the long slender neck with flared folded rim, the color of the glass graduating from darker to paler amber in places, 2nd half of the 2nd century A.D., 4¾in.

(Bonhams) **$10,400**

Daum post-war pâte-verre figure group by Amdrieu, loosely modelled as a schoolteacher, standing with his class, 33cm. diameter. *(Christie's)*

$1,920
▶

ges' No. 410, a clear, frosted and lescent bowl, molded on the underside low relief with a design of kneeling, ying angels, stencil mark *R. Lalique nce*, 37cm. diameter.
ristie's)

$2,880

set of three 2½ x 2in. lithophanes turing couples disporting themselves rously, complete with maker's box. *ristie's)*

$913

A Stourbridge amber triple gourd ewer, the neck applied with trailed decoration and each section with prunts, applied with bracket handle and short spout, on conical foot, late 19th century, 40cm. high. *(Christie's)*

$560

A pair of black suede gloves with shaped cuff decorated with gilt metal studs, labelled *Givenchy Paris*, the left glove signed in gold felt pen *Madonna*. *(Christie's)* **$688**

A pair of white kid gloves with deep cuffs white satin embroidered in silver thread a sequins, mid 17th century. *(Christie's)* **$4,8**

A pair of late 19th century American Woodlands Indian gauntlets of brown leather, probably Cree.
(Phillips) **$960**

A rare glove of knitted cotton, with finger tips to the index finger and thumb worked with pots of flowers at the knuck early 18th century. *(Christie's)* **$**

A pair of fingered gauntlets, late 16th/early 17th century, each with flared pointed cuff with inner plate, 11¾in.
(Sotheby's) **$6,900**

A pair of kid gloves, the ivory silk gauntl embroidered in colored silks, gilt thre and spangles, English, circa 1610.
(Christie's) **$2,5**

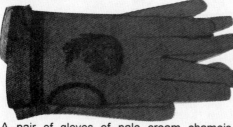

A pair of gloves of pale cream chamois leather, engraved under the thumb, *F. Bull & Co., Jan 4th 1791. (Christie's)* **$560**

A pair of north Indian embroidered rit hands, decorated with gold sequins and with ruby and diamonds with floral mo within borders of seed pearls, 6¼in. hi 19th century. *(Christie's)* **$8**

A 19th century Continental carved ivory group of a patriarchal gnome-like figure lecturing two similar squatting figures, on a rectangular base, 10cm. long.
(Bearnes) **$759**

...vo terracotta gnomes, one photographing ...e other who is holding a baby, 59cm.
...3onhams) **$1,600**

...vo terracotta gnomes with small bags, one ...odelled smoking a pipe, the other his ...nds on his sides, 64.5cm.
...onhams) **$1,600**

Cast iron doorstop, 'The Warrior', in the form of a gnome, 13½in. high.
(Eldred's) **$374**

A terracotta gnome leaning on pick axe, on hand shading his face, leaning against jardinière modelled as a tree stump, 84cm *(Bonhams)* **$960**

A Black Forest carved wood hall stand, late 19th century, modelled with a bearded figure holding aloft a branch, carved with two birds above, with a retaining rail and drip tray to the front, mounted on a raised oval plinth, 95in. high. *(Christie's)* **$12,110**

A pair of lead caricature figures, 19 century, 38in. high. *(Sotheby's)* **$6,0**

Captive golf ball with parachute attachment, circa 1905, being The Hopper. utta percha ball drilled and attached to a arachute for practice, with original tee and ox. *(Sotheby's)* **$960**

Ross's Patent 'Home' Press ball mold im press, circa 1900, in three pieces (the wer rotary arm with integral half ball old, the upper half ball mold, and the per rotary arm). *(Sotheby's)* **$1,195**

An Omnes Marker Co. Levy patent ball marker. *(Sotheby's)* **$480**

brass gutty golf ball mold for the 'Trophy' mple pattern golf ball, stamped *John White d Co., Edinburgh*, 3in. diameter. *hristie's)* **$1,489**

fine and rare gutty golf ball marker, amped *A. Patrick*, the hinged handle with ather-covered roller and enclosing two ooved metal rollers, circa 1870. *hristie's)* **$61,000**

A huge purpose made unique leather golf bag, together with a Bogey putter made by Foster Bros. Ashbourne and 17 other woods, irons and putters. *(Sotheby's)* **$557**

A silvered-wood 'Grotto' table, with a shell shaped top, on four scrolled dolphin legs joined by an undertier with four shells, the top: 35 x 23½in. *(Christie's)* **$9,200**

A carved, silvered, painted and parcel-gilt side chair, Italian, circa 1880, with a mussel shell and sea monster back, the seat in the form of a further shell, on sea horse legs. *(Sotheby's)* **$3,200**

A North Italian silvered and giltwood grotto armchair, late 19th century, the shell back and seat with dolphin arms 35in. high. *(Christie's)* **$6,440**

A North Italian silvered and giltwood grotto side table, late 19th century, the top modelled as a shell, on a naturalistic stem and tripod base entwined with a mythic sea creature, 33in. high. *(Christie's)* **$1,8**

A Hagenauer silvered metal face mask, of highly stylized smiling female, with curly hair and oval eyes, stamped marks *Franz, Hagenauer Wien*, factory monogram, 32cm. high. *(Christie's)* **$6,440**

A Hagenauer silvered metal mask, of highly stylized female with red enamel lips, holding splayed hand up to her face, on a circular base, stamped marks *Hagenauer Wien, Made in Austria,* factory monogram, 37cm. high. *(Christie's)* **$8,280**

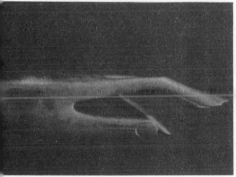

A Hagenauer silvered bronze paperweight in the form of a hand. *(Academy)* **$400**

▶

Hagenauer, oriental mask, 1930s, patinated metal and ebonized wood, cast as the stylized face of an oriental woman with sleek bobbed hair, the reverse stamped with VHW monogram, *Atelier Hagenauer Wien* and *Made in Germany*, 7¼in. *(Sotheby's)* **$3,457**

Pair of heads, 1930s, chromium-plated metal cast as a highly stylized male and female head in profile, each applied with angular features and tubular locks of hair, the female with an applied beaded necklace, on flat rectangular bases each with *WHW* monogram, *Hagenauer Wien* and *Made in Austria*, 55.5cm. (Sotheby's)

$19,200
▶

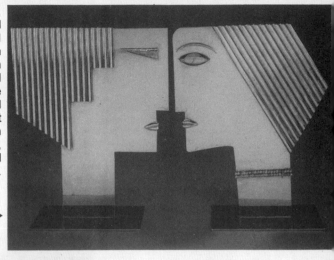

A Hagenauer brass head of a highly stylized young woman with wavy hair, elongated nose and slender cylindrical neck, stamped marks, 43cm. high. (Christie's)

$4,800

A Hagenauer wooden figure of an African warrior, wearing a necklace, kneeling with arms pressed against his body, a metal spear in one hand, 10¼in., impressed *Atelier Hagenauer Wien, Made in Vienna Austria, WHW.* (Bonhams)

$480

A lock of Wellington's hair set in a bracelet of Copenhagen's mane, Victor of Waterloo, Statesman and Politician, 1769-1852, the blondish white hair with characteristic darker flecks set in a hinged gold mount with engraved floral and foliate decoration on a plaited hair bracelet from the mane of the celebrated horse Copenhagen ridden by the Duke of Wellington at Waterloo; together with account of its sale and provenance dated 1906. *(Bonhams)* **$1,920**

Mary Queen of Scots (1542-1587), a lock of hair given by the Queen to John Hamilton of Udsden before the battle of Langside, 13 May 1568, together with a note in the hand of Lady Charlotte Campbell, *Friday November 30th 1816. Queen Mary's Hair given to me by Lord Belhaven and Stenton from out his Cabinet which said cabinet pertained also to Her Majesty. The Hair was sent to some of her adherents previous to the Battle of Langside*, the lock of fine red gold hair and the note affixed to a leaf of ivory paper, framed and glazed, a copy of the note written by Lady Russell, is included with the lot. According to a note by Lady (Constance) Russell, the lock of hair is a portion of a lock of Mary Queen of Scots' hair which came by descent to Robert, 8th Lord Belhaven and Stenton, from his ancestor, John Hamilton of Udsden. The larger portion and the cabinet in which it was kept, which had also belonged to the Queen, were presented by Lord Belhaven to Queen Victoria, and are now in the Palace of Holyrood.

The disastrous battle of Langside, fought shortly after Mary's escape from Lochleven, was observed by the Queen from a nearby hill. Many of her Hamilton supporters perished in it, and the defeat precipitated her flight to England and imprisonment. *(Christie's)* **$10,672**

A lock of Lord Nelson's hair, National Hero, Victor of Trafalgar, 1758-1805, the cutting of light brown hair with blondish strands wrapped in a sheet of paper with ink inscription *Lord Nelson's Hair*, together with a lock of the Duke of Wellington's hair, the yellowish strands with dark inclusions wrapped in a similar piece of paper titled in the same hand *The Duke of Wellington's Hair*, together with a trade card of Dimond, Hair Cutter, No. 1 Burlington Gardens, Bond Street. *(Bonhams)* **$1,920**

Two gray pottery models of a cockerel and a hen, Han Dynasty, the cock modelled standing on sturdy legs, the raised head with standing comb and short pointed beak, the long tail feathers arched, the hen modelled in a recumbent position with small head raised and long tail feathers, a brood of chicks applied to either side of her wings, 25cm. high. *(Christie's)* **$4,800**

A Chinese buff pottery model of a stick figure, the naked male figure standing facing forwards with serious expression and hair tightly pulled back, traces of black pigment remaining, 23¾in. high. Han Dynasty. *(Christie's)* **$400**

A gray pottery tricorn mythical beast, Han Dynasty, the beast heavily and powerfully modelled striding forward, the head lowered in an aggressive challenge with three pointed horns, the curled tail raised above the arched back, 13in. long. *(Christie's)* **$4,874**

A Han buff pottery model of a pot bellied drummer wearing breeches and a ha striding forwards with a comical expressio on his face, 18½in. high. *(Christie's)* **$1,28**

Cast bronze clad hands of Abraham Lincoln, each hand is inscribed *This cast of the hand of Abraham Lincoln was made from the first replica of the original made at Springfield, Ill. the Sunday following his nomination to the Presidency in 1860.* Originals by Leonard Wells Volk (American, 1828-1895), 6½in. long. *(Eldred's)* **$440**

A 19th century whale log stamp carved in the form of a clenched fist issuing from a silver studded cuff, the base with a whale carved in relief, 4½in. *(Sotheby's)* **$6,900**

A carved marble relief hand sign, American, late 19th century, the octagonal plaque carved in relief with a pointing hand with a checked cuff, 6½in. long. *(Sotheby's)* **$1,495**

A group of carved marbles, American, 19th century, comprising one marble sample stone, rectangular with four carved facades featuring a dove, a hand pointing to an open-faced book inscribed *Holy Bible*, a sleeping lamb, and two clasped hands; together with a carved marble baby's hand, inscribed at wrist *Anden;/ Austrian/ Gruppe/ 1876*, on a rectangular dark marble plinth, a man's hand, on rectangular marble plinth, marked *G. Chase*; a woman's hand, inscribed at wrist, *Ezekiel/ Rome/ 1891*, on rectangular marble plinth; and a woman's hand with bracelet and wedding rings, inscribed at wrist *1870*, on a rectangular pillow-carved plinth. *(Christie's)* **$5,520**

A straw bonnet with deep brim, trimmed later with satin with chine silk ribbon and artificial flowers, circa 1830.
(Christie's) **$480**

A gentleman's linen nightcap, embroidered in colored silks, gilt and silver gilt threads, with a repeating pattern of Tudor roses and pansies, English, circa 1600.
(Christie's) **$27,599**

A top hat of gray beaver, possibly 1829, labelled *M. Strieken*, 8in. high.
(Lyle) **$1,280**

A bonnet of black satin trimmed with a large bow and rouleaux, circa 1830.
(Christie's) **$520**

A child's or young lady's hat of ivory silk quilted with a scale design and trimmed with a rosette of ivory ribbons, circa 1820.
(Christie's) **$800**

Carved exotic burlwood English sailor's hat, 19th century, inlaid hatband, leather sweatband, 5in. high.
(Skinner) **$2,000**

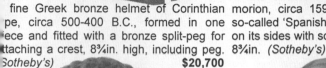

fine Greek bronze helmet of Corinthian pe, circa 500-400 B.C., formed in one ece and fitted with a bronze split-peg for ttaching a crest, 8¾in. high, including peg. Sotheby's) **$20,700**

A fine and rare Italian embossed parade morion, circa 1590, probably Milanese, of so-called 'Spanish form', the skull decorated on its sides with scenes of classical warriors, 8¾in. (Sotheby's) **$40,480**

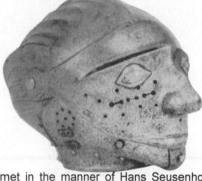

Important Itallan parade helmet by ippo Negroli of Milan, circa 1530-5, with unded one-piece skull, superbly nbossed and chased in high relief, except the brow and nape, with curly hair, 11½in. otheby's) **$178,400**

Armet in the manner of Hans Seusenhofer of Innsbruck, circa 1515-20, 9¼in. high.

This item belongs to the well-known group of helmets with grotesque visors produced in the Innsbruck Court Workshop by Konrad Seusenhofer and his brother Hans (Christie's) **$55,407**

Polish Hussar's winged Zischägge with mispherical one-piece skull embossed th radiating ribs, early 18th century, ¼in. high. (Christie's) **$4,250**

An unusual First World War cap, the interior with leather strap handle, the exterior with folding knife with leather and brass scabbard. (Locke & England) **$3,200**

Stoneware hot water bottle in the form of a Gladstone bag. *(Lyle)* **$80**

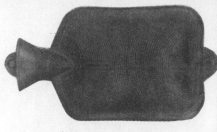

An early example of an English made Bet‍ hot water bottle. *(Lyle)* **$8**

'The Bungalow Footwarmer' by Denby Stoneware. *(Lyle)* **$65**

A decorative Victorian stoneware hot wate‍ bottle. *(Lyle)* **$3**

'The Adaptable Hot Water Bottle & Be‍ Warmer'. *(Lyle)* **$5**

A Staffordshire pottery footwarmer, the wedge-shaped two-handled warmer printed in green with vignettes of stylized Oriental palaces among palm trees within brown borders of scrolls, the top right hand corner with an aperture, with a cork stopper, circa 1860, 35cm. wide. *(Christie's)* **$920**

Late 19th century copper hot water bott‍ with screw plug, 7½in. diamete‍ *(Lyle)* **$4**

Junyao tripod incense burner, Northern Song Dynasty (960-1279), of compressed shape raised on three short cabriole legs, short neck and everted rim, all under a thick bubble-suffused grayish-blue glaze with random purple splashes, 4½in. diameter. (Christie's) **$28,800**

A Khorasan bronze incense-burner, Persia, 11th/12th century, in the form of a bird standing on four feet with closed wings, and head surmounted by a crest, the breast with a drawer, each wing with an openwork roundel and incised feather pattern, the head, back and tail also openwork, the drawer pierced with a short band of kufic inscription above, the large eyes with a hatched design, 19.3cm. high.
(Bonhams) **$19,200**

Chinese bronze censer and cover, in the form of a snarling kylin with its tail flicked up, wearing a bell-collar, 8¾in. high, 18th century. (Christie's) **$1,010**

A rare Ming Wucai ribbed tripod incense burner, Wanli six-character mark and of the period (1573-1619), the ribbed cylindrical body raised on tripod cabriole legs and enamelled with bands of classic scroll in yellow, green, iron red, black enamels and underglaze blue, 7¼in. diameter.
(Christie's) **$14,720**

A plated elephant's-head inkwell by Meriden Britannia Company, last quarter 19th century, the hinged cover with a cast figure of a monkey, 6½in. long.
(Christie's) **$1,540**

A parcel gilt bronze encrier modelled as helmet, late 19th century, the hinged cro⌐ surmounted with a dragon, cast in re⬛ overall with trailing foliage and mythi⬛ beasts, 7in. high.
(Christie's) **$1,3**

An unusual previously silver plated inkwell in the form of a helmet with movable visor, 4in. diameter, late 19th century.
(G.A. Key) **$80**

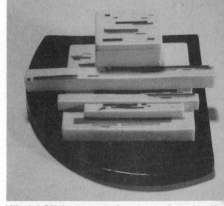

Nikolai Michailovitch Suetin, a Constructiv⬛ inkwell and cover, designed 1922-⬛ executed late 1920s by Alex Lutkin at ⬛ Leningrad porcelain factory, the geome⬛ glazed porcelain form with linear decorati⬛ of amber and lilac on cream field, on bla⬛ base, the underside with impressed hamm⬛ and sickle factory mark and make⬛ monogram, restorations, 5¾in. wide⬛

A 19th century French bronzed metal inkwell modelled as a setter's head, 6¼in. wide.
(Andrew Hartley) **$504**

(Christie's) **$12,6**

A late 19th century Continental novelty inkstand, realistically modelled as a tortoise, the hinged shell opening to reveal a pen rest, a recess for an ink bottle, and two hinged covers, one for stamps and one for four clips, nibs etc., with pseudo German marks, import marks for Chester 1900 and maker's mark of Bertholt Muller, 31cm. long, 35.5oz. *(Christie's)* **$5,150**

A 19th century French brass and bronze inkwell in the form of an eagle surmounting a globe on stand, 9in. high.
(Andrew Hartley) **$706**

A late 19th century inkwell globe, the 2in. diameter terrestrial globe, unsigned, made up of twelve with one overlapping paper gores, colored in pale blue, red, purple, yellow and green, the base flattened, the lid opening via a sprung button to reveal a glass inkwell with cover and sponge container.
(Christie's) **$480**

A 19th century French brass and coconut shell inkstand, satirically modelled as a seated Louis Philippe in barbarian dress holding a hatchet, 7in. high.
(Andrew Hartley) **$655**

An Edwardian gilt bronze lobster inkwell, circa 1890, the crustacean with hinged back, the interior with twin troughs, stamped on the underside *RD 136502*, re-gilt, 12in. long. *(Christie's)* **$1,197**

A French bronze elephant's head inkstand, late 19th century, modelled with a decorative ceremonial head-dress, the top of the head hinged to the interior recesses, with ivory tusks, 7in. high. *(Christie's)* **$6,400**

A Victorian carved oak cherub desk stand with inkwell, 9in. high, circa 1845. *(Russell Baldwin & Bright)* **$792**

A Victorian silvered bronze inkstand, modelled as a cat or 'Puss-in-boots' with feathered hat, standing on a naturalistic ground, the head hinged to the interior, 8½in. high. *(Christie's)* **$1,840**

A brass inkwell in the form of a crab standing on a heart-shaped oak plinth above a plaque engraved *PART OF THE RIVEN OAK LONGWOOD. (Christie's)* **$400**

A late Victorian parcel gilt and silvered bronze inkwell, late 19th century, modelled as a cat's head, with a bow tied to its neck, the head hinged to the cylindrical well, 4in. high. *(Christie's)* **$2,544**

A late Victorian gilt brass and silvered bronze desk piece, late 19th century, after a picture by Sir Edwin Landseer 'Islay and Tilco', modelled with a Macaw parrot bird on stand above a circular dish mounted with a spaniel and a terrier, the animals with hinged heads with inkwells with liners, 12½in. high. *(Christie's)* **$4,000**

A late Victorian silvered bronze inkwell modelled as a bear, late 19th century, shown seated on its haunches, with morion helmet, halberd and broadsword, on a later plinth, 7in. overall.
(Christie's) **$800**

A Black Forest carved wood inkwell, early 20th century, modelled as a terrier's head with inset glass eyes, with hinged cover and interior recess, 7in. high.
(Christie's) **$1,475**

A Wimshurst pattern electrostatic plate machine with six segmented glass contrarotating plates, 27in. wide.
(Christie's) **$4,950**

Shibukawa Harumi (1639-1715), a terrestrial globe, the image of the world painted on leather over a wooden base, diameter 55cm, the globe title [Translation], *The heavens are high yet one can sit and look at them, but although the earth is low it is impossible to visit every part of it. Because of our country's virtue people come here from all over the world. I have heard about their customs, followed what they have told me, and consulted the Sancai tuhui and the Tushubian to make this globe showing all the countries of the world. Someone asked me "The earth is flat, so why have you made it round?" I replied "I have simply relied on the Tushubian, which makes a single globe of the earth and the sea". Respectfully inscribed by Yasui Santetsu in autumn of the kanoe-inu year of Kanbun.* An important and magnificent globe, the earliest dated Japanese globe, 1670, one of only four recorded 17th century Japanese terrestrial globes. *(Christie's)* **$358,830**

Paint decorated kaleidoscope, 19th century, with a depiction of Lady Liberty in red, white, blue and gold, New Hampshire, 8in. high.
(Skinners) **$2,000**

A 19th century Italian wood polychrome decorated polyhedral sundial, unsigned, the seventeen dials painted in gilt with floral reserves in red, green, blue and brown, each dial drawn with the *Equatore*, with iron pin gnomons, on baluster turned support and shaped foot, 9in. high.
(Christie's) **$6,905**

A Doccia gilt metal-mounted etui, circa 1770, modelled as a baby wrapped in swaddling clothes, in a white lace-edged red bonnet, blue shawl tied with gilt-edged pink ribbon and a blue bow, the child's face lightly stippled in natural colors, 4¾in. long.
(Christie's) **$1,840**

▲

A chromium plated automatic traffic warner, stamped *Birglow Auto Signal Pat. 375944, Pat. 376564, Reg. design 767816*, 42in. long. *(Christie's)* **$400**

An unusual 17th century fruitwood simple microscope, the magnifying lens supported by three baluster-turned columns from the base, with threaded central support for the treen cup for specimen viewing, with turned column base, 4in. high fully closed.
(Christie's) **$1,008**

A late 19th century 'cabinet' microscope, the compound monocular body-tube with stage and mirror, supported on the arm of a standing gentleman with frock coat, on gilt and green-painted plinth base, 16.2cm. high, contained in a walnut case with brass carrying handle. *(Christie's)* **$3,300**

▲ An early 20th century German [? planisphere, unsigned, the 3-inch diamete wooden earth ball showing the tropics, Arcti and Antarctic circles, equator and prime meridian and stamped 26, held at the cente of a movable 12-inch diameter papere metal disc labelled with points of the compass and graduated around the edge ir degrees divided in four quadrants of 90°, the whole raised on an iron rod to turne fruitwood stand and circular plinth base with spirit level and inset compass, 22in. high *(Christie's)* **$1,19**

A rare 19th century lacquered-brass air-flow meter, signed on one of two cross bar *Biram's Patent Anemometer Davis Derb No. 63,* the suspension point with swin handle and enclosed dial mechanism, th two dials engraved *1-10,* one dial clockwise the other anti-clockwise, one labelled *C* the other *XS,* the twelve-blade fan drivin via spiral and pinion gear, the vertical sha running from the axis of the fan to the dia casing, with protective outer rings, overa height 9in. *(Christie's)* **$4,72**

An early Gothic flat iron with turned wood handle, circa 1500. *(Auction Team Köln)* **$11,508**

French slug iron with turned wood handle and serpent supports, circa 1800. *(Auction Team Köln)* **$4,795**

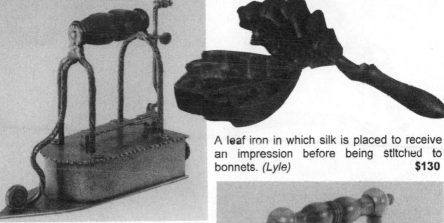

A leaf iron in which silk is placed to receive an impression before being stitched to bonnets. *(Lyle)* **$130**

An extremely rare and early slug iron with turned wood handle, circa 1720. *(Auction Team Köln)* **$7,992**

German flat iron with brass embellishments, circa 1875. *(Auction Team Köln)* **$1,918**

A very rare 18th century slug iron with brass embellishments and a turned wood handle, circa 1750. *(Auction Team Köln)* **$5,434**

A cast iron figure of a dog, probably American, late 19th century, with molded fur and curled tail, 24in. high. *(Sotheby's)* **$5,750**

A pair of cast iron cat andirons, American, early 20th century, each cast in the half-round seated on its haunches on a flaring pedestal, with green glass eyes, 16in. high. *(Sotheby's)* **$1,495**

A wrought iron scold's bridle, the mouthpiece incised with the maker's initials *I.G.*, and with rotating drum, possibly 17th century, 20.6cm. high. *(Christie's)* **$675**

A pair of cast iron satyr andirons, American, 20th century, each cast in the half-round with the head of a satyr with pierced eyes and mouth, 11³/₈in. high. *(Sotheby's)* **$1,035**

Cast iron painted figure of a black boy, last half 19th century, the standing figure wearing a hat, scarf, and vest, his right arm outstretched and his left hand in his pocket, 24½in. high, was used to hold a flag or lantern, depending on whether it was day or night. *(Skinner)* **$805**

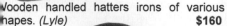

Wooden handled hatters irons of various shapes. *(Lyle)* **$160**

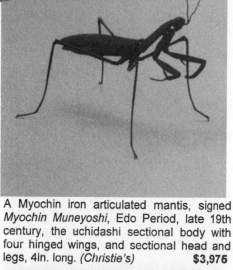

A Myochin iron articulated mantis, signed *Myochin Muneyoshi*, Edo Period, late 19th century, the uchidashi sectional body with four hinged wings, and sectional head and legs, 4in. long. *(Christie's)* **$3,975**

Imperial German sniper's body armor, a late Great War period example. The body plate is with a shaped side to fit the contour of the body, retaining the four smaller plates, the lower one shaped, these are supported by two contemporary webbing straps, the armor retains 85% of the original green painted finish. *(Bosleys)* **$1,200**

A Victorian cast iron walking stick stand, late 19th century, of Coalbrookdale pattern, modelled as a Chihuahua holding a riding crop to its mouth, the base with foliate cast drip tray, 23¼in. high. *(Christie's)* **$2,760**

A set of ten Austrian ivory and carved wood figures of musicians, late 19th or early 20t
century, each shown standing on turned ebonized plinths, 6¾in. overall.
(Christie's) $7,36

An Anglo-Indian gold, green and red-decorated solid ivory armchair, third quarter 18th century, Murshidabad, decorated overall with scrolling foliage, chevron and beaded patterns, the pierced oval back centered by an oval medallion with radiating rays and scrolling foliage, between straight uprights and a serpentine toprail enriched with scrolling foliage, each downswept arm with a lion-mask terminal facing outwards on a twisting serpentine support, each side filled with a pierced circle with foliage patera with rays, above a shaped oval padded seat covered with dark-blue velvet with a silver-thread border, on cabriole legs headed by foliage, and joined by an X-shaped turned baluster platform stretcher, 35¼in. high.
(Christie's) $143,172

A French carved ivory figure of a lady, m
19th century, shown standing holding a f
and handkerchief, wearing a wig benea
plumed head-dress and shawled bustier, h
hinged skirts opening to reveal a figurati
historical triptych, circular base, 8¾in. hig
(Christie's) $1,12

212

A Japanese ivory rectangular tray on four raised feet simulating bamboo, onlaid in mother-of-pearl, stained ivory, wood and horn with a crab, various exotic fish and crustaceans among reeds, 6¼in. wide. *(Christie's)* **$640**

pair of carved ivory groups, probably ıth German or Austrian, late 18th or early h century, one modelled as a woman ıcking a man, the other a man attacking a man, each on turned ebonized plinths, n. high overall.
ristie's) **$4,050**

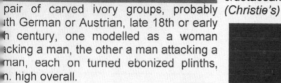

German carved ivory figures of itinerant sicians, late 18th or early 19th century, h shown playing bag pipes, on ebonized chip carved wood bases, 7in. high. *ristie's)* **$2,392**

Gabriel Argy-Rousseau and Pierre Le Faguays, seated dancer, 1920s, ivory and pâte-de-verre, modelled as a seated dancer with raised arms, the upper half of her body in ivory, the head heightened with staining, and adorned with gilt metal jewelry set with electric blue stones, the skirt in clear pâte-de-verre decorated in shades of green, pale and dark blue with circles, 20cm. high. *(Sotheby's)* **$24,000**

A French or German ivory comb, 15th century, one side carved with two jousting knights, 4⁷/8 x 5¾in.
(Sotheby's) **$28,750**

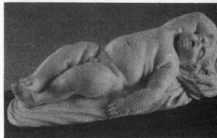

A pair of South German or Austrian ivory and fruitwood figures of peasants, in the manner of Simon Troger, 18th century, the man and the woman each with torn clothing and bare feet, each with ivory staff, on wood bases, 9¼in. high.
(Sotheby's) **$4,00**

A mid 19th century Dieppe ivory figure of François I, of 'Vierge ouvrant' type, the interior revealing a scene of François I and Charles V visiting the tomb of Saint Denis inscribed *François I et Charles Quint visitant le tombe ocu de Saint Denis*, raised on a cylindrical base, 31.5cm. high.
(Phillips) **$4,000**

A Flemish ivory figure of a reclining put late 17th century, the nude figure lying his back upon a creased blanket, his rig arm reaching back and resting upon head, the legs crossed, 6¼in. long, up molded, ebonized base.
(Sotheby's) **$6,9**

A Chinese ivory doctor's model of a reclining ▲ lady wearing only shoes and earrings on a draped throw, her head on a pillow, pigment traces, 12.4cm. long, 19th century. *(Christie's)* **$400**

A fine and rare carved and turned ivory Prisoner of War spinning lady mechanical toy, early 19th century, in the form of a stylized woman wearing a bonnet holding a spindle with thread, standing on a platform with spinning device, the lower platform with double wheel and crank, 5in. high. *Sotheby's)* **$3,737**

A Chinese erotic ivory group depicting a reclining couple lying side by side, the woman holding a puppy by a lead, all on a simulated mat base, the reverse incised with flowers, 3½in. high, 18th century. *(Christie's)* **$1,280**

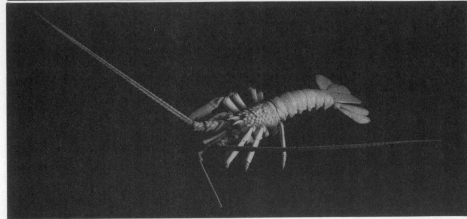

A Japanese articulated ivory model of a crayfish, second half 19th century, naturalistically carved and modelled with moving tail, legs and antennae, length 31.5cm. *(Sotheby's)* **$5,569**

An important Okvik ivory head, St. Lawrence Island 100B.C.-100 A.D., of oval form with large open mouth, long thin nose, protruding brow with narrow slit eyes, the back engraved with parallel spurred lines in the center, and two rows of small incisions at each side, 3¼in. high. This monumental head is from the earliest period of Okvik carving. It is one of the largest known. *(Christie's)* **$20,000**

An Austrian silver, ivory and enamel figur of a travelling clockseller, circa 1870, o square base with cut corners, enamelled i purple, orange, blue and green with ribbo bows, flowers and foliage, the standin figure holding a similarly decorated lanter and a halberd, with a watch hung around hi neck, the figure set with stones, 9¾in. high *(Christie's)* **$6,44**

Pair of spinach nephrite phoenix form vessels, each carved as a phoenix supporting an archaistic vase on its back, 7¼in. high.
(Butterfield & Butterfield) **$1,610**

A yellow jade mythical beast, Song Dynasty (960-1279), finely carved, seated on its haunches and looking up, the tail tucked between its legs and curling up to one side, the mane and fur incised, the stone of greenish-yellow tone with a russet inclusion over the mouth, 1½in.
(Christie's) **$4,800**

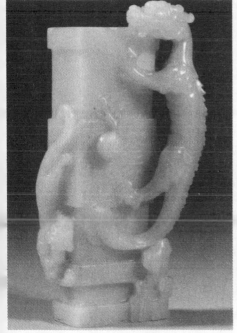

A celadon jade archaistic Fang Gu, Qianlong (1736-1795), carved with a large openwork chilong climbing past a flaming pearl towards the rim and a smaller chilong descending to the base, the central knop carved with a shallow-relief taotie mask, the stone of even pale greenish-gray tone with a well-used cream inclusion forming a cloud, 6in. high. *(Christie's)* **$11,200**

An unusual gray jade ewer and cover, 18th century, of flattened spherical shape with archaistic dragon handle and short cabriole spout emerging from a dragon head, the four legs emerging from lion heads and terminating in claw feet, the sides carved in shallow relief with dragons and a phoenix surrounded by water, rocks and trees, 8½in. wide. *(Christie's)* **$9,200**

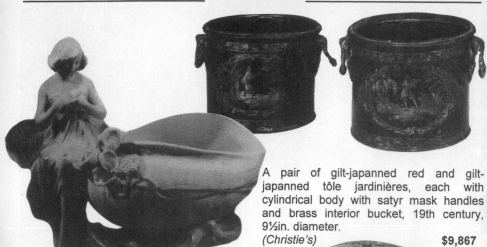

A pair of gilt-japanned red and gilt-japanned tôle jardinières, each with cylindrical body with satyr mask handles and brass interior bucket, 19th century, 9½in. diameter.
(Christie's) **$9,867**

A Royal Dux pottery jardinière modelled as a scantily clad maiden seated upon a blooming lily pad, beside a large conch shell, painted in shades of pink, sepia and gilt, applied pink triangle impressed *Royal Dux Bohemia E*, stamped *Made in Czechoslovakia*, impressed *2327*.
(Christie's) **$735**

A carved, silvered, painted and parcel-gilt jardinière, Italian, circa 1880, the upper part of hexagonal form with mussel shells, on three scrolled dolphin supports joined by a shell platform stretcher, 126cm. high.
(Sotheby's) **$4,800**

A ruby glass hexagonal jardinière, Yongzheng, four-character seal mark and of the period (1723-1735). The steep sides rising from a low foot to a flaring rim, the translucent glass of rich raspberry tone, 11.2cm. *(Christie's)* **$16,000**

A Chinese copper-red and cobalt blue decorated stag form jardinière, early 19th century, the sacred deer reclining with his head turned to one side, 11½in. wide.
(Christie's) **$8,625**

A pair of English stoneware jardinières, second half 19th century, modelled as naturalistic gnarled tree trunks with multiple branch plant holders, part-glazed in green and brown, with registration stamp for 8th June 1868 and indistinct patent numbers, 45¼in. high. *(Christie's)*

$800

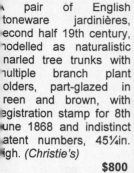

North Italian carved wood mer-boy jardinière, late 19th century, the large shell shaped bowl above a reclining figural support and naturalistic base, 33in. high x in. wide. *(Christie's)* **$16,000**

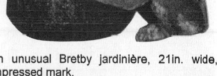

An unusual Bretby jardinière, 21in. wide, impressed mark. *(Dreweatt Neate)* **$546**

pair of majolica nautilus shell jardinières, 19th century, each naturalistically molded as a ge turquoise shell molded with yellow and pink seaweed, raised on a brown oval base lded with small snails, 45cm. high. *(Christie's)* **$3,680**

219

A carved pine jardinière modelled as a swan, late 19th or early 20th century, the body inset with a liner between the wings, on oval base, 31in. high.
(Christie's) **$3,634**

An unusual painted papier mâc rhinoceros jardinière, late 19th or early 2C century, standing, with a recess to t animal's back, 20in. long.
(Christie's) **$1,9**

A Le Nove jardinière naturalistically modelled as a cockerel above leaves and a footed scroll molded base, naturalistically colored and painted with loose sprays of flowers and lesser sprigs, blue comet mark, circa 1880, 68cm. high.
(Christie's) **$1,280**

A Singhalese padouk tripod jardinière, 1! century, the pierced foliate vase on waisted foliate column and supported three bird monopodia with paw feet, on concave-sided platform with scrolled fe brass castors, 38in. high.
(Christie's) **$5,1**

An unusual 18ct white and yellow gold brooch, of a woman blow-drying her hair, by Jeffrey L. Klein, 6.4cm. wide.
(Bonhams) **$400**

yellow gold brooch in the form of a llama, otted with turquoise and cabochon apphires, the eye with cabochon emerald. *Finarte)* **$2,167**

dual purpose clip brooch formed as an ephant, in yellow gold and multicolored amels embellished with an emerald and vé set brilliants, signed *Rivalta*. *inarte)* **$269**

Koloman Moser for the Wiener Werkstätte, brooch, 1912, metal, square, enamelled in black and white with a chess-board pattern against a gold colored background, the border enamelled with small white rectangles, the reverse stamped with *WW* monogram, 2.8cm.
(Sotheby's) **$3,784**

lip brooch as a stylized owl in yellow gold multicolored enamels with decorations vhite gold and brilliants, the eyes set with sapphires, brilliants 0.35ct, sapphires 5ct. *(Finarte)* **$1,614**

A clip brooch in yellow satin gold, in the form of a penguin with a cabochon nephrite in the center of its body and brilliant set beak. *(Finarte)* **$542**

A dragonfly brooch set with twenty nine diamonds & two rubies with blue enamel wings.
(Russell Baldwin & Bright) **$2,720**

An unusual H.G. Murphy gold 'tortois brooch, the creature having a green-stain chalcedony shell and garnet eyes, 3.5cr long. *(Phillips)* **$39**

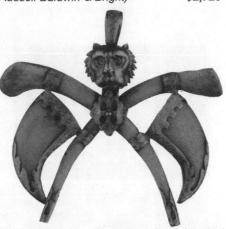

A late Victorian tiger claw bracelet and pendant, the bracelet formed of a graduated row of seven tiger claws in carved foliate mounts; the pendant formed of further mounted tiger claws surmounted by a tiger mask. *(Christie's)* **$800**

A clip brooch in the form of a stylized o head, in white and yellow gold with the ey set with two cabochon rubies and framed brilliants and strips of gold.
(Finarte) **$2,98**

A 14ct. gold and white gold brooch as a seated cat, the body set with pavé cut turquoises, the face with rubies and small diamonds. *(Finarte)* **$2,056**

Bakelite articulated figural pin, circa 19 black body and arms, brown legs, pain face, red topknot, holding a white stick i orange shield. *(Skinner)* **$£**

KEY BASKETS

Key baskets seem to be a particularly American phenomenon, with most examples coming from the Virginia area.

They are made of leather, decorated with stitching or tooling, and have a flexible handle.

A leather key basket, initialled *J.R. McK.*, probably Richmond, Virginia, circa 1830, 7¹/₈in. high. *(Sotheby's)* **$41,400**

leather key basket, probably Richmond, Virginia, early 19th century, the black oval basket decorated in silver and gold stitches, ¼in. high. *(Sotheby's)* **$2,070**

A rare tooled leather key basket, probably Shenandoah Valley, Virginia, mid 19th century, the shaped sides heightened with decorative tooling, 8½in. high. *(Sotheby's)* **$1,955**

KNIFE PISTOLS

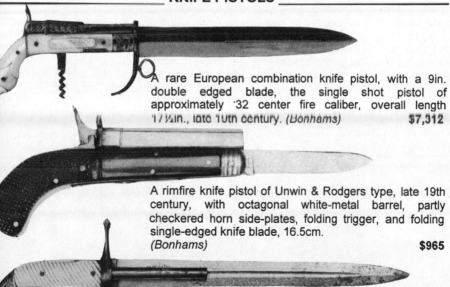

A rare European combination knife pistol, with a 9in. double edged blade, the single shot pistol of approximately ·32 center fire caliber, overall length 17½in., late 19th century. *(Bonhams)* **$7,312**

A rimfire knife pistol of Unwin & Rodgers type, late 19th century, with octagonal white-metal barrel, partly checkered horn side-plates, folding trigger, and folding single-edged knife blade, 16.5cm. *(Bonhams)* **$965**

A French dagger-pistol, by Dumonthier & Chartron, 194 Rue St. Martin, Paris, circa 1850-60, with tapering double-edged blade etched with scrollwork, plain barrels, 50cm. *(Bonhams)* **$3,054**

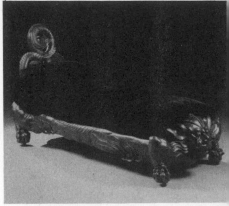

A rare red japanned day bed by Gabrie[
Viardot, Paris, dated *1887*, the upper part i[
the form of a scroll pierced scaly tail, the en[
with a grotesque chinoiserie mask in th[
form of a Chinese demon, on claw fee[
signed *G. Viardot Paris 1887*, 180cm. long
83cm. wide.

A lacquer okimono, Edo Period, late 19th century, of a Noh actor in the role of Shojo, standing with a dragon on his back, its head resting on top of the red wig, holding a stand on which is what appears to be a kogo, the stand loose in his hands, his clothes carved out in kijimakie with hiramakie, takamakie, gold and aogai kirikane and gyobu, the wood ground visible in the spaces, the hair in red lacquer, the mask carved from coral and the feet and hands in ivory.
(Christie's) **$3,374**

Gabriel Viardot started his career a[a wood carver and took over the family fir[from his father Charles in 1861. It wa[located at 36 rue Rambuteau where obje[d'art et de fantaisie were sold. Gabriel als[opened his own business in 1860 in rue d[Grand Chantier, but kept the workshops i[rue Rambuteau. He employe[approximately 100 workmen. The sho[moved several times before they final[settled at 36 rue Amelot where they staye[until the end of the century.
(Sotheby's) **$28,80[**

A pair of lacquer kogo, signed *Toyo saku*, Meiji Period (late 19th century) modelled a[oshidori [mandarin ducks] similarly decorated in red, gold, silver and black hiramakie, t[interior and base nashiji, with a box, 11cm. and 9.8cm. *(Christie's)* **$7,0[**

Lacquered wood sword stand, 19th century, fitted with tiers for three swords above a bi-level shelving unit containing four small drawers, 15⁵/8 x 7½ x 15in. *(Butterfield & Butterfield)* **$2,300**

A rare early Ming carved cinnabar lacquer box and cover, Xuande six-character mark and of the period (1426-1435), the top of the cover carved and incised through layers of red lacquer to a yellow ground with budding and blossoming peonies among dense leafy stems, the side of the box and cover similarly carved, the recessed base and interior lacquered black, the incised and gilt reign mark in a vertical line at the inner left side of the footrim, 4¾in. diameter. *(Christie's)* **$18,400**

A large Sino-Tibetan lacquer figure of Miyo Lobzangma, 18th century, the gilded goddess riding a tiger standing foursquare on a rockwork base, her right arm raised up, her left lowered, wearing a diadem, necklaces and strings of beads around her waist, her long hair and ribbons falling over her shoulders, the tiger growling and holding its snake-like tail up, 29¾in. high.

Miyo Lobzangma is one of the 'Five Sisters of Long Life', a group of ancient Tibetan deities converted to Buddhism by Padmasambhava. The five goddesses are mountain deities who reside in five glacial lakes at the foot of Mount Jo mo gangs dkar. *(Christie's)* **$32,000**

A pair of red cinnabar lacquer carved tripod vases, early 19th century, each of globular shape standing on three stout feet, deeply carved overall with archaistic taotie motifs, within scroll bands, all divided by three evenly spaced lion-masks at the waisted neck, the wide everted rim with wave-pattern and key-fret bands, 8½in. high. *(Christie's)* **$4,800**

A carved marbled lacquer stand of cinquefoil shape raised on five cabriole legs braced by a continuous cinquefoil stretcher, 17th/18th century, 23cm. wide. *(Christie's)* **$7,469**

A large Chinese lacquered zitan brushpot in the form of a tree section with irregular gnarled body, carved in relief with flowering prunus branches, 9½in. high. *(Christie's)* **$2,200**

A large Japanese polychrome, lacquered and gessoed wood model of a minogame with raised bushy tail, 37in. long. *(Christie's)* **$2,400**

An important 17th century ewer and basin decorated in gold hiramakie, the ewer 25.5cm. high. *(Christie's)* **$182,875**

A gold lacquer ground box and cover shaped as a persimmon decorated in hiramakie and kirikane, 19th century, 7.5cm. wide. *(Christie's)* **$1,693**

Marcel Louis Baugniet, lamp, circa 1930, thick glass shade in the form of a fish with round aperture as eyes, riveted to almost triangular brass 'fin', on rectangular nickel-plated metal base, the base with designer's monogram, 22.5cm.
(Sotheby's) **$4,865**

A Khorasan bronze zoomorphic oil-lamp, Persia, 11th/12th century, in the form of a feline, standing, each side with paired spouts, the tail with a further aperture, the head with naturalistic detailing, the flank with a rope pattern, 10.2cm. high.
(Bonhams) **$4,800**

An Italian serpentine marble model of an oil lamp, mid 19th century, in the Antique manner, the reservoir issuing twin branches carved with rams' head masks, the handle formed as a stylized horse's head, the cover carved with a lion mask within a border of further rams' heads, scarabs and acanthus ornament, the underside of the reservoir carved with human masks, intersecting ribbon tied laurel swags above a spray of stiff-leaf ornament, on tripod paw feet, 9¾in. high. *(Christie's)* **$6,400**

A Minton lamp base, modelled as an amphora resting on two rods, being carried by two putto wearing loose brown drapes, on stepped shaped rectangular base, shape 1517, impressed mark, year cypher for 1876, 36cm. high.
(Christie's) **$3,680**

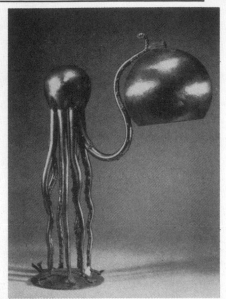

A Regency silvered-bronze colza-oil lamp, attributed to Messanger, in the form of a hunting horn, the flared rim with foliate handle, issuing from a boar-head with removable nozzle in its mouth, 7¼in. high. *(Christie's)* **$1,600**

A spelter table lamp, modelled as a stylized octopus holding semi-spherical shade, 54cm. high. *(Christie's)* **$773**

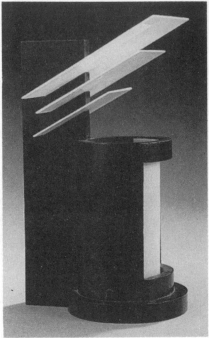

A pair of KPM Berlin lamps with swan bases, 16in. high. *(G.E. Sworder)* **$1,280**

Marcel Louis Baugniet and E. van Tonderen, lamp, before 1930, black painted wood, cylindrical body on stepped base with rectangular aperture with semi-circular opaque white glass shade, vertical support with three angled, stepped white glass panels, the underside with original paper label *Van Tonderen Ct Baugniet*, and inscribed in black ink *C* 75, 28.8cm. *(Sotheby's)* **$3,244**

Pierre Chareau, one of a pair of lamps 'La Fleur', circa 1924, nickel-plated metal bases, the shades composed of six removable alabaster panels, each 22cm.
(Sotheby's) **$12,880**

A bronze figural standard lamp, after the original by Gustave Gurschner, late 19th century, modelled as a nude male figure supporting a female companion holding a shade in open arms, all above a pendant drape and a second kneeling nude female upon the square section base, 60in.
(Bonhams) **$1,280**

A pair of bronze figural table lamps by Rudolf Marschall, circa 1914, caryatid maidens, their arms outstretched to support original shades, each lamp 13in. high. Marschall studied at the Academy of Decorative Arts in Vienna at the turn of the century and went on to become Director of the Vienna School of Engravers and Medallists. *(Christie's)* **$4,000**

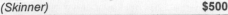

Streamline design airplane lamp, America, circa 1935, frosted colorless glass body, accented with silver paint, with nickel plated wings, tail, and base; resting on a looped metal support on a flat rectangular base with rolled ends, 11in. long.
(Skinner) **$500**

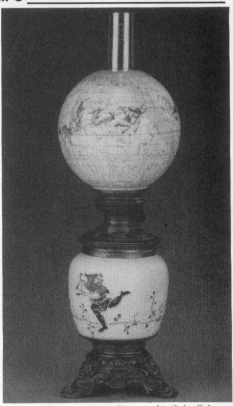

A late 19th century glass celestial oil lamp globe, the 7½in. diameter opaline celestial globe with the equator graduated in degrees and hours, the ecliptic graduated in days with symbols for the houses of the zodiac and large colorful pictorial representations of the constellations of zodiac, other constellations shown by dotted lines, stars shown to five orders of magnitude, fitting over a glass funnel engraved *Cristal H.S. 18in.* atop a brass oil lamp fitting, the reservoir set in a porcelain base decorated with three bearded gnomes dancing with drum, cymbals, · triangle and trumpet in stylized country setting, 23in. high.
(Christie's) **$1,288**

◀

An Italian polychrome wood and metal floor standing candelabrum, late 19th or early 20th century, the nine light fitting with beaded glass cresting, held aloft by a carved figure of a courtier, on a stepped hexagonal plinth, 82in. high. *(Christie's)* **$10,120**

230

A bronze lamp in the form of sandalled foot, an aperture at the ankle decorated with calyx leaves, Roman, circa 1st-2nd century A.D., 4³/₈in. long. *(Bonhams)* **$1,669**

Ingo Maurer, Germany, 'Bulb', manufactured by I. Maurer, circa 1980, giant bulb shaped hanging lamp in yellow, black and white plastic, 610mm. high. *(Bonhams)* **$551**

A Regency Döbereiner instantaneous light contrivance, circa 1825, the plinth circa 1780, the seated figure with outstretched hinged arms holding a cover over the nozzle, mounted on an associated earlier rectangular blue glass plinth, heightened in gilt with a lattice design, 5¼in. high. This type of instantaneous light contrivance was invented by Professor Döbereiner of Jena in 1823. *(Christie's)* **$800**

▶

Josef Hoffman for the Wiener Werkstätte, table lamp, circa 1905, brass, the square section stem decorated with four repoussé lozenges and with ball finial with U-shaped arm to hold shade, on square fluted base, stamped with designer's monogram, *Wiener Werkstätte* and *WW* trademark, 39.5cm. *(Sotheby's)* **$8,000**

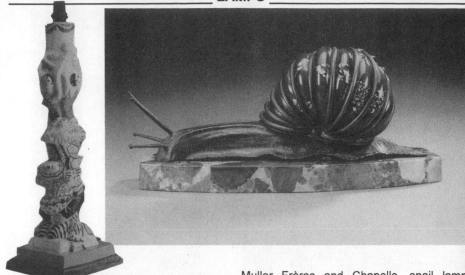

An important table lamp, designed by Dame Laura Knight, composed of clowns forming a human tower in support of five female acrobats with arms raised and hands joined beneath a cylindrical top hung with pendant garlands of puce outlined in gilt and all upon a triple stepped base of square section, 19in. high. overall.
(Bonhams) **$9,780**

Muller Frères and Chapelle, snail lamp 1920s, wrought iron armature cast as a snail with four horns, the body blown, with clear glass internally decorated with bright red and dark blue with silver foil inclusions shaped rectangular mottled gray and cream marble base, the glass marked *Muller F* *Lunéville,* the bronze marked *Chapelle Nancy* 15.5cm.
(Sotheby's) **$11,12**

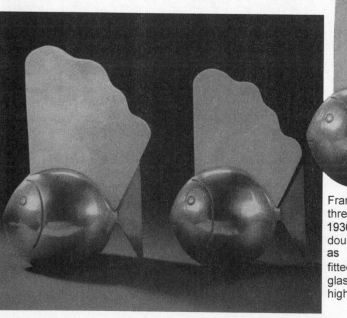

Frank Dobson, set of three table lamps, circa 1936, aluminum, one double sided, each cast as a stylized fish and fitted with opaque white glass fin shades, 41cm high. *(Sotheby's)*
$6,400

leather bottle, probably 17th century, of lobular form with flat ends, the buttressed neck with suspension holes, 9in. high. (Christie's) **$640**

vo leather wine vessels or costrels, obably English, 16th-17th centuries, the st with three pinnacles, one cylindrical and rving as the spout, another serving as the ndle, the second of barrel form and with movable panel, 10¾ and 9in.

The use of leather for such vessels as standard in the Middle Ages, rticularly in England, until the production metal vessels, followed by fine pottery d glass, superseded them. In the 16th d 17th centuries, barrel-shaped costrels d leather jugs, often known as 'black cks', were popular household items. otheby's) **$2,200**

The Ancient Order of the Boot, English, 1908, the leather boot with one penny stamp on toe and tri-color grosgrain ribbon bow ties along arch, below a faded typewritten letter dated *Nov. 14th 1908*, as follows:

I am desired by H.M. the king to inform you that he has been graciously pleased to bestow upon you of a companionship of the most ancient Order of the Boot, and at the same time to inform you that he considers no man as ever mor thoroughly deserved this distinction. His Majesty also desires to tell you that after your exit on the great scene in 'Doctor Johnson' Friday last that he had the greatest difficulty, such was the extraordinary diligence of your acts to refrain himself from leaping on the stage and personally invest you with the order. I have the honour to to ect. your obedient servant......

In a bow fronted mahogany case with domed top and dentil molding along the base, 61cm. high.

The boot was presented to an actor named Peter (unfortunately his surname has been forgotten), whose parents owned the Garrick or the Strand Theatre. Sadly, the actor died at an early age. (*Bonhams*) **$659**

A pair of Victorian ladies leather golfing boots, circa 1895, in good condition and with hammered-in studs. *(Sotheby's)* **$1,104**

A fine and very rare incised and gilt-lacquered leather travelling pannier, Liao dynasty, incised through a black lacquer layer and gold-filled on four sides, 16½ x 20½in. *(Christie's)* **$33,741**

A rare large J. Purdey 'The Audley' brass-mounted and bound oak and leather cartridge-magazine, for about 600 cases. *(Christie's)* **$1,920**

A 19th century four fold painted leather screen, depicting the 'Bombardment of Algiers, 1816', after the original canvas by George Chamber Snr. (1803-1840), 212cm wide. The bombardment took place on the 27th August, 1816, being a joint operation by the Dutch and British fleets to win Algiers from Barbary pirates. *(Bonhams)* **$4,72**

Arts and Crafts wastebasket, copper and leather decoration, 12½in. high. *(Skinner)* **$86**

A Kelly handbag of burgundy colored leather with gilt metal fastenings, Hermès Paris, 11¼in. base. *(Christie's)* **$70**

A Lenci Art Deco ceramic figure with box and cover, molded as the head, shoulders and torso of a young woman, 21.4cm. high. (Phillips) **$2,275**

A Lenci polychrome pottery figure of a young girl wearing floral sprig cream dress, seated on a bench holding an apple, beside two open books and an apple on a spotty cloth spread over a box, incised mark *AJR*, painted factory mark, 27.5cm. high. (Christie's) **$800**

A Lenci polychrome pottery figure of a naked young girl with head thrown back, reclining in a large green oval pool, a small duck pecking at her foot, painted factory mark, 41.5cm. diameter. (Christie's) **$1,280**

A Lenci Pottery jug in the form of a fierce rotund man with tall black hat being attacked by children, 30cm. high, inscribed under the base *Lenci, Made in Italy, 24-10-1930.* (Bearnes) **$1,107**

A Lenci head, 1936, designed by Helen König Scavini, polychrome glazed earthenware, modelled as the head of a young girl wearing a patterned headscarf, impressed mark *Lenci*, the reverse marked *Janetti, Lenci Torino, Made in Italy* and numbered *26.* (Sotheby's) **$720**

A pair of Lenci book ends each modelled as a naked young girl with short blond hair, kneeling between a book and a small dog, 23.5cm. high. *(Christie's)* **$1,431**

'Nella', a polychrome painted pottery figure modelled by Helen König Scavini for Lenci, circa 1931. *(Christie's)* **$3,078**

A glazed earthenware figure manufactured by Lenci, 1930s, modelled as a young woman seated coquettishly on a bookcase, 15¼in. high, painted mark *Lenci Made in Italy Torino 9.XI P.* *(Christie's)* **$4,800**

A polychrome ceramic ashtray, the central column as a nude woman holding a vase, factory marks and label, Lenci, circa 1930, 21cm. high. *(Finarte)* **$2,127**

A Victorian mahogany country house letter box, circa 1860, of octagonal form with domed top and brass letter slot. 12in. high. *(Bonhams)* **$640**

A Victorian stained pine club posting box, the molded cornice above a fielded panelled front bearing an enamel plaque *This is a private posting box. Letters and Packets posted in it will be treated in all respects as post letters, but proof of such posting will not be accepted in legal proceedings as evidence of receipt by the addressee by order of the Postmaster General*, with a panelled door below bearing a brass plate engraved *The Albany Club, Hours of Collection 9.45am-12.30pm 2.45-6.00pm*, 20½in. wide. *(Christie's)* **$1,806**

◄

An oak letterbox, 20th century, fitted with aperture and cupboard door, inscribed *Post Office Letterbox*, with further inscriptions, on plinth base, 19½in. wide. *(Christie's)* **$1,472**

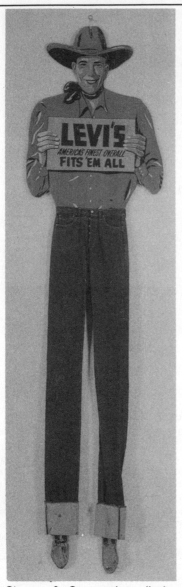

A Levi's denim jacket that won second place in Levi Strauss's oldest jacket contest, the jacket is believed to be circa 1910-1920s. Distinguishing itself from other jackets, this jacket features smaller buttons, a lower pocket, selvedge seams throughout the interior of the jacket, and the collar spreads out rather than coming to a V as on later 213 or 506 Levi jackets.
(Christie's) **$4,025**

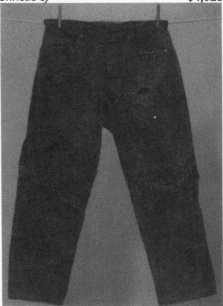

Levi Strauss & Co. cowboy display, this display, circa 1930s to 1940s, was used in stores for marketing purposes. It features a two-sided plywood cowboy wearing an actual oversized pair of Levi's 501s with plywood painted boots. The sign on the front states; *Levi's America's Finest Overall, Fits Em All.* On the back the sign states: *Look for the Red Tab.* 136in.
(Christie's) **$1,840**

A pair of brown duck cotton waist overalls circa 1890-1900s, believed to be one of the oldest pairs in existence. Distinguishing this pair from 501 jeans is the single stitch construction and a leather patch on the centre of the waistband.
(Christie's) **$30,000**

A rhinoceros horn libation cup, 17th/18th century, of conical shape, with ribbed spreading base and openwork double chilong dragon handle, 6¾in. wide. *(Christie's)* **$7,406**

A rhinoceros horn libation cup of tapered square shape, carved on the body with two pairs of confronted kui dragons, 17th century, 14.6cm. wide, carved fitted wood base. *(Christie's)* **$6,000**

A buffalo horn libation cup, Qing Dynasty, carved in high relief with an immortal standing beside a pine tree tempting the dragon emerging from the clouds above with the pearl he holds in his right hand, the translucent horn stained brown, 7¾in. high. *(Christie's)* **$1,725**

►

A rhinoceros horn libation cup, 18th century, carved in relief with a landscape depicting a boat in a mountainous river landscape dotted with pavilions, the handle formed by pine trees issuing from rockwork at one end, of deep honey tones, 5¾in. wide. *(Christie's)* **$7,475**

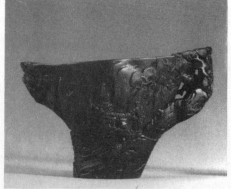

A set of George III oak library steps, the curved toprail terminating in finials above a pierced baluster gallery and above eight steps flanked by rails, above a conforming gallery terminating in the back with straight supports and shaped brackets joined by stretchers, the second step with concealed swivelling turned manoeuvring handles, on brass castors, 110in. high.

These library steps are likely to have been commissioned for Wentworth Woodhouse, Yorkshire, by William, 4th Earl Fitzwilliam (d.1833), who succeeded in 1782. *(Christie's)* **$28,800**

▶

A set of late Victorian oak library steps, the channelled hand rails and scrolling end supported by rope twist banisters on three spiral steps with linenfold panel decoration to the base, 55in. wide.
(Bonhams) **$3,520**

An oak easel/library steps with turned hand grips above a channelled frieze and adjustable rail for pictures opposed by seve shaped rungs forming treads to the ladde stamped *Hamptons Patent*, 76½in. high *(Christie's)* **$80**

A set of George III mahogany metamorphic library steps folding into a stool with padded rectangular green leather seat and hinged top opening to reveal a step with square legs, 18½in. wide. *(Christie's)* **$5,247**

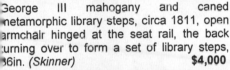

George III mahogany and caned metamorphic library steps, circa 1811, open armchair hinged at the seat rail, the back turning over to form a set of library steps, 36in. *(Skinner)* **$4,000**

A set of George III mahogany metamorphic library steps forming a table, inset with a tooled red-leather top, opening with red leather lined treads, on rounded and rectangular uprights, on ring-turned tapered feet, 36in. wide closed. *(Christie's)* **$1,920**

A set of oak library steps, 19th century, the bookrest and shelf above an arm rest with vertical slats and treads on rectangular supports united by stretchers, 50in. wide. *(Christie's)* **$2,400**

An incandescent lamp by Thomas Edison the blown-glass bulb with platina vice clamps and (detached) horse-shoe carbor filament, on turned wood stand, 7¼in. high circa 1880. *(Christie's)* **$7,831**

A Geissler pattern tube, the center section with sine curved section filled with yellow-green fluorescent liquid, with two Catherine wheel and scroll sections, terminating in elongated bulbs with electrodes, 21in. long. *(Christie's)* **$640**

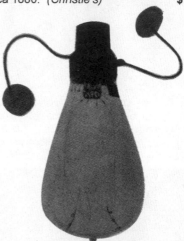

Dual Carbon Filament (dim/bright), circa 1905. *(Lyle)* **$65**

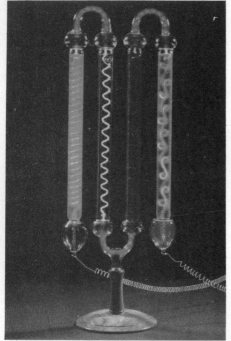

A double inverted liquid filled Geissler pattern U-tube, each column containing colored fluorescent liquids and enclosing multi-spiral and twist tubes, with six truncated spherical bulbs and two pear-shaped bulbs with electrodes, 26¼in. high. *(Christie's)* **$1,920**

Late 19th century 'Sunbeam Lamp' electric light bulb, with lobed element, 11in. high. *(Light)* **$480**

A pair of Geissler tubes, one with scroll and spiral section and elongated bulbs, the other with four uranium glass spheres and three scrolls, connected to two elongated bulbs, 15in. long. *(Christie's)* **$640**

double bulb fluorescent rock sample Crookes' tube, the two pear-shaped bulbs united by cross piece, on wood stand, 5¼in. high.
Christie's) **$640**

lacquered brass and vulcanite Geissler tube rotator, the twin coils with copperised magnetic ring, contact points and conductors, the Geissler tube locating arm with adjustment for length of tube, 13½in. high. *(Christie's)* **$1,600**

A Crookes' pattern vacuum tube with two electrodes, the elongated bulb containing phosphorescent mineral substances, on wood stand, 9¼in. high. *(Christie's)* **$827**

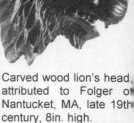

Carved wood lion's head, attributed to Folger of Nantucket, MA, late 19th century, 8in. high.
(Eldred's) **$605**

A pair of Luneville recumbent lions, circa 1780, modelled to the right and left, each with its tail curled over its back, their white bodies with blue markings and yellow manes, the blue paws, ears and faces with manganese markings, the mouths, nostrils and pupils picked out in red, the ears pierced, on rectangular green-sponged plinths, 18in. long.
(Christie's) **$8,000**

A very rare pair of figural redware lions attributed to John Bell, Waynesboro Pennsylvania, mid-19th century, 6½in high. *(Sotheby's)* **$9,775**

A Capodimonte (Carlo III) model of a crouching lion, circa 1750, incuse fleur-de-lys within circle mark, modelled by Giuseppe Gricci, the lion resting its head on its forelegs, naturally colored in brown and ocher, 2¾in. high.
(Christie's) **$4,800**

A soft-paste porcelain model of a lion, circa 1755, perhaps Longton Hall or Bow modelled standing to the left, fierce growling with his jaws agape, his tail curled beneath his back legs, on a rocky mount base, 7¾in. long.
(Christie's) **$8,000**

pair of verde antico and gilt-bronze rdinières, each in the form of Roman ths, 38cm. wide.
(Sotheby's) **$6,599**

A large model of a sandalled foot, in statuary and cipolino marble, in the Antique style, Italian, probably 18th century, 20in. long. *(Christie's)* **$11,450**

Roman Pentelic marble male torso, naked cept for a chlamys draped over his ulders, circa 1st century B.C./A.D., 17in. h. *(Bonhams)* **$11,016**

Bust of woman in shawl, circa 1900, white marble and painted wood, the marble carved as the pensive face of a woman resting her chin on her clasped hands, swathed in a patterned shawl of painted wood heightened with gilding, 30½in. wide.
(Sotheby's) **$19,200**

marble figural group, early 20th century, picting a nude couple in amorous position, n. high. *(Sotheby's)* **$3,450**

An Italian white marble group of The Wrestlers, after the Antique, the two naked athletes locked in combat, 19th century, 18¼in. high. *(Christie's)* **$4,138**

A grotesque bird modelled by Martin Brothers, 1904, removable head, the body with finely detailed plumage in olive green ice blue and brown, the head with splashes of brilliant Prussian blue, set on ebonized wood stand, 9in. high.
(Christie's) **$9,986**

A rare Martin Brothers saltglaze stonew 'Toby' jug, by Robert Wallace Martin Brothers. The figural form of a seated n with grotesque face, a pipe and drin horn, the strap handle formed as the bac the seat, light brown, green and wh incised *R.W. Martin & Bro.s, Lon Southall 10.10.1903.* Only three of th rare Toby Jugs were ever produced, 1 high. *(Bonhams)* **$9,4**

◄

A Martin Brothers saltglaze stonew 'Singing Imp' figure by Robert Wal Martin and Brothers, the seated figure an open songbook across his lap, underside incised *Martin Bro. Londo Southall.* Nine different musicians v produced for this group, 3¾in. h *(Bonhams)* **$1,9**

A Martin Brothers spoon warmer modelled as the broadly smiling head of a scaly fish-like creature, the tail looping to form a handle, covered overall with shades of brown and white dots on the scales, 18cm. long, painted on one side *R.W. Martin, London 1882*, incised and dated *1-9-82*. *(Bearnes)* **$2,400**

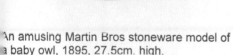

An amusing Martin Bros stoneware model of a baby owl, 1895, 27.5cm. high. *(Phillips)* **$4,800**

An unusual ceramic and pewter inkwell, cast in the style of a Martin Brothers bird with the head forming the hinged cover, 4¼in. high. *(Christie's)* **$341**

A grotesque bird modelled by Martin Brothers, 1901, removable head, the plumage decorated in shades of moss green, pale blue and sandy beige, set on ebonized wood stand, 8¾in. high. *(Christie's)* **$9,600**

A Martin Bros. stoneware tobacco jar and cover, modelled as a grotesque grinning cat, 1885, 22cm. high.*(Christie's)* **$12,800**

A Martin Brothers stoneware face jug, modelled in relief either side with a smiling face, in shades of white and brown on a buff ground, dated *1900*, 17cm. high. *(Christie's)* **$4,048**

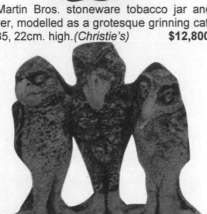

A rare Martin Brothers triple bird group of 'Two's company, three's none', circa 1906, modelled as a central, complacently smirking male bird with his wings about two females, 7½in. high. *(Sotheby's)* **$14,492**

A stoneware Martin Bros. grotesque double face jug, dated *1903*, 19cm. high. **$1,800**

An R.W. Martin and Brothers stoneware jug in the form of a grotesque animal squatting on four feet with scaled body, 12cm. high. *(Bearne's)* **$5,104**

'John Barleycorn' a Martin Brother stoneware flask, modelled in relief with a smiling face, glazed in black and white on a buff ground incised *Southall Potteries* 17cm. high. *(Christie's)* **$4,800**

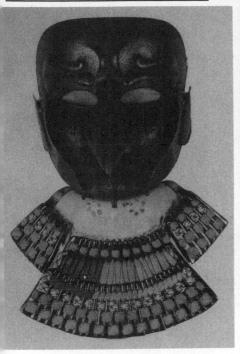

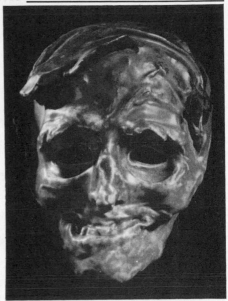

An earthenware mask, by Jean Desbois and Paul Jeanneney, 1904, the grotesque mask overglazed in shades of ocher, brown and green, 11¼in. maximum length. *(Christie's)* **$4,800**

An exceptional somen, late Muromachi/early Momoyama Period (16th century), this fine russet iron mask with its hooked beak of a nose is modelled on the mythical bird masks used in the gigaku dances, made in three pieces, the brow and nose joined by hinges whilst the ears are riveted on, the eyes are large and open beneath bold double eyebrows, there is no mouth, the piercing beneath the beak giving ventilation, the cheeks have standing flanges and beneath the chin are the shaped pegs and a short tube, on the point of the chin is an applied pierced plum blossom, the brow plate has a hood stitched to its upper edge and the interior is lacquered red, a two lame throat defense of black lacquered iron lamellae is laced closely with red, green and purple and is attached to the mask by a broad band of printed leather. *(Christie's)* **$25,600**

Carved and painted wood figural carnival mask, America, 19th century, in the form of a black man with hair wig, 14in. high. *(Skinner)* **$748**

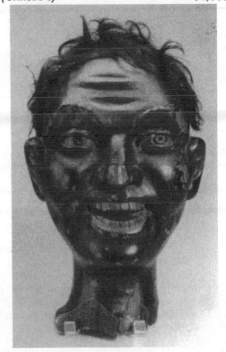

A Spanish painted wood mask of a man, 18th century, 6¼in. high.
(Sotheby's) **$1,092**

'Chahar', a rare Bizarre wall mask, painted in shades of red, yellow and black, printed factory marks, original Wilkinson paper label, 25cm. high.

This was one of the earliest Clarice Cliff facemasks, modelled around the same time as the Archaic series of vases. Like them it was clearly based on an Egyptian influenced theme, after designs in 'Grammar of Ornament' which had been published in 1856.
(Christie's) **$1,875**

Pende helmet mask, Giphogo, light wood with red, white and dark brown pigments, fiber cord beneath nose, slit eyes, 10½in. high. *(Butterfield & Butterfield)* **$690**

A Bizarre wall mask modelled as the head of an exotic woman with blue ringlets and a cap of green foliage, 9in. long.
(Christie's) **$521**

A wood noh-mask of Ko Beshima, with grimacing expression, gilt eyes, 8in. high, 18/19th century. *(Christie's)* **$1,280**

Venetian painted wood Commedia ll'arte mask, 18th century, with long rved nose 5¾in. high.
otheby's) **$3,162**

A wood Kitsune mask, Edo Period, late 17th/early 18th century, the striking mask decorated in white, red and black pigment, 20.8cm. long. *(Christie's)* **$8,000**

giltwood No mask of a demon, his face a grimacing expression, inlaid glass eyes, in., Meiji period.
nhams) **$998**

izarre' grotesque mask designed by Ron s, covered in a dark blue Inspiration e, the features picked out in red. *istie's)* **$2,656**

A Menpo [half mask], Edo Period (mid 18th century), the black lacquered iron mask with a long hair moustache, the three lame yodarekake of iron itamono laced kon ito sugare odoshi. *(Christie's)* **$2,062**

Beswick wall mask of a flaxen haired girl with green ribbons.
(Muir Hewitt)   **$500**

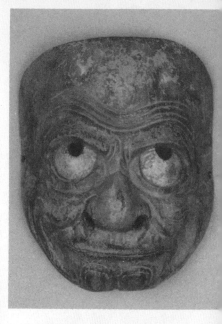

A Kyogen mask, Edo Period, 17th centu of a man with a rueful expression and double-lobed chin, colored in fle colored paint over gofun, with the lips red, the eyes white and the eyebrows dra in sumi, minor repairs, 21cm. lo *(Christie's)*   **$4,8**

A Gigaku style mask of Suiko, Edo Period, 18th/19th century, with a large protruding nose and stern expression, wearing a tall hat, decorated in red and black pigment, 18in. long.

Gigaku is considered the oldest form of dance performance with masks in Japan and was imported from the Asian Continent as early as the 7th century A.D.
(Christie's)   **$11,000**

Clarice Cliff Flora wall mask, large size 1 high. *(Muir Hewitt)*   **$2,7**

A rare Dukephone tin record player by Carl Lindstrom, Berlin, 1913.
(Auction Team Köln)   **$2,263**

A Mikiphone pocket watch form phonograph, System Vadasz, Swiss made, with Mikiphone soundbox, black resonator and nickel plated case, 4½in. diameter.
(Woolley & Wallis)   **$320**

A musical toilet paper dispenser, playing two melodies (including the national anthem!), by L.R. Paris.
(Auction Team Köln)   **$468**

Capitol Model EA phonolamp in Art Nouveau style by Burus Pollock Electric Mfg. Co., Indiana Harbor, USA, in octagonal case with two lamps under a pink fringe, on brass claw feet, 1919.
(Auction Team Köln)   **$3,795**

The Tango Two, an English printed cardboard dancing couple, who dance on the gramophone edge in time to the music.
(Auction Team Köln)   **$375**

A Seeburg Symphonola Type B early juke box by the Seeburg Co., Chicago, Art Deco style wooden case, for 12 shellac disks, 1936. *(Auction Team Köln)* **$1,219**

A Mikiphone Pocket Phonograph, wi Mikiphone soundbox, rectangular needle ti black composition resonator and nicke plated pocket-watch form case with red ar blue lettering, 4½in. diameter, with bilingu (French/English) instruction booklet, mahogany box. *(Christie's)* **$1,01**

A Nympho phonograph, with non-spin cylinder player, cast metal plate in the fo of a nymph, green and gold painted, 19 *(Auction Team Köln)* **$1,2**

An extraordinary American gramophone, Phonolamp 'Prairie Du Chien', circa 1920. *(Auction Team Köln)* **$2,877**

An early French Pathé Nr. 1 phonograp for standard cylinders and adaptor fc Pathé's Inter cylinders, with origina wooden cover, circa 1903. *(Auction Team Köln)* **$45**

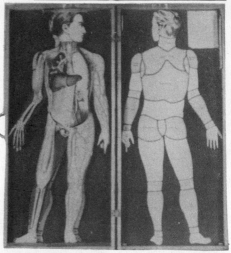

A rare plaster demonstration model of a womb with internal foetus, indistinctly signed and dated *ANZ - Doctr Fecit anno 1875*, probably French, 6½ x 5in. *(Christie's)* **$1,128**

Anatomical teaching device, 'Smiths New Outline Map of the Human System, Anatomical Regions, No. 2', manufactured by American Manikan Co., Peoria, Illinois, 1888, 44in. high. *(Skinner)* **$900**

late 18th century pewter commode, with screw-on handle, the underside impressed with the touchmarks of Stynt Duncombe London (circa 1766) 11¾in. diameter. *Christie's)* **$360**

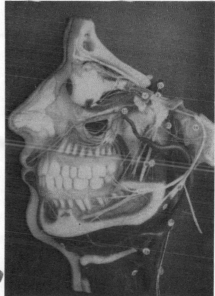

Patent 374091 – 1887, truss, Thomas Emmons, Hartford, CT, leather, canvas, wood and nickel-plated brass, 9in. diameter. *Christie's)* **$920**

A late 19th century wax model of the nerves, arteries, veins and muscles of the human head, by Lehrmittelwerke, Berlin, the various nerves, arteries and muscles with numbered labels to correspond with a printed list contained in the ebonized case with glazed door, 10¼in. high. *(Christie's)* **$560**

A Chinese doctor's ivory anatomical model of a young woman, with finely carved hair colored in black, both wrists with bracelets, and wearing shoes, 9¾in. long. *(Christie's)* **$1,195**

A fine late 19th century composition anatomical figure, of the human male, the front of the body arranged so as to be removed revealing the internal organs for instructional purposes, 23½in. high. *(Christie's)* **$1,036**

A late 19th century colored plaster mode of the human leg, the areas of muscles arteries and bone structure numbered to correspond with a printed list applied to the plinth base, contained in a glazed wood grained finished case with hinged front, 50in long. *(Christie's)* **$1,74**

A prepared skull of Homo Sapiens Sapiens, prepared circa 1900, the principal parts of the lower half identified in India ink. *(Bonhams)* **$240**

Late 19th century sectional model of the eye, the plaster body decorated in color and with glass lenses, 6¾in. high *(Christie's)* **$80**

A fine late 19th century electro-medical coil, unsigned, the burnished-iron magnet with adjustable sector, the quadrant stamped 0-60, the gilded brass winding handle in the form of a dolphin, with ivory finial, the driving wheel and supports for the rotating twin coils decorated with vines and other foliage, on three decorated ball feet and marble plinth base, contained in a mahogany case, 13¾in. wide, with glazed door.
(Christie's) **$736**
▶

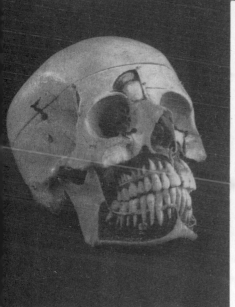

A fine articulated human skull, sectioned and hinged with hooks and eyes, the cranium decorated in colors on the inside with areas of nerves and veins, the jaw complete with nerve ends for the teeth, the left side of the cranium drilled with numerous holes, contained in the original colored paper card covered box, 9in. wide. *Christie's* **$1,000**

A model eye, the decorated plaster model with numbered areas for identification, mounted on an ebonized stand, 9¾in. high. *(Christie's)* **$735**

An ivory anatomical model attributed to Stephen Zick, of a pregnant woman with articulated arms, the woman with removable torso revealing internal organs, 7½in. German, late 17th/early 18th century. *(Christie's)* **$8,769**

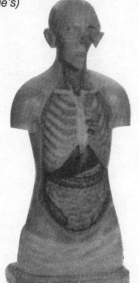

A novelty ivorine and simulated tortoiseshell ear cleaner, unmarked, modelled as a woman, wearing a dress, movable limbs, 7.5cm. long. *(Bonhams)* **$160**

An anatomical teaching model, on painted wooden base, some organs removable, 93cm. high.
(Auction Team Köln) **$295**

'Improved Magneto-Electric Machine', and electro-therapeutic instrument, with attached original leads.
(Auction Team Köln) **$468**

A 19th century fruitwood and ebony vaginal dilator, unsigned, with teardrop-turned handles, 8in. long. *(Christie's)* **$736**

McConnell dental folding chair with curved headrest and footrest, American, circa 1900. *(Auction Team Köln)* **$268**

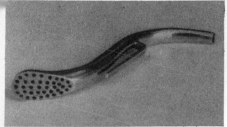

A sick syphon, double curved with a plain tong, unmarked probably early 19th century, 13cm. long overall length, 1oz. *(Christie's)* **$350**

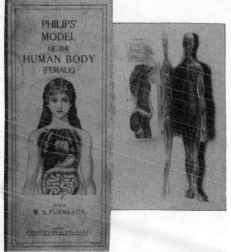

Philip's Model of the human body (female), edited by W. S. Furneaux, published by George Philip & Son Ltd., 32 Fleet St., London E.C.4., 19 x 7¾in. *(Christie's)* **$258**

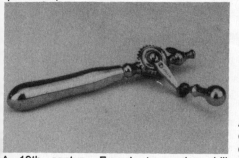

A 19th century French trepanning drill, signed *Collin*, with ball-socket handle and chuck for trepanning accessories, 7¼in. long. *(Christie's)* **$480**

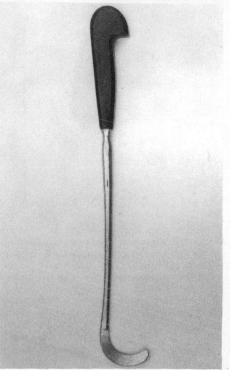

A late 19th century nickel-plated steel decapitating hook, stamped *H. Naertel*, with lignum-vitae pistol-grip shaped handle, 15in. long. *(Christie's)* **$515**

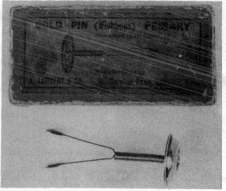

A rare gold pin 'wishbone' pessary contraceptive device, English, early 20th century, in original case titled *GOLD PIN (Wishbone) PESSARY Warranted 15ct Gold Manufactured by A. LAMBERT & CO. 16 DALSTON LANE LONDON E.8.* *(Bonhams)* **$379**

A pair of Meissen porcelain figures of Bolognese hounds, after J.J. Kändler, with brown and white patch decoration, 8¾in. high. *(Canterbury)* **$1,650**

An early Meissen pagoda figure, as a seated Chinaman with distinct fixed grin and holding a tea bowl and saucer in his right hand with a further tea bowl and saucer and teapot to the shaped base, he wears a robe, open to the waist with scattered floral decoration, crossed swords mark later added, circa 1730, 11cm.
'Tennants) **$4,000**

A Meissen Kakiemon spoon stand and four coffee spoons, the stand circa 1735, the spoons of later date and with blue crossed swords marks, the central stem fitted for six spoons and with blackamoor finial, the basin decorated in colors with Kakiemon flowers beneath a band of iron-red scrolling flowers and a gilt line edge, 5¼in. diameter. *(Christie's)* **$12,650**

A Meissen squirrel teapot, circa 1735, modelled by J.J. Kändler, as a squirrel nibbling an acorn, a green bow-tied collar around its neck, 6in. high. *(Christie's)* **$3,220**

A large Meissen group of Count von Bruhl's tailor after a model by J.J. Kaendler, typically modelled astride a goat wearing black tricorn hat, gilt spectacles, blue sash, yellow flowered coat, striped waistcoat and black knee length top-boots, blue crossed swords reverse punkt mark, incised *107* and Pressnummern, circa 1930, 43cm. high. *(Christie's)* **$11,960**

A Meissen box and cover modelled as a tortoise, probably by George Fritzsche, with a yellow head and tail with black and iron-red markings and four yellow feet with black claws, circa 1725, 19.5cm. long. *(Christie's)* **$38,000**

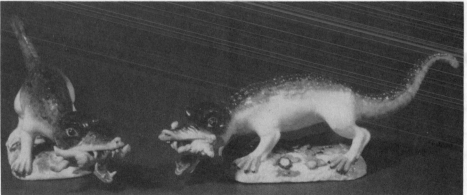

Two Meissen models of crocodiles devouring infants, circa 1745, blue crossed swords marks, modelled by J.J. Kändler, the reptiles naturalistically modelled and colored with their tails raised and each with a baby in its jaws, their bodies molded and incised with scales on oval mound bases applied with flowers and foliage, 11in. long. *(Christie's)* **$3,200**

A pair of Meissen figures of bulldogs, seated with a pup, having black and brown glazes, 7in. high.
(Russell, Baldwin & Bright) **$1,500**

A Meissen Bacchanalian figural group, modeled as a dandy seated on a barrel raising his glass in a toast, a boy and girl at his feet joining in the revelry, a horn blowing faun behind resting one hand on his shoulder, 20.7cm. *(Bonhams)* **$1,530**

A pair of late Meissen busts, after the models by Kändler, of Prince Louis Charles de Bourbon and the Princess Marie Zephirine de Bourbon, 23cm.
(Phillips) **$1,836**

A pair of Meissen figures of rabbits, late 19th century, each seated on its haunches, one with right foot raised, 7in.
(Bonhams) **$3,498**

A Meissen allegorical group of a gallant and an old lady, the young man wearing a puce coat and striped breeches, the old lady wearing a mob cap and flowered dress, seated in a high backed chair, the flatterer kissing her hand, at their feet a chest and faun, on a mound base, 15cm. high.
(Christie's) **$1,650**

A menu holder with two white mice playing double-base and a cornet, inscribed *Doulton Lambeth*, circa 1880, 3¾in. high. *(Lyle)*   **$1,360**

An Edwardian cased set of six novelty menu card holders on round bases, each surmounted by a pair of owls on a branch, maker's mark *M & C*, Birmingham 1905, 3.5cm. high, loaded.*(Christie's)*   **$1,250**

A pair of silver gilt and enamel menu holders, each disk with a game bird, on elled circular loaded bases. Makers Levi & alaman, Birmingham 1910. *(Woolley & Wallis)*   **$270**

A silver menu card holder, London *1901*, modelled as a monkey, on a raised circular base, 4.3cm. high. *(Bonhams)*   **$160**

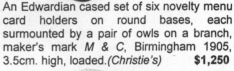

A set of six Edwardian silver menu holders, the double disks passed with a De Dion Bouton automobile, Chester 1907, 166 grammes total. *(Phillips)*   **$314**

A set of six silver menu holders, modelled as standing owls with glass eyes, by S. Mordan Co., Chester, 1906. *(Bonhams)*   **$640**

Marianne Brandt for Ruppelwerk, Gotha, menu holder, circa 1930, lime green painted sheet steel, 5¼in. *(Sotheby's)*   **$1,462**

1893 menu, shaped as artist's palette.
(Lyle) **$35**

Wedgwood Room menu, Waldorf-Astoria
January 25 1950. *(Lyle)* **£35**

Menu for Les Tuileries Restaurant, 16
September 1934.
(Lyle) **$65**

Menu for Piccadilly Hotel, New Year's Eve
1916. *(Lyle)* **$16**

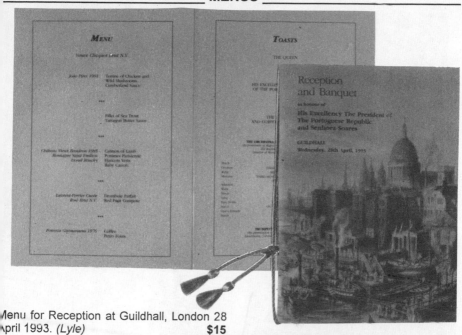

Menu for Reception at Guildhall, London 28 April 1993. *(Lyle)* **$15**

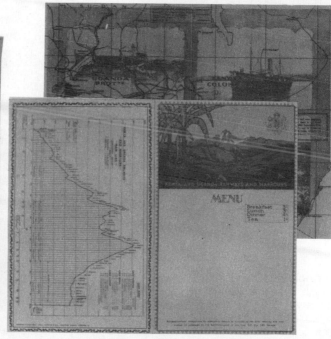

shmongers Hall menu, 16 June 1927. *yle)* **$40**

Menu for Kenya and Uganda Railways and Harbours for Breakfast, Lunch, Dinner and Tea. *(Lyle)* **$65**

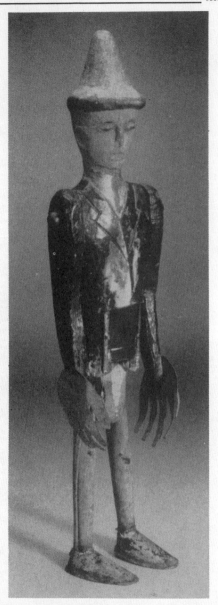

A Hagenauer carved wood and metal bust c
a woman in profile, 12½in. high.
(Christie's) **$1,34**

Hagenauer figure of a piano player, nicke
finish, flat stylized representation, impresse
with Wiener Werkstätte mark, 8½in. hig
(Skinner) **$1,10**

Carved painted wood and tin erotic figure of
a man, America, early 20th century, the full
figure with a silver painted pointed hat and
wears a black suit jacket, his carved arms
with applied sheet metal legs and shoes, a
tin sliding panel opens to reveal a spring
representation of a penis, (pants missing),
19in. high. *(Skinner)* **$3,000**

A novelty table bell, Chester *1912*, maker
mark of Grey and Co., modelled as
tortoise, silver shell, the body electroplate
14.5cm long. *(Bonhams)* **$96**

A massive Victorian metal figure of a swan, circa 1880, standing with wings aspread, 42in. high. *(Sotheby's)* **$11,500**

Articulated sheet metal figure of a man, 19th century, 13¼in. high. *(Skinner)* **$518**

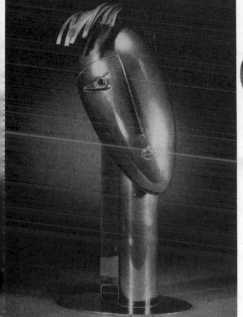

Set of six late 19th century shaped pastry cutters. *(Lyle)* **$65**

A Hagenauer silvered metal mask, of highly stylized oval face with cylindrical neck, on an geometric features and stylized fringed hair, on an oval base, stamped marks *Franz, Hagenauer Wien, Made in Austria,* factory monogram, 41cm. high.
(Christie's) **$16,560**

A 19th century Continental gilt metal inkwell, modelled as a seated bear with glass eyes and hinged head holding a tree stump pen holder, 4in. high.
(Andrew Hartley) **$269**

A sheet metal bust of Liberty, American, late 19th/early 20th century, in several joined pieces: the female head with backward flowing and molded hair, articulated eyes, nose and mouth, wearing a laurel wreath collar centered by a six-point star, with a later five-point star at head, 25in. high.
(Christie's) **$1,500**

Robert Mallet-Stevens, pair of waste paper baskets from the Villa C. at Croix, 1931-32, chromium-plated metal, cream painted interior and underside, cylindrical, on waisted base, each approximately 34.5cm.
(Sotheby's) **$10,812**

Female nude, 1930s, brass, modelled as a stylized female torso, her tress of hair sweeping over her head and dropping down to curl around her hips, on a rectangular base, with martelé finish, the underside with *WHW* monogram, *'Franz'*, *Hagenauer Wien* and *Made in Austria*, 34in.
(Sotheby's) **$6,400**

A complete stony meteorite with almost complete fusion crust, from the celebrated fall at L'Aigle, Orne, France, weight approximately 1.55 kilograms, 5in. wide.

Jean-Baptiste Biot (1774-1862), one of the most polymathematical French scientists of his period, was professor of astronomy at the Faculté des Sciences in Paris, a member of the Académie Française, a commander of the Légion d'Honneur, and author of the influential textbook Traité Élémentaire d'Astronomie Physique (Paris, 1802), a book from which Sir George Airy acquired his interest in astronomy. On April 26 1803, after the appearance of a fireball and detonations, a shower of stones weighing a total of about 37 kilograms fell near L'Aigle. Biot visited the area immediately afterwards and wrote his famous report which first proved beyond doubt the fact of a fall of stones from outer space. Until the beginning of the 19th century scientists were sceptical of stones falling from the sky, and much material was probably discarded or lost. Biot's report gives details of the stones he could find, eye-witness accounts, and such details as the fact that the freshly fallen stones taken into houses gave out such a disagreeable smell of sulphur that they had to be taken outside. Most of the stones he found at the time are now in the Natural History Museum in Paris. *(Christie's)* **$19,200**

An extremely rare fragment of lunar meteorite, Dar al Gani 262, 0.7g in weight, 1.75cm. long.

The Dar al Gani 262 meteorite was found in the Sahara Desert of Libya on 23 March 1997. Lunar meteorites are very rare, the first having been found in the Antarctic in 1982. Since then only eighteen separate rocks have been identified as being of lunar origin, some of which undoubtedly originated from the same blasted-off rock source.

The Dar al Gani 262 meteorite originally weighed 513g, and preliminary study was carried out by Bischoff and Weber, who determined that the rock was of lunar origin, based on its texture, types of mineral, glass and lithic clasts, mineral composition and bulk composition. The fragment has also been examined by professors at the Department of Earth and Planetary Sciences, Washington University, St. Louis, Missouri, USA, where examinations were made of mineral, matrix and fusion crust compositions. Comparison was also made with lunar meteorite QUE93069, which, it has been suggested, is from the same point of origin. *(Christie's)* **$14,536**

A mouse group molded with three minstrels on a green mound, by George Tinworth circa 1885, 3¾in. high. *(Lyle)* **$2,560**

George Tinworth (1866-1913) was the illiterate son of a Walworth wheelwright who became an artistic genius with a world famous reputation. He studied sculpture at Lambeth School of Art and was one of the first students to work for Henry Doulton who quickly recognised his talents. He produced many terracotta panels with religious themes as well as humorous figures of people and animals and incised and painted vases and jugs.

Play Goers by George Tinworth; the group glazed pale brown with a blue and brown shaped base, 1886, 5¼in. high. *(Lyle)* **$3,520**

A menu holder with a little mouse about to steal an apple from a stall, circa 1885, 3in high. *(Lyle)* **$2,080**

A menu holder with a white mouse playing a harp and a little mouse playing a double bass, by George Tinworth, 1885, 3¾in. high. *(Lyle)* **$1,920**

A tea party with pale green mice seated on brown chairs, by George Tinworth, the hollow oval base inscribed *Tea-Time Scandal,* circa 1885, 3½in. high. *(Lyle)* **$3,040**

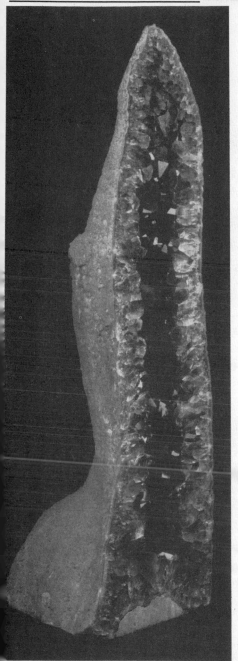

A brown polished geode with blue and white agate bands and protruding quartz crystals. *(Lyle)* **$640**

Part of the trunk of a fossil tree probably related to extinct plants in the Cardaites, probably 290-323 million years old, 16in. wide. *(Christie's)* **$320**

An amethyst geode, from south Brazil, cut and polished, the outer surface of greenish/blue hue, 32¾in. high. *(Christie's)* **$3,634**

A mass of Rhodochrosite of an attractive pink color. *(Lyle)* **$360**

Late 1920s tinplate money box in the form of a tiled fireplace by John Wright & Co. *(Lyle)* **$225**

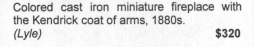

Colored cast iron miniature fireplace with the Kendrick coat of arms, 1880s. *(Lyle)* **$320**

Cast iron miniature fireplace embellished with a Victorian coat of arms, circa 1880. *(Lyle)* **$400**

Scottish cast iron miniature fireplace with thistle decoration, circa 1880. *(Lyle)* **$280**

19th century pewter miniature fire grate with classical embellishments and gadrooned borders. *(Lyle)* **$175**

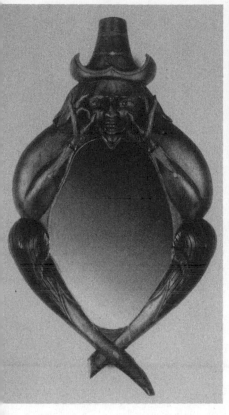

A Venetian carved walnut and micro-mosaic inlaid mirror, late 19th century, the bevelled shaped-oval mirrorplate within a frame carved with a maiden with raised arms and inlaid with blossoming foliage and a shooting star encircling a Venetian scene with gondola in the foreground, 57¼in. high.
(Christie's) **$27,600**

Polychrome decorated carved pine figural mirror, America, late 19th century, in the form of a court jester, 21in. high.
(Skinner) **$3,737**

▶

Carlo Bugatti, cheval glass, circa 1900, vellum covered wood, almost oval, the whole painted in gilt and red with stylized flowerheads and dragonflies, the back with tall thistle stems, U-shaped base, decorated with beaten black patinated brass panels, 84 x 110cm. wide.

This mirror features in the catalog of the Turin Exhibition of 1902 at which Bugatti's exhibit of furniture entirely covered with decorated vellum marked the highpoint of his career.
(Sotheby's) **$24,000**

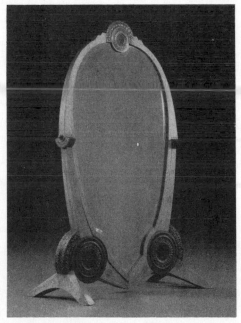

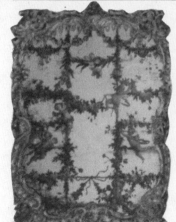

A George II giltwood and painted mirror, the painting attributed to Andien de Clermont, the cartouche shaped plate in sixteen sections and painted with winged putti climbing amidst a trellis of floral garlands, 111 x 79in.
(Christie's) **$190,720**

An Italian giltwood table mirror, mid 18th century, with a domed overhanging canopy, the shaped mirror within a pierced and carved frame, on a shelf base, 30in. wide.
(Bonhams) **$5,600**

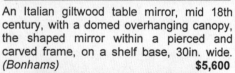

A Chinese Export reverse-painted mirror picture, the border mid-18th century, the later cartouche shaped central plate in a border with a scene of three Chinese figures seated in an extensive river landscape, 23 x 20¾in.
(Christie's) **$13,363**

A Meissen oval mirror frame surmounted by two loosely-draped putti holding a garland of flowers, molded with ovolos and flowerheads above a band of stiff leaves, the lower section applied with leaves and berries tied with a bow, 57cm. high.
(Christie's) **$4,40**

A model of the Leominster ducking stool, English, 1920s, the oak model with silver plaque inscribed *MODEL OF THE LEOMINSTER DUCKING STOOL last used in 1809. (Bonhams)* **$192**

An early Victorian cork model of a house, with quarter framed glazed windows to the front, flanking a double arched portico entrance, with figures of a man and woman, lozenge shaped glazed windows to the sides below the sloping roof, later applied with card, decorated with a printed pattern simulating tiles, the initials and date branded above the entrance *W. C. 1867*, 17in. high. (Christie's) **$800**

A wooden butcher's shop, English, mid 20th century, the shop with open shelf front and open door, top rail with a selection of hanging meats, three wooden carved and brightly painted butchers, two chopping boards and a hook stick, 22in. wide, 8¼in. deep. (Bonhams) **$800**

A French wood and iron model of a guillotine, 19th century, the rectangular frame with pulley and blade, 48½in. high. (Christie's) **$1,372**

A polychrome wood model of a butcher's shop front with carcasses and joints of meat hung to the façade, with three figures beside their carving blocks, 20 x 28in. overall. *(Christie's)* **$11,885**

A shadow box paper collage of an Adam-style Scottish public building, circa 1770, the five-part broken façade with quoined lower story, the central columnar portico surmounted by a balustrade and central domed clock tower with bird-form weather vane, flanked by a faux slate-tiled roof, a watercolor painted sky behind, glazed in a gilt-wood frame, 10¾in. x 15½in. *(Sotheby's)* **$1,840**

Mahogany model of a spiral staircase, wi finely-turned balusters, 24½in. high. 16½ diameter. *(Eldred's)* **$1,15**

A rare J & E Stevens Co. 'Girl Skipping Rope' clockwork bank, cast iron, place coin in squirrel's paws and wind mechanism, pressing the lever activates the revolving rope, as girl skips, her legs move, head turns and coin is deposited, circa 1890. *(Russell Baldwin & Bright)* **$24,000**

Late 1950s papier mâché 'Oliver Hardy' money box, 8in. high. *(Lyle)* **$65**

J. & E. Stevens reclining Chinaman cast iron money bank, American, bearing patent date 1882, 21cm. long. *(Sotheby's)* **$6,139**

A fine Mickey Mouse mechanical bank, German, early 1930s, possibly made by Saalmulmer and Strauss, 7in. high. *(Sotheby's)* **$18,285**

A Victorian cast iron money bank 'Stump Speaker'. *(Greenslade Hunt)* **$735**

A cast iron 'I Always Did 'Spise a Mul
mechanical money bank, American, 1880
with black jockey sitting on a mule. E
placing the coin in the rider's mouth, whe
the latch is pressed the mule will kic
sending the jockey flying and depositir
the coin into the bank, 25.5cm. lon
(Bonhams) **$56**

A J & E Stevens Paddy & the Pig bank, cast
iron, Irishman with pig held between his
legs, 18cm. base length.
(Christie's) **$439**

A cast iron dentist mechanical bank, wh
coin is inserted the dentist pulls the toc
(Auction Team Köln) **$3**

A Dinah mechanical bank by John Harper &
Co., Willenhall, Staffs., long sleeved version,
17cm. high, 1911.
(Auction Team Köln) **$432**

A cast iron Indian and bear mechan
money bank, American, 1880s, knee
Indian with rifle aimed at a standing be
place coin on the gun, press the lever a
the Indian will aim and shoot the coin i
the bear. *(Bonhams)* **$8**

An unusual wood okimono of a seated Japanese macaque monkey, (nihonzaru) or ape (Saru) holding a two case inro with Daikoku's lucky mallet netsuke, 5in. high, Meiji Period. *(Bonhams)* **$960**

A large Bing & Grondhal porcelain figure, modelled as a monkey, seated contemplating a tortoise held in his hand, printed factory marks, numbered *1545 4*, 22.2cm. high. *(Christie's)* **$1,100**

An extremely rare push-button mechanical monkey, 1930s, the mechanical toy comprising a black painted metal tube with four sprung buttons to the left side, activating the arms and yes-no head movements of the monkey, with cinnamon mohair head with felt ears, flock covered tin face with spectacles and painted eyes behind, the arms and top of tube with red felt tailcoat covering, with painted black buttons to front, pale blue cloth neck bow, painted tin hands, 6¾in. high. *(Sotheby's)* **$1,560**

A silver and onyx dish by Fabergé, workmaster Julius Rappoport, St. Petersburg, circa 1890, oval, the hardstone dish surmounted at each end by a realistically cast and engraved monkey, one pulling the other's tail, 18.2cm. long. *(Christie's)* **$11,523**

A majolica monkey jug, possibly English, modelled seated, his hands behind his back, before overlapping palm leaves, the handle branch-molded, circa 1900, 17cm. high *(Christie's)* **$560**

A famille rose waterdropper modelled as a monkey seated holding a peach with leafy tendrils, 11cm. long, 18th century *(Christie's)* **$960**

A Portuguese pottery model of 'Sloth and Mischief' after L.A. Malempré, modelled as a gray monkey riding atop a mottled brown and ocher tortoise, using his tail for reins, on shaped rectangular base with canted corners, painted in colored glazes, impressed marks, circa 1895, 41cm. high. *(Christie's)* **$3,200**

A Meissen monkey band group, modelled as a monkey seated on the back of another and playing the piano, on gilt scroll base, blue crossed swords and Pressnummern, 20th century, 13cm. high. *(Christie's)* **$1,470**

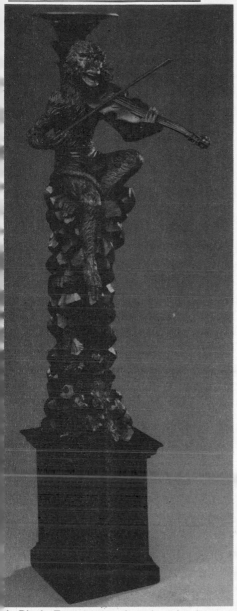

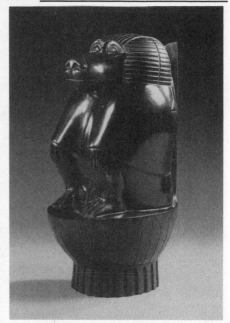

French, baboon, 1940s, black slate, carved as the figure of a baboon, seated on a base decorated with stylized leaves, 15¼in. high. *(Sotheby's)* **$3,229**

A Black Forest carved and stained wood figure of a monkey, late 19th century, shown playing a violin and seated on a raised rockwork plinth, the rectangular ebonized pedestal with retailer's stamp *Bellman, Ivey & Carter, by Appointment To The Queen, New Bond St.,* 60¾in. high. *(Christie's)* **$7,728**

A Continental majolica candlestick modelled as a monkey wearing a top hat and waistcoat, seated on its haunches holding a pipe, on a wickerwork base, impressed numeral, circa 1890, 13.5cm. high. *(Christie's)* **$480**

An unusual oriental table base, the single piece of teak well-carved with eight monkeys clambering through branches, approximately 72.5 x 120 x 110cm. *(Bristol)* **$4,800**

A charming wood okimono of a seated Japanese macaque monkey (nihonzaru), holding a fruit or pumpkin, 3½in. high, signed in an oval reverse *Mitsukuni*, Meiji/Taisho Period. *(Bonhams)* **$1,120**

Two painted cast iron monkeys, American early 20th century, each seated with left hand under chin and tail curled in front of feet with traces of polychrome, the first fitted as a bank, the second a doorstop, heights 8½in. and 9½in. *(Sotheby's)* **$2,300**

A wooden figure of a stylized monkey, probably Hagenauer, seated on one leg, one arm hanging by his side the other raised scratching his ear, on rectangular metal base, 6in. indistinct factory marks and *London, Made in England.*

Victorian novelty claret jug, formed as a monkey with dimpled glass body and plated ounts, 11in. high.

hristie's) **$1,076**

(Bonhams) **$480**

▶

very rare pair of inese famille rose onkeys, circa 1770, ouching to look uisitively to the left and ht, each hunched over green and pink peach ld out in a forepaw, the outh and ears pink amelled, the head and olt fur markings dotted caramel brown, the est fur paler, all on eaked blue rocky base.

Figures of monkeys re imported into Great tain early in the 18th ntury and many erences can be found British shipping records various sizes of nkey figures from circa)4 onwards. They re frequently depicted ding a peach, a symbol ongevity. *(Christie's)*
$28,800

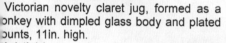

A Schuco monkey novelty perfume bottl the removable head fitted with a sm. internal glass flask, 3½in. high.
(Bonhams) **$24**

A Copeland model emblematic of 'Sloth and Mischief' after L.A. Malempré, naturalistically modelled as a brown monkey riding atop a large brown and green tortoise, the monkey using his tail as a harness, on an ocher mound and cobalt-blue canted rectangular base, impressed title and marks, date code for 1879, 44cm. high.
(Christie's) **$6,400**

A Minton majolica garden seat modelled as a crouching monkey holding a yellow pomegranate with green foliage in one hand, circa 1870. *(Christie's)* **$12,512**

An ivory netsuke, signed *Masatsugu*, E Period (19th century), of a finely render monkey, seated scratching his left leg, e inlaid in light and dark horn, age cra 1¼in. high.

Kaigyokusai Masatsugu (18 1892) was a superb carver, self-taught a who made studies for his carvings from l He worked in many materials choosing o the finest, and his designs encompassec very wide range of subject matter.
(Christie's) **$15,0**

rare pair of famille rose 'monkey and vase' roups, Qianlong, each modelled with a onkey clutching a hexagonal vase, its fur nely enamelled in sepia, chips to fingertips f one hand and chips infilled to one vase, n. high. (Christie's)　**$19,200**

A Meissen monkey-ewer and a cover, circa 1738, blue crossed swords mark and Dreher's incised double-lined cross, modelled by J.J. Kändler, with incised fur, orange muzzle and eye-lids and ears, gray face and shoulders and gray markings to arms, back and feet, wearing a yellow-belled red collar and yellow-edged red belt applied with a chain, with two young, one clasping its neck and forming the spout, the other forming the handle and climbing on its back and holding a fruit, 7½in. high. overall. (Christie's)　**$6,400**

erracotta figure of a monkey, seated and serving the frog in his hand. nhams)　**$480**

A Chinese blue and white brushwater modelled as a monkey seated on rockwork before a large peach and coiled guei dragon, 3¾in. high, 18th/19th century. (Christie's)　**$640**

'Avro Tutor', this model aeroplane wa
manufactured in Britain and only given out t
pilots who had trained on this particular typ
of aircraft. Chrome plate with the prope
red, white and blue markings.
(Lyle) **$1,00**

'Coq Nain' a Post War clear and frosted
mascot, modelled as a cockerel, on a
circular base, stencil mark *Lalique Fance*,
20.3cm. high.
(Christie's) **$480**

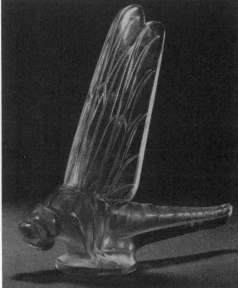

A frosted glass car mascot in the form of
erotic couple – the lady with long flowi
hair, being held by a kneeling gentleman,
square base, 9in. high.
(Canterbury) **$5**

'Libellule' no. 1145, a clear and frosted car
mascot, modelled as a dragonfly, with a faint
violet hue, molded mark *R. Lalique* and
engraved mark *R. Lalique France*, 20.5cm.
high. *(Christie's)* **$4,800**

'The Dummy Teat', nickel plated masc
manufactured by J. Grose & Co., 1926,
the Austin 7, fondly known as the Ba
Austin. *(Lyle)* **$5**

gallows mousetrap with two holes, 1920. *(Auction Team Köln)* **$48**

Late 19th century dual end ash and wire dead fall rodent trap, 11½in. long. *(Lyle)* **$32**

mouse trap, oak, of triple dead-fall type, 18th or 19th century, 14½in. wide. *(Christie's)* **$1,518**

An American automatic mouse trap with guillotine action, circa 1905. *(Auction Team Köln)* **$160**

mouse trap, oak with ash block, of rectangular dead-fall type, first half 19th century, 11¼in. wide. *(Christie's)* **$303**

A mouse trap, English, first half 19th century, pine and ash, of rectangular dead-fall type, 27.5cm. wide. *(Christie's)* **$184**

Pierrot serenading the Moon, a composition-headed clockwork musical automaton, with fixed brown eyes, metal hands, orange waistcoat and black tights, 22in. high, by G. Vichy. *(Christie's)* **$54,071**

A hand-operated musical automaton, of a cat and dog with composition heads and glass eyes, playing instruments, in original clothes, 12in. wide. *(Christie's)* **$968**

A Commodaphone gramophone built into the seat of a wooden armchair, circa 1920. *(Auction Team Köln)* **$800**

A Swiss chalet musical box with clock, in typical carved wood case with balconies, beehives, flower-pots, timber stacks and high plinth, two-train clock movement striking on wire gong and musical movement playing six airs, with tune-sheet on back of case, 21¼in. wide, the cylinder 6in. circa 1890. *(Christie's)* **$2,400**

A musician and clown automaton, French, late 19th century, probably made by Gustave Vichy, the Negro musician with composition head, moving mouth and neck, playing a banjo while tapping his foot, 33 x 28in. *(Sotheby's)* **$24,000**

A 'Toothache' musical automaton, the hunched papier mâché figure bending as the music plays, 30 tone cylinder mechanism, 1920s. *(Auction Team Köln)* **$35**

An automaton musical picture of a forge, of painted lithographed card, framed and glazed, 24¾ x 32¼in. *(Christie's)* **$4,600**

A hand operated automaton, of five figures with bisque heads, two seated playing stringed instruments and three dancing, the box 42cm. wide, German. *(Christie's)* **$1,875**

German Komet penny in the slot upright disk musical box, circa 1900, 30in. wide. *(Bearne's)* **$9,200**

A rare Monopol chalet disk musical box, model 45Sch, with double-comb 11¾in. movement beneath hinged roof, the walls painted with half-timbering, door and windows, with coin-slot in front drawer in the rocky plinth and plaque *Mettez une Pièce de 10 Centimes*, 18in. wide, circa 1890, with six discs. *(Christie's)* **$4,048**

An E-flat helichon, by Boosey & Co., and engraved *Solborn class A* and numbered *9908. (Christie's)* **$300**

Painted and decorated tambourine, America, early 20th century, painted in polychrome, pressed brass bells, 9½in. diameter. *(Skinner)* **$1,400**

An English serpent (Schlangenrohr), circa 1830, by F. Pretty, the body of hard wood with overpainted light canvas or hide covering, overall length 30in. *(Phillips)* **$2,496**

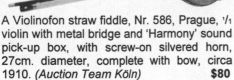

A Violinofon straw fiddle, Nr. 586, Prague, ¹/₁ violin with metal bridge and 'Harmony' sound pick-up box, with screw-on silvered horn, 27cm. diameter, complete with bow, circa 1910. *(Auction Team Köln)* **$80**

A Q.R.S. Playasax, self-playing saxophone with three rolls.
(Auction Team Köln) **$338**

The Tanzbär (Dancing Bear) automatic concertina, an original self-playing accordeon for interchangeable cylinders by A. Zuleger, Leipzig. The notation is by pressed tin paper rolls, the roll driven by a hand lever on the right side of the instrument which operates a ratchet drive with flywheel in square case, 26 x 29 x 22cm., with around 18 rolls and rewinding crank, in original box with instructions in English, circa 1900, in working order.
(Auction Team Köln) **$1,741**

Trombino, a rare plated tin 18 tone mechanical trumpet by M. Winkler & Co., Munich, with four paper rolls, circa 1900. *(Auction Team Köln)* **$1,775**

A Triola zither with twenty-five note roll action, six manual chords and thirty-seven rolls. *(Christie's)* **$1,011**

A Tanzbaer automatic accordion with trigger-operated twenty-eight key mechanism, in grained wood casing, with fourteen rolls. *(Christie's)* **$3,272**

Classical mahogany and mahogany veneer harmonica, probably New England, 1830s, the rectangular hinged top with rounded corners banded in veneer, opens to an interior with rounded open painted glass vessels identified by stencilled letters and musical notations, these produce music with the addition of water, 34in. high x 41in. wide. *(Skinner)* **$2,300**

A rare Hohner Trumpet Call harmonica with array of trumpet horns. *(Auction Team Köln)* **$240**

A Victorian mustard pot formed as Mr Punch, maker JBH, London 1878, 10cm. high, 6.5oz. *(Christie's)* **$966**

A Victorian parcel-gilt novelty three piece chinoiserie condiment set, mustard pot and two pepperettes modelled as monkeys, by E.C. Brown, 1867, the larger monkey 10.5cm. high, 8oz. *(Phillips)* **$15,960**

A pair of Edward VII mustard pots in the form of miniature tankards, 7.5cm. high, Elkington & Co. Ltd., London 1908, 7.8oz. *(Bearne's)* **$526**

A Victorian silver novelty owl mustard pot by Charles Thompson and George Fox, the body with textured plumage and red and black glass eyes, the hinged cover and large, hooked beak with traces of gilding, concealing the mustard spoon with a cast field mouse finial. London 1865, 4in. high, 6oz. *(David Lay)* **$3,662**

A Victorian novelty three-piece condiment set modelled as turrets engraved with brickwork, by Edgar Finlay & Hugh Taylor, 1891, 5oz. *(Phillips)* **$2,191**

Nakamura Takakazu, known as Kuya (1881-1961), Neck wrestlers, netsuke, ivory stained details, 3.5cm. diameter, signed *Kuya*. (Christie's) **$2,530**

A wood netsuke, signed *Tanaka Minko*, Tsu school, Edo Period, (18th century), of an octopus and a monkey standing and embracing on an awabi shell, eyes inlaid, 5.4cm. high.

This is a reference to the fairy tale Saru kurage ni noru [The Ride of the Monkey on the Jellyfish] in which Otohime, the daughter of the Dragon King, becomes ill and is prescribed a monkey's liver by the King's doctor, the octopus, in order to recover. *(Christie's)* **$4,444**

A wood netsuke, carved as a skeleton kneeling beating a large mokugyo, ivory hole rims, signed.
(Lawrence Fine Art) **$387**

An ivory netsuke, signed *Moriharu*, Edo Period (18th century), a well sculpted group of eight masks, the masks are those of Gigaku and Noh, the two groups of four comprising, on reverse Oji, Hannya, Bishamon and Saruto?, the signature at the side, on the ear of the scowling fox, 2.8 x 5 x 4.1cm. *(Christie's)* **$4,000**

Late 19th century wood netsuke of a wasp inside a rotten pear, signed with a kao. *(Christie's)* **$6,048**

A coral and iron netsuke, Edo Period (19th century), of an iron Myochin School fly resting on a coral branch, 5.3cm. long.
(Christie's) **$1,583**

An ivory netsuke of Okame, the mirthful goddess kneeling over to trim her toenails, signed *Shinsan*, Meiji Period, 1½in. high.
(Butterfield & Butterfield) **$862**

An ivory netsuke of Gama Sennin with mouth agape as he pulls a toad off his head, Meiji Period, 4cm. high.
(Butterfield & Butterfield) **$1,150**

Ivory netsuke, 19th century, in the form of a Dutchman with a hailing trumpet.
(Eldred's) **$3,500**

A wood netsuke, Toshinaga (Juei), Tokyo School, Edo Period, 19th century, of an elderly oiran sitting face to face with Emma-o, the regent of the Buddhist hell, who, with his two assessors, administers judgements and punishments in the nether regions, here he appears to have bitten off more than he can chew as, having pronounced his judgement on the prostitute, she is attempting to extract his tongue with pincers for doing so, 1¾in. wide.
(Christie's) **$2,438**

An ivory netsuke, carved in the form of Daruma, with arms stretched above his head and standing on a torn piece of cloak, signed *SHOSHI*, Meiji, 11cm. *(Bearnes)* **$823**

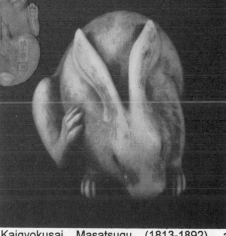

Kaigyokusai Masatsugu (1813-1892), a superb ivory netsuke of a seated rabbit, scratching its neck; its fur delicately engraved and stained and worn smooth in places, the eyes inlaid in amber, signed in a polished rectangular reserve *Kaigyokusai* with seal Masatsugu, Osaka School. *(Bonhams)* **$32,000**

ory netsuke, 18th century, depicting a rly-haired foreigner in the pose of an hinaga using a monkey as his fishing rtner. *(Eldred's)* **$6,500**

A fine ivory netsuke, signed *Tomotada*, Edo period, 18th century, of a wolf, seated and holding down a frightened crab, 1¹³/₁₆in. long. *(Christie's)* **$31,867**

A wood netsuke depicting a human skull entwined by a snake, its body passing through the left orbit, its head with black inlaid eyes, unsigned, 19th century, 3.5cm. high. *(Christie's)* **$2,600**

A wood netsuke, signed *Masakuni*, Edo Period (late 18th century), of an octopus in a tsubo with its tentacles stretched around it, eyes inlaid in horn, 1½in. high. *(Christie's)* **$3,284**

A well-detailed ivory netsuke of a rat sittir holding a candle with its forepaws, its eye inlaid in black horn, signed *Tomokazu*, 19 century, 3cm. high. *(Christie's)* **$1,40**

A wood netsuke, Edo period, 19th century, carved as a group of nine noh masks including Okame, Hyottoko, and Hannya, 1½in. wide. *(Christie's)* **$1,405**

An ivory netsuke of a wolf with bared teet hunched over the severed head of a beau inscribed *Tomochika*, 19th century, 3.2c high. *(Butterfield & Butterfield)* **$86**

A chalkware nodding cat, Pennsylvania, 19th century, the hollow molded figure of a standing cat with brown, red, and yellow-paint decoration, 4½in. high.
(Christie's) **$2,500**

A pair of late 19th century German porcelain nodding figures 'Grandma & Grandpapa', in. high. *(Lyle)* **$360**

large pair of Chinese-export polychrome-painted plaster nodding-head figures, 19th century, each in the form of a man with a detachable weighted head, wearing long multi-layered robes with floral decoration nd holding hands raised to the chest, anding on a rectangular base, 31½in. high. *Christie's)* **$6,992**

A nodding dog, Eastern European, late 19th century, the black and white plush dog standing on hind legs, with glass eyes, papier mâché mouth and lolling tongue, when head nods eyes flit from side to side, 21in. tall. *(Bonhams)* **$320**

A pair of nodding head seated figures, one of a Japanese nobleman holding a cup in one hand and a fan in the other, the other of a scribe holding out a scroll, 8in. *(Woolley & Wallis)* **$1,600**

◄

Emile Gallé crouched nodding cat, circa 1880, pale pink colored tin glazed earthenware decorated with flowered jacket and a medallion, 15.5cm. *(Sotheby's)* **$10,750**

A French carved wood nodding head donkey, Gustave Bayol of Angers, circ 1885, the figure with carved short man saddle and tail, 49in. long. *(Christie's)* **$5,12**

Pair of 19th century Continental glazed and decorated stoneware nodding figures, 'Policeman' and 'Woman', 12in. and 11in. tall. *(Lyle)* **$240**

A late 19th century French automaton in the form of a bulldog with natural hide body glass eyes, nodding head with growler and fiber and leather collar, on casters, 70cm *(Bearnes)* **$578**

A pair of cast brass 19th century nutcrackers, the top in the form of a cockerel's head, circa 1800, 5¾in. long. (Lyle) **$160**

Squirrel cast iron nutcracker, America, late 19th century, the full-bodied silver painted squirrel with a hinged tail mounted on a walnut molded base, 7in. long. (Skinner) **$460**

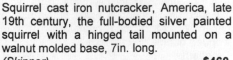

A carved treen caricature nutcracker, early 18th century, of Humpty Dumpty, the lower jaw with lever action, with traces of polychrome, 7½in. high. (Christie's) **$800**

A fine boxwood nut cracker, 17th century, of thumbscrew type, the spherical body carved overall in high and low relief with interlacing foliate ornament and a cartouche with the date 1631, the screw handle carved with addorsed heads flanking a gloved hand and a palm frond, 3in. high. (Christie's) **$1,120**

Cast iron painted dog nutcracker, America, late 19th century, standing figure with a hinged tail on a platform base, old light brown paint. (Skinner) **$115**

A Virotyp, small pocket edition of the French pointer typewriter by Kavalleristen Viry, 1914. *(Auction Team Köln)*   **$535**

A check-writing machine, circa 1890, with gilt decorated japanned base, brass disk to punch Fr. M. $ and numerals 1-0 with wooden handle, 17cm. wide.
(Bonhams)   **$190**

The Abbott Automatic Check Perforator, 1891, a very early American check writer, with 'fraud-proof' printing of the check amount, 1891, conforming to US Patent of 23 April 1899.
(Auction Team Köln)   **$502**

An Addo rare original version of the popular Swedish 10 row adding machine with direct display, with original base and case, 1920.*(Auction Team Köln)*   **$937**

A Marion's pencil cutter and sharpener, of brass with adjustable steel blade, adjustable anthropomorphic arms grip, detachable bone handle, instruction sheet (in French and English) and maker's carton, marked *Registered 5th September 1851* on sharpener and lid, the lid inscribed in pencil with indistinct initials and date *1852*, the carton 2¼in. *(Christie's)*   **$542**

An extremely rare Pathépost machine for recording and playing 11 and 14cm. wax discs, French, 1908.
(Auction Team Köln) **$3,880**

A J.M. Paillard French rotary pencil sharpener in attractive Art Nouveau case, circa 1920.
(Auction Team Köln) **$505**

The Brical round calculator for addition in British currency, wlth peg entry, in elegant velvet case, with pegs, 1905.
(Auction Team Köln) **$502**

A Ludwig Spitz & Co T.I.M. ("Time is Money") calculator, German, early 20th century, with japanned tin cover, 55cm. wide. *(Bonhams)* **$800**

A very early Reynolds Envelope Sealer letter sealing machine, attractive design, US Patent of 4 January 1910 by the Reynolds Envelope Sealer Co., Chicago.
(Auction Team Köln) **$96**

A Gould & Cook pencil sharpening machine, with rotary sandpaper wheel as sharpener, circa 1886.
(Auction Team Köln) **$678**

A four function XxX step-drum arithmometer by Seidel & Naumann, Dresden, with lever insertion, 1906. *(Auction Team Köln)* **$4,427**

A Webster Electronic Memory Model 80-1 RMA 375 tape recorder, with microphone, cable, three tapes and instruction booklet, circa 1935. *(Auction Team Köln)* **$213**

A Jowei German rotary pencil sharpener, in original condition, with original shavings container. *(Auction Team Köln)* **$201**

A Russian Original Odhner Model 1 Arithmometer, produced by the Swedish pioneer Willgodt T. Odhner in Tsarist Russia, the first mass produced cylinder calculating machine in the world, insertion to 9 places, results to 13, 1886. *(Auction Team Köln)* **$5,060**

A demonstration model Brunsviga Model A four-function calculator, 1899. *(Auction Team Köln)* **$813**

An Agaphone tape recorder by Haycraft of England, circa 1955. *(Auction Team Köln)* **$135**

Ivory okimono of three rats, Meiji Period, the rodents standing in a row on a wooden floor board, happily eating a stash of peanuts that they have found, their eyes enhanced with red and gray inlay, the underside signed, 7¼in. long. *(Butterfield & Butterfield)* **$1,000**

An ivory okimono of Fukurokuju and Daikoku, the latter holding the top of the former's head bent forward, the robes decorated with mallets and cloud-scrolls, 5½in. wide, 19th century, signed. *(Christie's)* **$2,760**

A large Japanese okimono, with twenty six ivory monkeys playing in and on a gnarled root, early 20th century, 24in. long. *(Woolley & Wallis)* **$1,680**

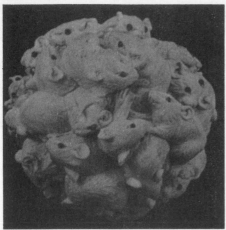

Ivory study of a skeleton holding a skull, 19th century, the kneeling skeleton wiping off the skull he holds in front of him, 1³/₈in. high. *(Butterfield & Butterfield)* **$546**

An ivory spherical okimono of a group of rats clambering over one another, the details well defined, the eyes inlaid in horn and coral, 2½in. diameter, 19th century. *(Christie's)* **$1,280**

An ivory okimono of a group of seven skeletons, seated and standing on a rocky base, drinking saki and one holding a fan, 4¾in. wide, signed Ichiryusai Hiroyuki, 19th century. *(Christie's)* **$2,400**

A wood okimono of two wrestlers grappling, one holding the other's loin cloth, the other with grimacing expression, horn inlaid eyes, 5in. high. *(Christie's)* **$1,120**

Three ivory okimono studies, 19th century, depicting the simians in their humorous 'See-no-evil, speak-no-evil, hear-no-evil' poses, 1³/₈in. high. *(Butterfield & Butterfield)* **$2,070**

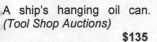

An extremely rare Kayes Patent miniature oil can with *K* on the copper body and *Meccano* on the lid. *(Tool Shop Auctions)* **$465**

A ship's hanging oil can. *(Tool Shop Auctions)* **$135**

. An early all copper oil can of Portuguese origin, 12in. overall.*(Tool Shop Auctions)* **$70**

Gamage's Motor Oil, one gallon tin. *(Lyle)* **$225**

Coolie Motor Oil tin from Lagos, Nigeria. *(Lyle)* **$80**

Cross Country Motor Oil pourer, USA. *(Lyle)* **$80**

A 10in. diameter copper oil filler.*(Tool Shop Auctions)* **$192**

A lovely Victorian copper oil can with brass top, punch decorated with a floral array. *(Tool Shop Auctions)* **$285**

A very rare half-gallon Kayes oil can in the form of a kettle, the first of its kind to be found. *(Tool Shop Auctions)* **$180**

E. Reynauld, Paris, a hand-cranked Praxinoscope and a quantity of picture strips. *(Christie's)* **$1,096**

A collapsible Kinora viewer with metal body section, single lens, hand-cranked mechanism, on a wood base with one Kinora reel. *(Christie's)* **$91**

J. H. Steward, London, a fine wood and lacquered-brass fitted triunial lantern, dividing into two sections, the upper single lantern with side door, decoratively gilded japanned metal chimney and lens mount. *(Christie's)* **$50,625**

Zoetrope, the drum and base with colored paint and gilt decoration and a quantity of picture strips. *(Christie's)* **$759**

A Praxinoscope by Emile Reynaud, Paris, post 1878, Reynaud's improvement on the zoetrope, whereby, using a mirrored drum, the picture sequence runs more smoothly and without dark flashes. *(Auction Team Köln)* **$1,03**

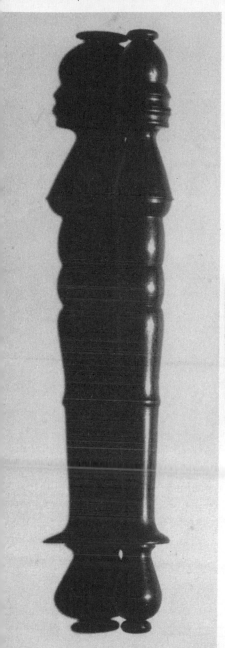

A 7½ x 5¼in. five-part peep view, the front section printed in German, French and English. *(Christie's)* **$1,320**

A cardboard body The Cinématograph-Toy with five picture strips, metal hand crank and marble weight, in original box. *(Christie's)* **$457**

laburnum 'shadow form' optical toy, turned form, via a shadow, the outline of a lady's ad and body, 8in. long. *Christie's)* **$720**

A gilt-metal photograph viewing ball, each half with six 1¼in. diameter apertures and one 2¼in. diameter, circa 1870. *(Christie's)* **$720**

A Japanese glazed model of a snail, la
19th century, modelled crawling on a bran
with large yellowish-brown glazed shell ov
a white body, 25in. long.
(Christie's) **$3,68**

A pair of Chinese Guangdong figures
mythical three-legged toads, modelled wi
wide open mouths, seated on pierced wave
form bases, 11½in. high.
(Christie's) **$5,98**

A rare molded Yueyao funerary jar and a
cover, Hunping, Three Kingdoms/Western
Jin Dynasty, the well-potted ovoid body
applied with rows of molded decoration
including seated Buddhas, turtles, dragons,
male and female phoenixes, cockerels, qilin,
llama-like creatures, and bearded Central
Asian equestrians with soft caps, the ridged
shoulder supporting a three-tiered temple
entrance flanked on either side by a pagoda
containing a seated Buddha, and encircled
by mischievous monkeys and bearded
Central Asian entertainers at various
pursuits including juggling, playing the flute,
strumming on the pipa, singing, fishing and
preparing food, the tall, tapering neck
applied with globular pots and numerous
birds below the lipped rim, 19in. high.
(Christie's) **$79,800**

A Chinese white glazed biscuit cens
modelled as a toad, with stippled decorati
overall, 11in. long, 18th century.
(Christie's) **$2,4**

A famille rose green-ground 'Nine Boys' baluster vase, Jiaqing, applied to the shoulder and body with a long iron-red enamelled ribbon knotted to one side and suspending tassels, with figures of boys in high relief clambering up the sides, dressed in colorful short robes over loose trousers, the long neck elegantly flaring at the gilt rim, the interior plain white, 36cm. high. *(Christie's)* **$6,400**

rare model of a roistering Dutchman, Edo ariod (late 17th/early 18th century), seated stride a Dutch gin cask, one arm held high utching a bottle as if to pour its alcohol into e goblet held in front of him, his coat olded in relief and painted in iron-red, een and pale aubergine and gilt with eony and scrolling foliage, his breeches d leggings decorated with cherry blossom, e scroll base molded and painted with a arashishi, 14¼in. high. *Christie's)* **$40,000**

famille verte 'Laughing twins group', Hehe xian, Kangxi, one figure modelled anding and leaning with outstretched ands on the shoulder of the other seated oy, the faces with lively smiling xpressions, the bodies naked except for ort colorfully enamelled tunics, 4¾in. gh. *(Christie's)* **$6,400**

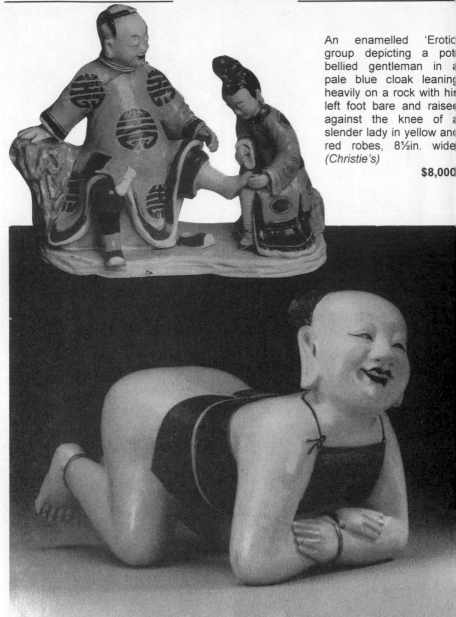

An enamelled 'Erotic group depicting a pot bellied gentleman in a pale blue cloak leaning heavily on a rock with his left foot bare and raised against the knee of a slender lady in yellow and red robes, 8½in. wide *(Christie's)*

$8,000

A rare enamelled pillow of a kneeling boy, Qianlong, naturalistically modelled in a liv pose resting on the knees and folded forearms, the head cocked slightly to the right, mouth open to a little laugh, the chest and belly tied with a gilt and iron-red vest, extrem chips and cracks, 16½in. long.

Pillows of this form were almost certainly inspired by dingyao and qingbai pillo from the Song dynasty. *(Christie's)* $12,8

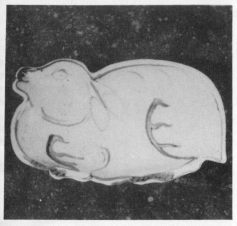

A combination Satsuma mask and bowl, the mask in the form of a chubby face, the jet black hair decorated with flowers, 22.3cm. high. *(Bearne's)* **$2,309**

A rare late Ming blue and white Ko-sometsuke 'hare' dish, the shallow dish with rounded sides modelled in the shape of a crouching hare, supported on three short feet, painted at the interior and the underside with details of the animal and splashed pale blue speckles, 6½in. long. Very typical of Ko-sometsuke are small dishes, called mukozuke. These were used for wafers and cakes served during the tea ceremony and were made in sets of five, often depicting or in the shape of, animals, birds and fish, as well as leaves, shells, fruit, flowers, fans etc. *(Christie's)* **$9,600**

Pair of Kakiemon cockerels standing on rockwork bases, circa 1680, 28cm. high. *(Christie's)* **$35,200**

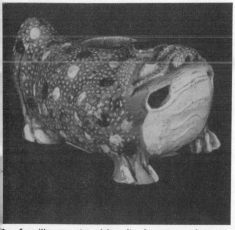

A Chinese Pottery cat night-light, the crouching feline with brown and cream glazed coat and painted facial detail with later inset glass eyes, pierced aperture on its back, Qing, 12.5cm.

A famille verte biscuit incense burner modelled as a mythical three-legged toad, looking upwards, the body well molded to simulate scales, 6¼in. long, Kangxi. *(Christie's)* **$1,010**

(Tennants) **$800**

A pair of ostriches, Dresden, circa 1880, in 17th century style, chased silver mounts, the bodies of ostrich eggs wrapped in the finely chased plumage, with hinged wings and applied bands on the backs and wings, 19in high.

The neck mountings bear the arms of Augustus I & II, Electors of Saxony and Kings of Poland in the first half of the 18th century. These pieces were probably inspired by the ostrich egg cups from the Electors' collections, now in the Grünsgewölbe, Dresden, attributed to Elias Gever and mentioned in the Cabinet inventories of curiosities of 1610. *(Christie's)* **$7,360**

An amusing silvered metal mounted ostrich egg box modelled as a frog, the cover with malachite finial and the head with inset glass eyes, 8¾in. high. *(Christie's)* **$700**

A pair of ostrich egg and horn ornaments with silvered metal mounts and on fluted socles with ebonized bases, the eggs with malachite bosses, 19¼in. wide. *(Christie's)* **$883**

A set of four silvered metal mounted ostrich egg goblets, with pierced gallery rims and on claw feet, the larger 7½in. high, the smaller 6in. *(Christie's)* **$348**

A pair of novelty condiments, London 1964 and 1965, maker's mark of R. Comyns, comprising a salt shaker and a pepper pot, modelled as standing owls, glass eyes, approximate weight 6oz. 7.5cm. high.
(Bonhams)   **$320**

A cast iron lantern, 20th century, modelled as an owl, 10¾in. high.
(Christie's)   **$1,179**

A pair of long-eared-owl silver-mounted claret jugs, possibly American, one green and one ruby, each mounted with silver neck rim and head stamped with simulated plumage and set with glass eyes, on silver feet, English import marks and hallmark for 1967, 28cm. high.
(Christie's)   **$4,600**

A late Victorian silvered bronze inkwell, late 19th century, in the form of an owl, with hinged head to the cylindrical liner, on a later domed base, 13cm. overall.
(Christie's)   **$4,000**

A pair of English porcelain brown owl lamp-bases, late 19th century, impressed design registration lozenges, each with applied glass eyes, their plumage picked out in shades of brown, modelled seated on flower encrusted rocky mound bases enriched in colors, 17¼in. high.
(Christie's) **$10,480**

A Staffordshire slipware owl-jug and cover, circa 1700, of lead-glazed red earthenware slip-decorated in cream and brown, the cover modelled as the owl's head with dark brown eyes set in wide cream sockets within dot borders beneath a raised ridge crest, the back of the head decorated with zig-zags, the oviform body with allover scrambled combed decoration, the tear-shaped wings with zig-zag and other geometric ornament within dot borders, the reverse with a short protruding tail and striped loop handle, the base modelled as two three-toed claw feet gripping a circular socle, 9in. high.
(Christie's) **$39,974**

◄

A brass lantern in the form of a pierced owl, a hinged opening to one side, late 19th/early 20th century, 13in. high.
(Christie's) **$5,634**

A Victorian parcel gilt, novelty three-piece 'owl' condiment set, modelled as a pair and one larger owl, by Charles Thomas & George Fox, 1849/51/53, the largest 9.5cm. high, 12oz. weighable.
(Phillips) **$9,300**

Nove maiolica owl jug naturalistically modelled perched on a branch, his chest painted with loose sprays of flowers, with branch handle, 20th century, 24cm. high. *(Christie's)* **$330**

Doulton Silicon ware modelled owl with brown wings and feet, the detachable head and the body decorated with applied blue, green and white motifs, circa 1880, 7½in. high. *(Lyle)* **$2,240**

A pair of English porcelain white owl lamp-bases, late 19th century, both with blue script *WR* marks, one with indistinct impressed design registration lozenge, each with applied glass eyes, modelled standing on flower encrusted rocky mound bases enriched in colors, 17in. high.
(Christie's) **$7,176**

Two Meissen models of owls, circa 1750, the first modelled to the right, its ocher plumage with dark-brown markings, the second modelled to the left, its pale-brown plumage with dark-brown markings and with large white patches about its eyes, both perched on shallow circular mound bases, 2in. and 1⁷/₈in. high.
(Christie's) **$2,400**

Two Victorian novelty owl peppers wi colored glass eyes, by Charles Thoma Fox and George Fox, 1860, 8cm. hig 3.25oz. *(Phillips)* **$96**

A Swiss white metal novelty timepiece, Cloche Frères, Paris Londres, first quart 20th century, 5in. high.
(Christie's) **$10,6**

A German stoneware jug modelled as an owl, circa 1900, incised L to base, the cover modelled as the bird's head, on a hinged pewter mount, incised all over the head and body with plumage enriched in manganese, the eyes picked out in yellow, 8in. high.
(Christie's) **$588**

A Staffordshire saltglaze owl jug and cov circa 1760, with applied ridged pluma enriched with brown slip spots, 8¼in. hig
(Christie's) **$55,0**

A pair of painted cast iron 'Dr. Owl' andirons, American, 20th century, each cast in the half-round with inset yellow and black glass eyes, 21½in. high.
(Sotheby's) **$2,070**

pair of Chinese painted pottery vessels nd covers modelled as owls, 18¼in. high.
Christie's) **$2,400**

Austrian pottery model of an owl, late th century, modelled perched on an open ook, on which rests an inkpot and quill, aturalistically colored in tones of brown, t with glass eyes, 22in.
otheby's) **$1,600**

A Black Forest carved and stained wood model of an owl, early 20th century, possibly an inkstand, with hinged head and interior recess, shown standing on a naturalistic base, 12¼in. high.
(Christie's) **$2,180**

A pâte de verre paperweight by Daum, circa 1910, modelled with a frog seated on a rock amongst leaves and a snail, the lime green circular base streaked with olive green, 3¼in. high. *(Christie's)* **$2,194**

A Clichy blue-ground sulphide weight, mid 19th century, with Louis Philippe facing to the right, in military uniform, 3in. diameter. *(Christie's)* **$614**

A Bohemian faceted engraved weight, the translucent amber-flash ground engraved with a lady riding her mare side-saddle in a wooded landscape, 2½in. diameter. *(Christie's)* **$460**

Two Saturday Evening Girls paperwights, sailboat and windmill design, one unmarked, one signed, 2½in. diameter. *(Skinner)* **$632**

A pâte de verre paperweight by Almaric Walter, after a model by Henri Berge, circa 1920, modelled with a hermit crab on a pentagonal base covered with fronds of seaweed, 2½in. high. *(Christie's)* **$3,264**

A Baccarat faceted sulphide weight, the clear glass set with a sulphide of a hunter and his dog standing in a wooded landscape, on a translucent ruby red ground foot, 3½in. diameter. *(Christie's)* **$3,450**

A Baccarat faceted garlanded sulphide weight, mid 19th century, Louis XIV facing to the right within a garland of green and white and pink and white canes, 3in. diameter. *(Christie's)* **$775**

A Saint Louis camomile weight, the flower composed of numerous rows of white recessed petals about a blue, red, yellow and white cane center, 6.6cm. diameter. *(Christie's)* **$2,300**

A Baccarat garlanded butterfly weight, the insect with deep-purple body with shaded gray-blue eyes and antennae, multi-colored marbleized wings, 7.3cm. diameter. *(Christie's)* **$4,025**

A New England free-blown pear weight, the naturally modelled pear in shades of pink and yellow resting on a clear glass circular base, circa 1870, 7cm. diameter. *(Christie's)* **$747**

A Saint Louis Marbrie weight, the bright red loops forming a quatrefoil festoon with a central composite cane in shades of salmon pink, blue and white, 6.6cm. diameter. *(Christie's)* **$2,990**

A Paul Ysart dragonfly weight, the insect with long shaded blue body with yellow markings, on a translucent mottled purple ground, 2¾in. diameter. *(Christie's)* **$978**

A pâte de verre paperweight by Alméric Walter, after a model by Henri Berge, circa 1920, modelled as a brown and russet speckled shrimp clinging to a rock with stylized waves, the base pale lime green tinted, 4½in. wide. *(Christie's)* **$4,571**

Alméric Walter, butterfly paperweigh 1920s, pâte-de-verre, in shades of yellow blue and brown, marked *AWN*, 11.5cn *(Sotheby's)* **$3,089**

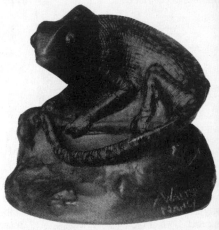

A pâte de verre paperweight by Alméric Walter, after a model by Henri Berge, circa 1920, modelled as a mouse in shades of cornflower blue and pale turquoise on a mottled green base, 2½in. high. *(Christie's)* **$4,225**

A rare Alméric Walter pâte-de-ver paperweight, designed by H. Berge, 8cr high. *(Christie's)* **$15,33**

A Saint Louis molded lizard weight, naturalistically molded with a coiled lizard enriched with gilding lying on top of a hollow bulbous base, the entire weight with a blue and white jasper ground overlaid in clear glass, 3¼in. diameter. *(Christie's)* **$1,840**

Tiffany bronze and favrile paperweigh swirling wave designed dark bronze fram on green iridescent damascene glass inse 3¾in. long. *(Skinner)* **$2,07**

Unic, a black 'Duocolor' Zerollo double pen, with Unic nibs, Italian, for the French market, 1930s. *(Bonhams)* **$1,120**

D.D. Zerollo, a gold plated Zerollo double pen, with chevron design and D.D. Zerollo nibs, Italian, 1930s. There are very few other recorded examples of overlaid Zerollos such as this. They are the rarest versions of this already rare and unusual pen. *(Bonhams)* **$1,920**

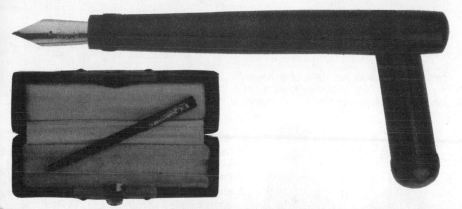

Waterman, a black 'Smallest Pen in the World', with gold nib, American, circa 1910. *(Bonhams)* **$2,880**

Mont Blanc, a Rouge et Noir No. 12 safety pen, with No. 12 nib, German circa 1915-18. *(Bonhams)* **$9,600**

OMAS, a black celluloid Colorado double pen with 'scissor' mechanism, two pump-filling reservoirs, and OMAS nibs, Italian, circa 1945. *(Bonhams)* **$2,080**

A fountain pen shop display sign, 20th century, the turned ebonized body with iron nib and clip, 59in. long. *(Christie's)* **$1,472**

An Edwardian silver novelty pepper pot, Birmingham 1908, maker's mark of H. W. Ltd., modelled as a seated bear, pull-off cover, 3.5cm. high. *(Bonhams)* **$240**

A silver pepperette in the form of a seated smiling cat, 2½in. high, Birmingham 1911. *(Russell Baldwin & Bright)* **$575**

A late Victorian silver novelty caster, import marks for London 1890, importer's mark of Lewis Lewis, modelled as a standing bird, the pull off head reveals a pierced cover, engraved feather decoration, red eyes, approximate weight 3oz., 14.7cm. long. *(Bonhams)* **$400**

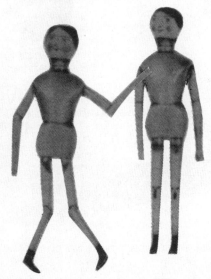

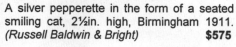

A pair of Edwardian novelty peppers, the articulated bodies with porcelain heads, 13.5cm. long, 1905. *(Phillips)* **$2,400**

A Victorian novelty pepperette, modelled as a knight's helmet, the hinged visor engraved with a crest, George Unite, Birmingham 1879, 2½in. *(Christie's)* **$267**

A pair of Edwardian novelty casters, modelled as ventilator chimneys with hooded cowls and bayonet fitting bases, Samuel Jacob, 1909, 18.5cm. high, 13.5oz. *(Christie's)* **$1,713**

Carlton cat pepper pot. *(Goss & Crested China)* **$22**

A pair of Victorian novelty pepperettes, modelled as a seated pug dog and a seated cat, dated 1879 to 1882, E.H. Stockwell, London 1877, 2½in. high. 6oz. *(Christie's)* **$2,456**

A late Victorian novelty cast pepperette, in the form of a fox with detachable head, by William Hornby, 1898, 11cm. long, 5oz. *(Christie's)* **$1,104**

A pair of American silver casters, Dominick & Haff, New York, 1879, realistically formed as seated pugs wearing collars, 5oz. 6dwt., 2¾in. high. *(Sotheby's)* **$4,887**

A novelty silver pepper pot, import marks for London 1925, importer's mark of I.S. modelled as a Dutch girl, in standing position, approximate weight 1½oz., 7.2cm. high. *(Bonhams)* **$160**

A pair of cotton bell-bottom style pants worn by Janis Joplin, designed in a multi-color flower motif.
(Christie's) **$10,350**

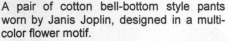

Saturday Night Fever, 1977, the white suit worn by actor John Travolta as he portrayed Tony Manero in the classic film, handwritten in blue ink on the interior lining, *To Gene, So here's to a classic, your friend, John Travolta.*
(Christie's) **$145,500**

A hair-miniature relic of Nelson, National Hero, Victor of Trafalgar 1758-1805, the oval gold brooch with watercolor miniature of Nelson with verre eglomise border on the obverse, the reverse mounted with a lock of light brown hair with blondish strands tied with gold wire and 'matched by another lock of brown hair with blondish strands tied with gold wire and 'matched' by another lock of brown hair to form an 'S' set within a border engraved, *Earl Nelson Duke of Bronte, Nelson of the Nile Copenhagen, Trafalgar obt at the Moment of Victory Oct 21 1805*, with brooch back and suspension loop, 6.8cm. high.

After Nelson's tragic death at Trafalgar his hair was given to his beloved Emma Hamilton and subsequently his daughter Horatia. Both Emma and Horatia gave locks of hair to friends and colleagues of Nelson, other hair was passed to members of the Nelson-Ward family. However the majority of Nelson's hair is in Greenwich and it was Horatia's special wish that this should be the case and this important relic was presented to Greenwich after Horatia's death in 1881. It is probable that this present locket was made at the time of the centenary of Trafalgar in 1905 by the division of a larger lock of hair, hence the need to 'match' another lock of hair to fill such a large and impressive brooch.
(Bonhams) **$3,200**

Rocky Marciano, gloves by Goldsmith of Cincinnati (from Mickey Duff via the National Sporting Club).
(Bonhams) **$1,750**

Elvis Presley's black cowboy shirt, the black cotton dress-shirt embroidered on front and back in white cotton.
(Bonhams) **$2,212**

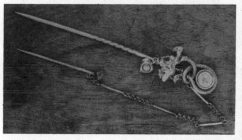

A gold cravat pin containing locks of Wellington's and Napoleon's hair, Wellington's hair in a locket surrounded by a coiled rope, and engraved on reverse *Wellington's Hair Died 15 Sept 1854*, gold nugget below attached with heart shaped pendant containing Napoleon's hair engraved *Napoleon*, 9cm. high.
(Bonhams) **$659**

Madonna, a stage dress of aquamarine silk and net embroidered with rhinestones, with shawl collar, made for Madonna for her stage performance of True Blue and Pappa Don't Preach.
(Christie's) **$7,360**

General George A. Custer's campaign shirt, made by Elizabeth Custer, circa 1873, navy wool bib front shirt with white trim and pearl buttons, and worn by General Custer on the Black Hills expedition of 1874.
(Butterfield & Butterfield) **$46,750**

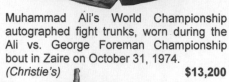

Muhammad Ali's World Championship autographed fight trunks, worn during the Ali vs. George Foreman Championship bout in Zaire on October 31, 1974. *(Christie's)* **$13,200**

Hermann Goering's wallet. A rare item of historical importance belonging to Hermann Goering, head of the Luftwaffe, Reichsmarschall and Adolf Hitler's heir apparent. It was given by Goering to his defence lawyer at the International Military Tribunal at Nuremberg, Dr. Otto Stahmer. Superior quality, silk lined maroon pigskin wallet bearing remains of gold tooled Vienna maker's name. Contains a postcard size photograph of Goering in Reichsmarschall uniform with his second wife Emmy and his daughter Edda; it bears ink signatures of all three. The reverse of the photograph bears a censor's ink stamp and a signed ink dedication in Goering's own hand, roughly translated to *To my defence council Dr. Stahmer with sincere and heartfelt appreciation. Hermann Goering Nurnberg Sept 1946*. The wallet also contains a dried pansy and a pencil written note in Goering's own hand, roughly translated to *We have to hurry up with our application otherwise Funk will be finished and the application will be made difficult.* (Walther Funk was President of the Reichsbank and was sentenced to life imprisonment at Nuremburg.) *(Bosleys)* **$1,600**

A dress worn by actress Julie Andrews as Maria in The Sound of Music, the sturdy heavy brown homespun jumper is constructed with a wheat colored blouse underneath an attached matching fabric jerkin. *(Christie's)* **$29,900**

Oliver Hardy, the comedian's trademark black felt bowler hat, *O. Hardy* is typed on a 20th Century Fox tag on the inside lining, with two signed photographs. *(Christie's)* **$7,475**

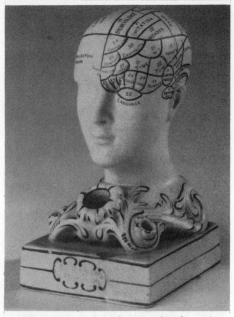

...ainted and molded plaster phrenological ...ead, 19th century, with labelled sections, ...e front with label inscribed ...HRENOLOGY, Approved by Fowler & ...ells, New York, the back stamped ...UBLISHED BY AL VACO, GRAY'S INN ...ONDON. (Sotheby's)   **$1,500**

A 19th century glazed ceramic phrenology head, by Bridges, the cranium decorated with the areas of the sentiments, the upper torso formed as an inkwell with blue decoration on plinth base, 13.7cm. high. (Christie's)   **$1,000**

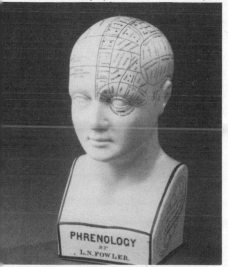

...porcelain phrenology head, inscribed L.N. ...owler Ludgate Circus London, Phrenology ...y L.N. Fowler., Entered At Stationers Hall., ...e back side with an inscription by Fowler, ...e cranium outlined with areas of the ...entiments and corresponding indentations, 1¾in. high. (Christie's)   **$1,300**

A Staffordshire earthenware phrenological head inkwell, stamped F. Bridges Phrenologist, 19th century, the head painted in black with numbered sections above three wells surrounded by blue scrolls, the rectangular base stamped By F. Bridges Phrenologist, 5½in. (Sotheby's)   **$747**

A Spanish 17th century carved, gilded and painted frame, with stepped outline and pierced scrolling acanthus leaves, overall size 39¼ x 33in. *(Christie's)* **$10,533**

A Roman parcel gilt ebonized frame, circa 1680, of ribbed molded form with large associated pierced scrollwork clasps at the corners, 81cm. high.
(Sotheby's) **$2,691**

A jewelled gold-mounted enamel frame, marked *Fabergé*, St. Petersburg, 1899-1903, the aperture within a border of seed pearls, 3¹/8in. high.
(Christie's) **$63,000**

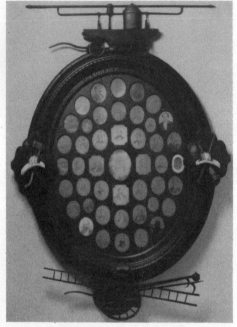

An impressive carved mahogany 'Lady Washington Fire Company' frame, probably Pennsylvania, late 19th century, the deeply carved and molded oval frame inset with numerous oval tin types of the honorary members of the Lady Washington Fire Company, the frame incised with stylized floral motifs and surrounded by a carved wood hose set with fire related trophies including helmets, hatchets, picks and a full fire engine wagon with pumper, hooks and ladders, 47in. wide.
(Christie's) **$17,250**

A Wiener Werkstätte giltwood mirror, designed by Dagobert Peche, decorated with overlapping stylized leaf design, 48 x 46.6cm. *(Christie's)* **$18,183**

A Wemyss pig, modelled seated and glazed overall in puce, 9.7cm. impressed marks.
(Bonhams) **$480**

An unusual painted sheet iron pig weathervane, probably Pennsylvania, circa 1880, the silhouetted figure painted white with brown spots, 34½in. long.
(Sotheby's) **$7,475**

An Edwardian pin cushion in the form of a standing pig, Adie and Lovekin Ltd, Birmingham 1906, 6.5cm.
(Christie's) **$480**

A German carved wood pig, jumper, by Friedrich Heyn, circa 1900, the figure with a sweet expressive face and wagging tongue, 29½in. long.
(Christie's) **$794**

A French bronze model of a pig, late 19th century, shown standing, on a naturalistic base, indistinctly signed 12½in. long.
(Christie's) **$1,920**

Paint decorated sheet metal pig weather vane, America, 19th century, 42in. long.
(Skinner) **$2,070**

Paint decorated tin pig trade sign, 19th century, 16 x 35in. *(Skinner)* **$3,105**

An attractive Wemyss (Bovey Tracey) model of a pig in the usual squatting pose, with ears pricked, painted all over the back and ears with sprays of flowering clover, 46cm. *(Phillips)* **$3,785**

'Middle White Sow: Wharfdale Royal Lady' a gilt bronze figure, cast from a model by Herbert Haseltine, American, late 19th/early 20th century, 5¼in. high. *(Christie's)* **$16,100**

A mid Victorian Rye pottery pig, the green body applied with white tail and inscribed *Wint be Druv*, the hog's head forming a cup to the vessel body, 20cm. long. *(Dreweatt Neate)* **$480**

English sterling silver pig-form shaker, 20th century, with hallmarks, 4½in. long. 1.8 troy oz. *(Eldred's)* **$33**

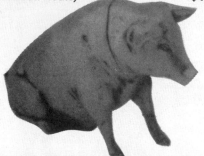

A Continental model of a pig, the detachable head with an appealing quizzical expression, Berthold Muller, bearing import marks for Chester 1899, 5¼in., 7.75oz. *(Christie's)* **$1,126**

A Roullet and Decamps musical pig, French circa 1905, the skin covered toy in cream and brown, with white and black glass eyes, papier mâché snout and trotters, when curly tail turned it plays music, original pale blue ribbon, 11in. long. *(Bonhams)* **$960**

Wemyss style container, modelled as a pig, decorated in dark green with foliage, on a paler green ground, one leg with indistinct impressed marks, 3½in. high.
(G.A. Key) **$94**

A Continental pottery green-glaze flower-holder modelled as a seated pig, the back pierced with three lines of apertures, 19th century, 8in. long. *(Christie's)* **$95**

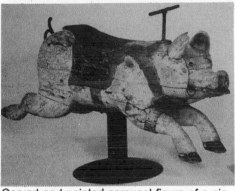

Carved and painted carousel figure of a pig, late 19th/early 20th century, the white painted running pig with protruding tongue, glass eyes, yellow bridle, carved red and blue saddle and blanket, 44in. long. *(Skinner)* **$2,300**

A carved and painted pine and gesso 'pig' butcher's trade sign, American, 20th century, carved in the round, length 30in. *(Sotheby's)* **$3,450**

A Continental electroplated novelty money box, maker's mark of WMFB, modelled as a seated pig, hinged lockable base, with key, height 8.5cm. *(Bonhams)* **$320**

A large Wemyss pig, the seated animal painted with pink leafy roses, 43.5cm. from snout to tail.
(Lawrence Fine Arts) **$5,420**

Felipe Archuleta black and white pig, carved and painted wood, 16 x 30in. *(Sotheby's)* **$5,000**

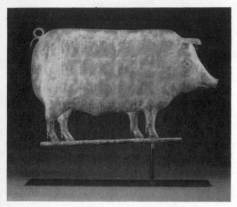

A Sussex pottery flask in the form of a pig, naturalistically modelled standing on all fours with detachable head, 19th century, 26cm. wide. *(Christie's)* **$1,280**

A molded and gilded copper pig weathervane, attributed to L. W. Cushing and Sons, Waltham, Massachusetts, late 19th century, standing profile with articulated eyes, snout, and curly tail, on a rectangular stand, 21in. high.

This full-bodied, double-chinned, handsomely-hocked testimony to American porcine beauty was a popular model of the firm of L.W. Cushing and Sons and its antecedents, I. W. Cushing & Co., and Cushing and White. It is illustrated in a circular printed by the firm between 1865 and 1872, and was in demand for a long time thereafter.
(Christie's) **$25,000**

A Wemyss pottery model of a seated pig, produced for Plichta, brightly painted with sprays of clover, the snout, trotters and tail tinged in pink, 29cm. long, inscribed *Nekola, Pinxt. (Bearnes)* **$2,160**

An Edwardian pin cushion in the form of a standing cow, Levi and Salamon, Birmingham 1907, 5.5cm. *(Christie's)* **$480**

An Edwardian pin cushion in the form of an elephant, Adie & Lovekin, Birmingham 1907, 6.5cm. *(Christie's)* **$590**

A novelty pin cushion in the form of a brick wall, Levi and Salamon, Birmingham 1910, 7.5cm. *(Christie's)* **$950**

A Continental pin cushion in the form of a mythical fish with large gaping mouth, import marks for London 1901, 9cm. *(Christie's)* **$809**

An Edwardian pin cushion in the form of a crouching frog, Birmingham 1907, 5.4cm. *(Christie's)* **$640**

A William IV silver-gilt pin-cushion, maker's mark of Paul Storr, London, 1835, formed as a duchess' coronet, with central silver-gilt tassel rising from foliage, fitted with red velvet cushion, fully marked, 3½in. high, the base: 8oz. *(Christie's)* **$5,623**

A silver pin cushion in the form of a rabbit with ruby eyes, Birmingham 1901, 2½cm. wide. *(Russell Baldwin & Bright)* **$690**

An early 19th century pin cushion designed as a crown, of turned wood, inscribed *King George the fourth crowned July 19 1821.* *(Phillips)* **$202**

An Edwardian pin cushion in the form of a standing lamb, Adie and Lovekin Ltd, Birmingham 1909, 5cm. *(Christie's)* **$480**

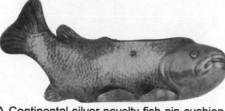

A Continental silver novelty fish pin cushion, bearing French import marks, modelled as a swimming fish, lacking cushion, 13.5cm. long. *(Bonhams)* **$336**

A late Victorian large novelty silver pin cushion, London 1900, maker's mark of William Comyns, modelled as a shuttlecock, with realistically cast feathers, inscribed *Fürstenstein 1900*, 12cm. high. *(Bonhams)* **$1,120**

An ivory pin cushion with hot needle decoration in the form of a wheelbarrow, English, early nineteenth century. *(Christie's)* **$120**

A novelty silver pin cushion, in the form of a fish, Chester, date letter worn, maker's mark of S. Mordan & Co. *(Bonhams)* **$240**

An Edwardian pin cushion in the form of a standing camel, Spurrier & Co., Birmingham 1906, 7cm. *(Christie's)* **$48**

An Edwardian pin cushion in the form of a fish, Sampson Mordan and Co, Chester 1908, 5.5cm. *(Christie's)* **$560**

An Edwardian novelty silver pin cushion, in the form of a bulldog, Birmingham 1908, maker's mark partially worn.
(Bonhams) **$240**

An Edwardian silver novelty pin cushion, modelled as a hedgehog, Birmingham 1904, maker's mark probably that of Levi & Salamon. *(Bonhams)* **$400**

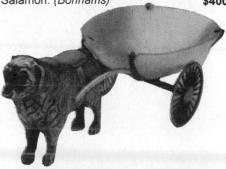

An unusual pin cushion, woven with silks and metallic thread, edged with metallic braid and fine scrolling copper wire, English, late seventeenth century, 5.8cm. square.

This pin cushion was probably designed to attach to a chatelaine, hence the ring at one corner.
(Christie's) **$240**

A silver dog pin cushion harnessed to cart of mother of pearl, 4¾in. wide, Birmingham 1909. *(Russell Baldwin & Bright)* **$810**

An Edwardian pin cushion in the form of a standing elephant, A.B. & Co., Birmingham, date letter indistinct, 4.7cm.
(Christie's) **$400**

An Edwardian pin cushion in the form of a standing pig, the side engraved, *From the Hyde Park Hotel*, Levi and Salamon, Birmingham 1909, 7cm.
(Christie's) **$370**

Flirty, Daring, Thrilling, Exciting, 1940s.
(Lyle) **$25**

Wink – A Whirl of Girl, 'Silk Stockings and High Heels'. *(Lyle)* **$25**

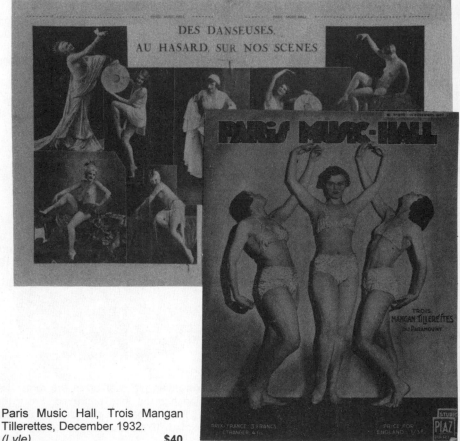

Paris Music Hall, Trois Mangan Tillerettes, December 1932.
(Lyle) **$40**

La Vie Parisienne, January 1928.
(Lyle) **$40**

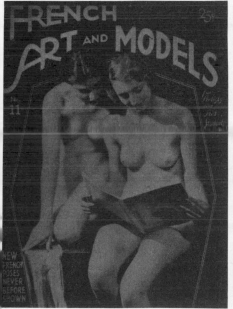

French Art and Models, New French Poses
Never Before Shown, 1930s.
(Lyle) **$32**

The Stocking Parade, Fotos, Fiction, Fun,
December 1938.
(Lyle) **$32**

Gay Book Magazine, November 1937. *(Lyle)* **$25**

Paris Sex-Appeal, August 1935. *(Lyle)* **$25**

Paris   Magazine,   February   1932 *(Lyle)* **$3**

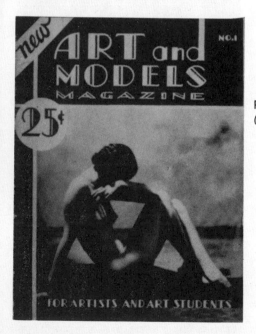

Art and Models Magazine – For Artists and Art Students, No.1. *(Lyle)* **$32**

L'Amour,   August   1902,   French *(Lyle)* **$2**

An unusual novelty Meerschaum pipe, modelled as a skull and crossbones, with an amber mouthpiece, in a fitted case. (Bonhams) **$320**

An unusual carved burl wood pipe, probably American, 19th century, a large knot of burl carved and polished in the form of a grinning stylized man's head fitted with a hollowed root pipe stem painted with a spiralling band, overall length 21in. (Sotheby's) **$2,500**

A pearlware pipe modelled as a man seated astride a green barrel, perhaps Yorkshire, circa 1800, 15.5cm. high. (Christie's) **$1,000**

A Meissen pipe bowl modelled as a recumbent sheep-dog with hinged neck, circa 1745, 8cm. long. (Christie's) **$1,303**

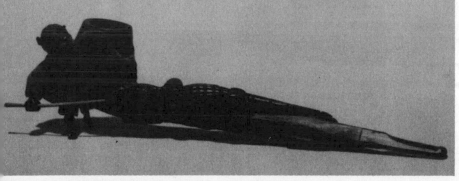

A rare and unusual American folk art pipe, early 20th century, in the form of a black boy clinging to the pipe bowl and fending off an alligator with a stick, 12¾in. long. (Eldred's) **$385**

A Victorian silver-mounted hookah pipe maker's mark of Edwin Charles Purdie London, 1882, on cylindrical base with three stud feet, the spherical water-bowl on three scroll supports, the detachable stem formed as the standing figure of a nude slave gi with rings around her ankles, wearing turban and with her hands raised above he head, supporting a detachable associate baluster shaped tobacco container with pierced domed cover, 32¾in. high.

This hookah or narghile wa probably produced for the Turkish marke The custom of smoking tobacco, ofte flavored, in a water-pipe is supposed t have originated in India. It then passe through Iran and became popular in Turke and the Eastern Mediterranean countrie during the first years of the 17th century. became so popular in Turkey that the Sulta Murat IV (1623-1640) banned smoking c pain of death. However, this only drove underground and the law was repeale some years later.

(Christie's) $6,40

A large silver tobacco pipe, unsigned, Meiji Period (late 19th century) elaborate decorated with two shishi among tree-peonies and rocks training and toughening a cu 28.5cm. long. *(Christie's)* $2,52

A rare American gold pipe, first half of the 19th century, the elongated stem with ove bowl and flattened triangular-shaped mouthpiece, engraved band of scrolling leaves bowl rim and end of stem; one side of bowl with inscription *From L.F. to M.F.*, the oth side of bowl with March 21st. 1856, 9¾in. long; gross weight 1oz. 10dv *(Christie's)* $3,45

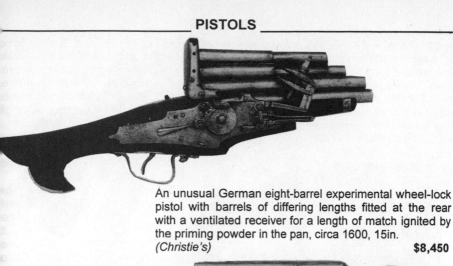

An unusual German eight-barrel experimental wheel-lock pistol with barrels of differing lengths fitted at the rear with a ventilated receiver for a length of match ignited by the priming powder in the pan, circa 1600, 15in. *(Christie's)* **$8,450**

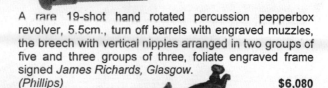

...ercussion knuckleduster combination pistol, the brass ...ame, marked *The Sure Defender*, with attached folding ...ip/knuckleduster, 2in. barrel with spring hammer ...ounted underneath.
...utterfield & Butterfield) **$1,360**

A rare 19-shot hand rotated percussion pepperbox revolver, 5.5cm., turn off barrels with engraved muzzles, the breech with vertical nipples arranged in two groups of five and three groups of three, foliate engraved frame signed *James Richards, Glasgow.*
(Phillips) **$6,080**

...rare flintlock box-lock 'duck's foot' pistol with turn-off ...se-hardened barrels numbered from 1-4, signed and ...graved case-hardened action, later steel with rollers, ...ed belt-hook, thumbpiece safety-catch, by Southall, ...ndon, London proof marks, early 19th century, 9in. ...ng. *(Christie's)* **$5,630**

A composite well made French 4 barrelled 50 bore flintlock boxlock 'duck's foot' pistol, converted from a pocket pistol of circa 1820, 6½in. overall, barrels 1¾in. numbered 1 to 4, the frame engraved with a stag and a wolf, engraved hidden trigger, top safety, ring neck cork, chequered and carved walnut butt. *(Wallis & Wallis)* **$3,200**

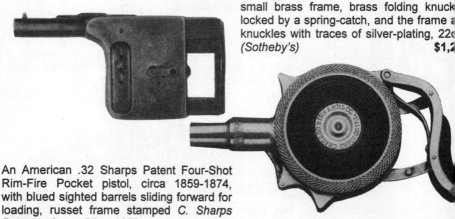

A very rare 6-shot double action 7mm. pinfire Continental harmonica pistol 5½in., barrel group 2¾in., No. 821, plain wooden grips to bird's head butt.
(Lyle) **$3,200**

An unusual percussion under-hamr knuckleduster knife-pistol, 'The S Defender', No. 517, late 19th century, v flat-sided sighted barrel fitted with bar-spr hammer with knurled head directly engag the trigger, wavy blade pivoting on the l small brass frame, brass folding knuck locked by a spring-catch, and the frame a knuckles with traces of silver-plating, 22c *(Sotheby's)* **$1,2**

An American .32 Sharps Patent Four-Shot Rim-Fire Pocket pistol, circa 1859-1874, with blued sighted barrels sliding forward for loading, russet frame stamped *C. Sharps Patent Jan. 25. 1859* on one side, checkered hammer with revolving nose, bird's head butt with rounded walnut grips, and traces of original finish, 12.5cm. *(Bonhams)* **$704**

Chicago Firearms Co. protector palm pis caliber ˙32 rimfire, standard model v nickel plated finish and hard rubber ins *(Butterfield & Butterfield)* **$1,3**

This was a variation on the art of decalomania which was so popular in the late Victorian period. Again it was a parlor craft, whereby a plain glass jar or vase was decorated with bright and colorful designs and pictures.

The term comes from the French word *potiche*, used to describe what was originally a Chinese vase shape, but one which was regularly adopted by English potteries such as Worcester.

The technique was to paste the same scraps as one would use for decalomania on a colored ground and then stick it to the *inside* of a transparent glass vase. It would then be varnished to hold it in position. The result, according to Sir William Harrington, 'outvies all Dresden and excels St. Cloud'.

As with the shape, so with the content. Potichomania tends to an oriental theme, perhaps as a result of exhibitions in London and Paris in the 1860s, which brought japonaiserie to the attention of the fashionable world and made it all the rage.

Two potichomania covered baluster vases, late 19th century, each with potichomania depicting floral sprays, birds, pagodas and mandarins, 13½in. high.
(Christie's) **$1,747**

A pair of Victorian potichomania vases, of ovoid form with shaped lids, each with polychrome chinoiserie transfers on a white ground, 16¼in. high.
(Andrew Hartley) **$4,719**

A wicker and bentwood baby carriage, labelled *Whitney*, raised on wooden wheels, America, circa 1895, 55in. long. *(Skinner)* **$560**

An interesting Victorian child's horsedrawn carriage, the wicker seat lined with buttoned leatherette cushions, 150cm. long *(Phillips)* **$2,720**

1930s German wickerwork pram with alloy wheel arches and bumpers. *(Lyle)* **$160**

A rare T. Trotmans patent 1854 folding pram with carpet back seating and wood and brass wheels. *(Lyle)* **$800**

A fine Landau baby carriage, circa 1870, by S.H. Kimball, Boston, Mass., featuring a turned push bar, 40in. long. **$4,500**

A baby carriage with maker's name plate attached, A. Mitchell, Margate, height to hood 31in. *(Worsfolds)* **$640**

George Cruickshank, A Scene In The Farce Of 'Lofty Projects' As Performed With Great Success For The Benefit & Amusement Of John Bull Ano D 1825, hand colored etching published by G. Humphrey London July 17th 1825, a good impression, 25 x 35cm. *(Bonhams)* **$2,560**

N. Currier (Publisher), The Life of a Fireman, 'Take Up', 'Man Your Rope', hand colored lithograph, with touches of gum arabic, 1854, L. Maurer del., 435 x 660mm. *(Sotheby's)* **$1,150**

◄

James Gillray, The Fashionable Mamma or the Convenience of Modern Dress, colored etching, published 1796 by H. Humphrey, wove paper, with margins, 35½ x 25cm. *(Christie's)* **$550**

A print of 'The Reward of Cruelty' by William Hogarth (1697-1764). *(Lyle)* **$280**

19th century print by Aubrey Vincent Beardsley (1872-1898). *(Lyle)* **$320**

'Love in a Tub' by Thomas Rowlandson, circa 1802. *(Lyle)* **$640**

lliam Heath, *Take care of your pockets, The Slap up Swell wot drives when ever he
es, The Cad to the man wot drives the sovereign, The guard wot looks arter the
vereign*, hand-colored etchings, published 1829 by T. McLean, 11¼ x 15¾in.
hristie's)   **$735**

fore and After by William Hogarth, the first shows how precarious it is for Frailty to strive
h Opportunity: and the second, how useless it is for Importunity to solicit Impossibility.
le)   **$640**

James Gillray, Metallic-tractors, hand-colored aquatint, published by H. Humphrey, wove paper, with margins, slight discoloration to sheet edges, 25 x 32cm. *(Christie's)* **$560**

N. Currier (Publisher), Arguing the Point, hand colored lithograph, with touches of gum arabic, 1855, after the painting by Arthur F. Tait, framed, 467 x 606mm. *(Sotheby's)* **$4,600**

James Gillray, Brisk Cathartic, hand colored etching, published 1804 by Humphrey, wove paper, with margins, 25 x 20cm. *(Christie's)* **$40**

blue-green ceramic Jumbo radio in the
rm of an elephant before a palm tree, with
tegral detector radio.
Auction Team Köln)   **$450**

A radio lamp, by Radio Lamp Company of
America, Chicago, of bronzed metal with
baluster stem, five-valve chassis in base,
speaker concealed in the 'reservoir', electric
lamp, 25in. high. *(Christie's)*   **$686**

e first German transistor radio by
efunken in its original case.
ction Team Köln)   **$3,197**

Ballantine's Whisky bottle radio complete
with original box, 9in. high, circa 1965.
(Lyle)   **$65**

National Panasonic for Matsushita Electric Industrial Co. Ltd., Japan, portable radio model 'R-725', circa 1969, plastic. *(Sotheby's)* **$187**

A Zenith Golden Triangle radio alarm, rotates on its base. *(Auction Team Köln)* **$171**

Emor globe radio, circa 1947, in a chromium plated case with black metal stand, 43in. high. *(Lyle)* **$1,600**

A Kuba Komet 1523 de Luxe combined radio and television, in working order, 1962. *(Auction Team Köln)* **$8,408**

A transparent plastic Bubble television by Zarach, UK, circa 1970, Sony colour television elements housed in and visible through a brown tinted plexiglass sphere, 68.5cm. high. *(Bonhams)* **$1,702**

A very early de Forest Spherical Double-Wing Audion radio tube, circa 1906. *(Auction Team Köln)* **$1,340**

A green Ekco circular casing, Type AD 65, with (distorted) semi-circular dial, circular central speaker grille with three chromium-plated strips, 15½in. diameter, and a G.E.C. speaker cone. *(Christie's)* **$5,265**

A Loewe OE 333 local receiver with Dr. Lertes reel and battery cable, 1927. *(Auction Team Köln)* **$1,084**

7th century child's rattle bearing the dinburgh date letter for 1681. .yle) **$3,200**

Unusual Edwardian child's silver rattle/teether with double child's mask to top, Birmingham 1908. *(G.A. Key)* **$276**

An Edwardian child's rattle in the form of Mr. Punch. *(Phillips)* **$210**

silver novelty rattle, depicting the bust of a entleman, wearing a hat, suit and bow tie, ith four dependant bells, mother of pearl andle, Birmingham, date letter worn, aker's mark of *A.M.* 3onhams) **$290**

orthwest coast polychromed carved wood ven rattle, carved in two sections, 12¼in. ng. *(Lyle)* **$8,000**

A 19th century beechwood rattle for bird scaring, 10½in. long. *(Lyle)* **$160**

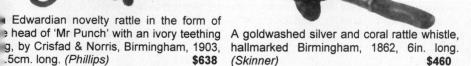

Edwardian novelty rattle in the form of e head of 'Mr Punch' with an ivory teething g, by Crisfad & Norris, Birmingham, 1903, .5cm. long. *(Phillips)* **$638**

A goldwashed silver and coral rattle whistle, hallmarked Birmingham, 1862, 6in. long. *(Skinner)* **$460**

A molded redware figural group, attributed to the 'Master Hobo Potter', Pennsylvania, 19th century, depicting a dog resting on an alligator atop a turtle, 5in. high.
(Christie's) **$13,800**

A glazed redware figure of a dog, probab Pennsylvania, 19th century, molded in th form of a seated dog with basket in mou with articulated fur, the glazed red body wi daubs of brown, 5¼in. high.
(Christie's) **$2,50**

A glazed redware figure of a bird, possibly American, 19th century, molded in the form of a perched upright peacock, with articulated crest, head, body and tail, on a stylized tree stump base.
(Christie's) **$1,500**

A glazed redware pig rumme Pennsylvania, 19th century, in the form of pig with articulated ears, eyes, snout, ar tail and incised body on bent legs, wi spout at rear, all in clear glaze with brov daub highlights, 5in. high, 9in. wid
(Christie's) **$6,00**

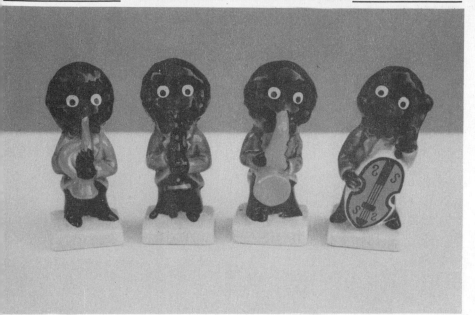

Wade, Robertson's Golly musicians, circa 1960. *(Ian Pendlebury)*   (Four)   **$640**

Robertson's Golly musician hardboard display figure. *(Ian Pendlebury)* **$240**

Robertson's Golly china teapot. *(Ian Pendlebury)* **$120**

Robertson's Golly bandstand by Carltonware, circa 1985. *(Ian Pendlebury)* $320

Golly musician trinket boxes by Do-Do Designs. *(Ian Pendlebury)* (Each) $96

Robertson's 'Golden Shred' showcard, circa 1960. *(Ian Pendlebury)* **$50**

Robertson's Golly light up counter display 'Golly it's Good'.
(Ian Pendlebury) **$640**

Robertson's Golly pottery dish. *(Ian Pendlebury)* **$16**

Robertson's Golly china cruet set. *(Ian Pendlebury)* **$80**

A small 1960s Robertson's showcard. *(Ian Pendlebury)* **$50**

Robertson's Golly shop showcard, circa 1970. *(Ian Pendlebury)* **$80**

Robertson's Mincemeat showcard, circa 1950. *(Ian Pendlebury)* **$130**

Robertson's Golly puzzle by Gamecraft Ltd. *(Ian Pendlebury)* **$32**

Robertson's 'Lemon Curd' showcard, circa 1950. *(Ian Pendlebury)* **$160**

Nando, the mechanism activated by air pressure through remote control, moveable legs and head, with box, by Opset, Italian, circa 1948, 13cm. high.
(Christie's) **$3,200**

Rudolph, a robot light fitting, designed by Frank Clewett, 149cm. high.
(Christie's) **$3,484**

Dyno Robot, battery operated, moveable legs, opening mask to reveal a flashing red dinosaur's head, with box, by Horikawa, Japanese, 1960s, 28.5cm. high.
(Christie's) **$1,280**

A Masudaya 'Machine Man' Robot, the rarest member of the 'gang of five' robot series, battery operated red lithographed tinplate with blue, pale blue and silver details, on/off switch to front of chest, green translucent plastic eyes and mouth panel and amber translucent plastic convex ear panels, 15in., late 1950s.
(Christie's) **$47,840** ▶

An Asakusa Thunder robot, Japanese, 1960s, finished in brown, with plastic sleeves and hands, 11¼in. high.
(Sotheby's) **$1,215**

Sparky Jim, battery operated with remote control, moveable legs and flashing eyes, Japanese, 1950s, 19.5cm. high.
(Christie's) **$1,600**

A rare Nomura tinplate battery operated 'Robby Space Patrol' with mystery action, clear plastic dome and light dishes, 1950s, 12½in. long.
(Christie's) **$2,323**

A Masuyada battery-operated lithographed tinplate Target robot, red target on chest causing evasive action, 1950s, 15in. high.
(Christie's) **$1,549**

A rare 1960s Jupiter Robot, The Space Explorer, by Yonezawa.
(Lyle) **$4,800**

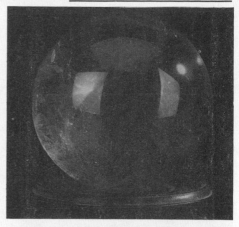

A Chinese rock-crystal ball, 5in. diameter, wood stand. *(Christie's)* **$1,600**

A silver-gilt mounted rock-crystal model of a lion, the head possibly 17th century with outer flange struck with unidentified marks, the body modern, formed as a lion sejant, the crystal body carved to simulate a lion's pelt, the detachable silver-gilt cover chased as the animal's head, the cover 4¾in. high, overall length 8¼in. the cover 8oz. *(Christie's)* **$17,480**

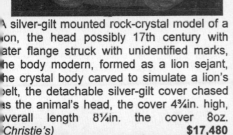

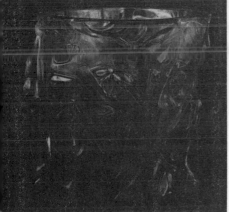

A Chinese rock-crystal brushpot in the form of a tree section carved in relief with bamboo, pine and prunus issuing from rockwork, 5¼in. high. 18th century. *(Christie's)* **$2,880**

A Continental silver-gilt and copper-gilt mounted rock-crystal cup, unmarked, the mounts possibly Austro-Hungarian, 17th century, on lobed spreading oval foot and openwork stem, the shaped oval bowl carved in the form of a hen with applied head, the mounts with foliage borders, the front applied with an openwork scroll and floral festoon cartouche, engraved with a coat-of-arms, in fitted leather case, 7½in. high. *(Christie's)* **$8,000**

Rocking chairs conjure up the image of down-home evenings on American stoops listening to the crickets and puffing on a briar pipe, and there are plenty of hickory and bentwood examples which perfectly fit that picture.

At the upper end of the market there are also plenty of more elegant versions, among them those made by the famous Thonet company of Vienna. These are still mostly made of bentwood, and may have caned seats and backs. When designed by prestige names such at Marcel Breuer they can fetch many thousands of pounds.

Oak and leather platform rocker, late 19th century, all over geometric forms, square crest rail over trapezoid-shaped back with leather insert, flat arm over vertical dowel shaped supports, comforming seat with leather insert. *(Skinner)* **$862**

Rustic bentwood armed rocking chair, probably America, late 19th/early 20th century, the shaped coiled back jointed to the bent arms on splint seat and legs on rockers with arched and coiled seat supports, 41½in. high.
(Skinner) **$920**

▶

A fine and rare painted and smoke-decorated plank-seat rocking chair, Pennsylvania, circa 1820, the horizontal crest flanked by projecting 'bamboo'- turned stiles centering six similarly turned spindles, the compass-form plank-seat below, on turned flaring 'bamboo' legs joined by stretchers, on shaped rockers with scrolled terminals, overall height 32in.
(Sotheby's) **$8,625**

360

The earliest rocking horses had a boat shaped structure, consisting of two parallel semicircular panels held vertically by a small wooden seat between them. By the late 17th century, horses with free standing legs on a panel attached to bow-shaped rockers had become popular. These were now accoutred with saddles and bridles and had a prancing rather than a galloping stance. Gallopers came in around a century later, beautifully and realistically carved. Dapple gray was the favored shade.

Earlier gallopers tended to be narrow, with irregular spots and steep bow rockers. Later, however, they became broader with more regular dapples and shallower rockers.

It was for safety reasons that the trestle base was developed in the 1880s, to prevent the accidents caused by over-exuberant riders. Legs were now attached to a pair of boards which swung on metal brackets mounted at the ends of a trestle base.

Painted wood spring horse, American, late 19th century, in the form of a dapple gray horse, 43¼in. high. *(Skinner)* **$3,450**

A black- and gray-painted child's rocking horse, New England, 19th century, gazing forward with peaked bars, the padded seat below on carved legs and shaped rockers. *(Sotheby's)* **$1,610**

The first commercial makers of rocking horses were probably those who made fairground gallopers, wooden saddle trees, etc. It was thus that G. & J. Lines began in the middle of the 19th century. Other notable manufacturers were the Liverpool Toy Industry, Woodrow & Co. of London, and Norton & Baker of Birmingham.

The points to look for when buying an old rocking horse are a well-carved, lively head, original paintwork and trappings, and a luxuriant mane and tail of real horsehair. Superficial damage indicative of a well-loved, well-used toy is not necessarily prejudicial to the value. Look out in particular for three footed horses on trestles, which are very sought after.

A painted wooden dapple gray rocking horse, on swing stand, 44in. long, by Lines Bros. *(Christie's)* **$1,600**

A Japanese gnarled rootwood bowl naturalistically carved, with two tapering carrying handles and metal liner, the bowl 10½in. wide, 19th century.
(Christie's) **$560**

A Chinese gnarled wood brushpot of irregular form with pierced sections to the body, 9¼in. high, 19th century.
(Christie's) **$400**

A pair of Chinese rootwood models of a Mandarin duck and drake, one looking ahead and the other with its head turned to look behind, 6¾in. long, 19th century.
(Christie's) **$1,380**

A suite of rootwood furniture formed of links, comprising: a pair of chairs with planked seats and a pedestal table with planked top, late 19th century. *(Christie's)* **$7,623**

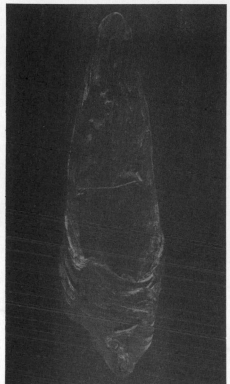

A boxwood root tea caddy, probably Scottish, late 18th or early 19th century, of naturalistic form, with a hinged cover, 6¾in. wide. *(Christie's)* **$3,997**

A rare and early kake hana-ike [hanging flower vase], late Momoyama/early Edo Period late 16th/early 17th century, of gnarled wood, perhaps formed from a section of an ancient creeper, a portion of a branch removed to form a cavity for a flower arrangement, simple copper hook-and-eye provided to support a flower spray, 41cm. high.

This is probably the work of a tea master of the Momoyama period at the end of the 16th century. This was when Sen no Rikyu, tea master to Hideyoshi, purged the tea ceremony of the showy extravagances of its recent past, and nurtured in his pupils an appreciation for utensils of humble beauty and elegantly simple surroundings in which to conduct the ceremony. The tea masters of the time often made their own vases, usually from bamboo, and their products are characterised by a sophistication of taste and the use of curious natural forms such as this, simply adapted to their purposes. *(Christie's)* **$5,249**

A hardwood root sculpture, cut off at the base of the stem and trimmed at the end of the roots, shaped by the top of a rocky outcrop from where it grew, to be displayed upright on its natural axis and viewed from one side only, the sinuous roots of polished honey tones, 28½in. high. *(Christie's)* **$6,000**

Royal Dux figure, of a snake charmer, printed and impressed marks, 22cm. high. *(Christie's)* **$205**

Czechoslovakian Royal Dux wall mask of a red haired lady, 1930s. *(Muir Hewitt)* **$500**

Royal Dux wall mask of a young girl with bonnet, 8in. high. *(Muir Hewitt)* **$570**

'Tango Dancers', a Royal Dux group of two dancers, they both wear blue and gilded costumes, he supports his female companion in a highly stylistic arched pose, 21.50cm. high. *(Phillips)* **$1,300**

A large Royal Dux group in the form of a scantily clad female welcoming the returning hunter, 70cm. high. *(Bearne's)* **$1,888**

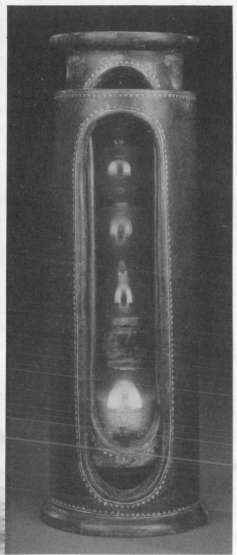

A rare 17th century four-section brass sandglass, the upper and lower frames with punched decoration of flowers and beads, impressed with the maker's mark of a running stag, the upper section secured by four brass clips from the decorative frieze, both upper and lower sections united by eleven barley-twist rectangular section columns, the glasses filled with white sand, bound with wax and cord, with gilt decoration, the reverse fitted with a brass plate for turning the glasses, 7½in. high. *(Christie's)* **$8,000**

A rare late 17th century five-bulb hour glass, the upper series of four bulbs united with the base bulb, the joint protected by green plush binding, contained in a leather-covered wood sliding cylinder within an outer cylinder, both fitted with longitudal apertures to enable the glass to be read and then turned for concealment and protection, the leather-covered wood cylinders decorated with repeating gilt motifs, 11¼in. high. *(Christie's)* **$12,719**

A rare 17th century four double-bulb sand glass, the gilt-brass frame of rectangular polygonal form and finely engraved with strapwork, foliate decoration, the center reserve on both upper and lower faces engraved with a vase containing flowers, edged with a molded section, 9in. wide. *(Christie's)* **$14,536**

Scagliola work is essentially imitation marble, composed of marble chips, isinglass, plaster of Paris and coloring substances and has been practised in Italy since Roman times. It enjoyed a notable renaissance in the early 18th century in Tuscany, where leading exponents worked in the monastery of Vallombrosa under the patronage of Grand Duke Cosimo (1670-1723). Enrico Hugford (b. 1696), the son of an English Catholic exile who became abbot in 1737, perfected the art and his work was renowned throughout Europe.

Pietro Seyter (fl.18th century), one of a set of six panels, with views of Rome and the Campagna, scagliola on slate, 45 x 55cm. *(Finarte)* *(Six)* **$7,714**

An Italian scagliola inlaid Siena marble paperweight, late 18th or early 19th century, of rectangular outline, the scagliola panel depicting a partially clad woman on the back of a centaur, he with hands tied and she attacking him, 6½ x 4¾in.

Used since Roman times to imitate marble, scagliola is composed of pulverised gypsum mixed with pigments and then applied to a gesso ground. *(Christie's)* **$3,200**

A rectangular surface in polychrome scagliola, with trompe l'oeil decoration imitating a game table with cards, coins, documents, weapons and other objects, 162 x 88 x 4cm. *(Finarte)* **$7,02**

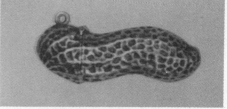

A late 19th century/ early 20th century silver novelty scent bottle, modelled as a monkey nut, the hinged cover opening out to reveal a screw-off top, 1¾in. long. *(Bonhams)* **$416**

Lucretia Vanderbilt 'Lucretia Vanderbilt', the bottle of cobalt blue glass and disk form with butterfly stopper, 4¾in. high. *(Bonhams)* **$1,440**

Amusing mid Victorian Samuel Mordan double scent flask in the form of a pair of opera glasses, 3in. high. London, 1868. *(Prudential)* **$878**

Jury – Jasmin, clear cylindrical bottle with black button stopper, in original open bowerhead amber silk display case, 3in. high. *(Bonhams)* **$416**

A George III 'Chinese Market' gold-mounted enamel and paste-set scent-bottle with watch by James Cox, the watch signed, circa 1780, silver bottle, coated with translucent blue guilloché enamel and applied with a pierced gold cagework chased with scrolls and foliage, a pavilion chased and embossed on the reverse, paste and seed pearl set screw top and hinged base, the watch with gilt-brass verge movement, striking and repeating on a bell, 5½in. high. *(Christie's)* **$24,000**

Lubin 'Enigma', 1921, designed by Julien Viard, the clear bottle and stopper of pyramidal panel form, intaglio molded and heightened in gilt with a sphinx and pillar, 3½in. high. *(Bonhams)* **$2,080**

Baccarat for Guerlain 'Coque d' Or', the cobalt blue glass gilt and modelled in the form of a bow tie with button stopper titled in black, 3¹/8in. high. *(Bonhams)* **$288**

A pair of Gallé scent bottles, decorated in the Persian manner, of stepped bowed rectangular section, sepia tinted glass enamelled in colors and gilt, 13.5cm. high. *(Christie's)* **$4,500**

Rosine 'Le Bosquet de Apollon', 1923, the clear bottle of cigar case form with gilt metal half cover embossed with a young woman' head, 3½in. high. *(Bonhams)* **$2,56**

'Voltigy', a Baccarat clear bottle for A. Gravier, modelled as a butterfly with outstretched wings, the body stained in pink and black, 3⁵/8in. *(Bonhams)* **$31,500**

Rosine 'Aladin', a gray metal bottle of arched panel form cast in relief with rearing horses, 2½in. high. *(Bonhams)* **$80**

Eerie Mysteries, August 1938, featuring City of Stone Corpses by Ralph Powers, first issue. *(Lyle)* **$200**

Tops in Science Fiction with features by Ray Bradbury, Ross Rocklynne and Isaac Asimov, Spring 1953, first issue. *(Lyle)* **$80**

Startling Stories featuring The Black Flame by Stanley G. Weinbaum, January 1939, first issue. *(Lyle)* **$130**

Two Complete Science-Adventure Books featuring Pebble in the Sky by Isaac Asimov, Spring 1953, first issue. *(Lyle)* **$72**

Air Wonder Stories, July 1929 edited by Hugo Gernsback, first issue. *(Lyle)* **$175**

Planet Stories, Winter 1939, Strange Adventures on other Worlds, first issue. *(Lyle)* **$320**

Fantastic Science Fiction, August 1952 featuring The Day New York Ended, first issue. *(Lyle)* **$80**

Captain Future, Wizard of Science, Winter 1940, first issue. *(Lyle)* **$240**

A pair of mahogany table firescreens, one George II and one of later date, each with a rectangular back with twin-hinged semi-circular flaps, 20in. wide.
(Christie's) **$13,579**

Alvar Aalto, manufactured by Oy. Huonekalu Ja Rakennustyötehdas AB 'Screen No. 100', 1935-36, executed circa 1945, rolled pine wood slats strung with wire, 130cm. high. *(Sotheby's)* **$5,520**

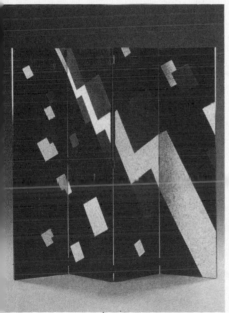

Paul Etienne Saïn, decorated by Bernard Boger and Herbst, four panel abstract screen, circa 1930, the front lacquered in midnight blue and decorated with a bold geometric design in eggshell and shades of rust, the reverse lacquered in black, 68½ x 7¾in. each. *(Sotheby's)* **$9,600**

Piero Fornasetti, four panel screen, 1950s, hand painted and transfer-printed wood, one side decorated with a book shelf containing various vessels and busts, the other side showing a tall garden fence with a seated cat, a violin and a red scarf, 200.5 by 50cm. *(Sotheby's)* **$12,800**

A brass folding fan-shaped spark guard, 39½in. wide. *(Christie's)* **$789**

Paul Etienne Saïn, decorated by Bernar Roger, four panel screen, circa 1930 th front lacquered in Chinese orange an decorated in eggshell with black, yellow an gilt details with a tiger and her cubs, th reverse lacquered in black, 175 x 62cn *(Sotheby's)* **$9,60**

A painted four-leaf screen decorated with a scene in the manner of Francis Barlow of a spaniel and a goose arguing in an idyllic pastoral landscape with other birds, each leaf 86¼ x 26½in.
(Christie's) **$13,552**

A French painted canvas four-fold screen, mid 19th century, the screen painted with an interior with a woman at a piano and a young man leaning against it, 6ft. wide. *(Butterfield & Butterfield)* **$6,325**

A 19th century Rowland Ward scree display, containing stuffed birds, the bambo surround set with approximately twenty fiv exotic birds, the whole raised on outswe bamboo feet, the interior with Rowland Wa and Co. Piccadilly, London paper labe 77cm. wide. *(Bonhams)* **$2,48**

gold-mounted ivory desk seal, unmarked, nglish, circa 1840, carved as a hand asping a baton, the leaf-chased 'cuff' ushion inset with an amethyst matrix, ⁄₂in. high. *(Sotheby's)* **$4,609**

A gold musical fob seal, with typical barillet movement in oval base with répoussé floriate frieze, similarly répoussé arched upper section and winding shaft with modern watch-winder cap. *(Christie's)* **$1,379**

nineteenth century gold and enamel sical erotic automata seal, the base ged to reveal the painted enamel tomated erotic scene, 30 x 25mm. *hristie's)* **$8,800**

A rare Imperial ivory square seal, Kangxi (1662-1722). The upper half deeply carved and pierced in high relief with a five-clawed full-frontal scaly dragon surrounding a flaming pearl amidst clouds above two confronting dragons above breaking waves on each side, the base carved to form a positive seal reading Kangxi yu lan zhi bao, 3¾in. high. *(Christie's)* **$35,000**

varicolored gold musical fob seal with mmemorative portraits of Napoleon I and sephine and an erotic automaton, Swiss, ly 19th century, 42mm. high. *ristie's)* **$17,600**

A Korean gilt bronze seal, the square base surmounted by a tortoise standing foursquare with head raised and cast with a bulbous snout and incised with fangs, Yi dynasty, 15th/16th century, 9.6cm. square. *(Christie's)* **$20,273**

A nineteenth century silver mounted iv◄ desk seal, unmarked, modelled as a ha▼ holding a baluster shaped seal, flu▼ terminal, foliate mounted matrix, initiall◄ 7.6cm. long. *(Bonhams)* **$6**

An historical gold fob seal owned ▶ Thomas and John Hancock, circa 176◄ the citrine matrix carved with the Hanco◄ arms within a rococo cartouche. *(Christie's)* **$6,05◄**

A Continental silver novelty seal, with import marks for Chester 1907, importer's mark of Berthold Müller the handle modelled as a cherub surmounted on an upright signet ring, with a monogrammed oval cartouche, 5.8cm. high. *(Bonhams)* **$240**

A jewelled gold desk seal, unmarked, la◄ 19th century, formed as an India▲ rhinoceros with baroque pearl body, a◄ chased gold head and legs, 2¾in. long. *(Sotheby's)* **$6,53◄**

An unusual gold musical and erotic seal in oval case, the movement wound by the pendant and operated by a slide in the band, 30 x 25mm. *(Christie's)* **$8,800**

Early 19th century Swiss gold and enam◄ musical fob seal. **$1,6◄**

A German made tinplate sentry box, with 120mm. sentry of the Foot Guards, in original box, 1890. **$470**

A late Victorian novelty silver and enamel vesta case, London 1887, maker's mark overstamped, possibly that of Henry Jackson, modelled as a sentry box, hinged cover, enamelled with a Life Guards sentry, striker to base, 5.7cm. high.
(Bonhams) **$3,200**

blue painted sentry box, 20th century, the edimented gabled roof above an arched ntrance, the weatherboarded sides and ack each fitted with glazed windows, re-ecorated, 39in. wide, 114in. high. Acquired om Buckingham Palace, London. Christie's) **$4,000**

A German made tinplate sentry box with 60mm. mounted sentry of the royal Horse Guards, in original box, 1890. **$640**

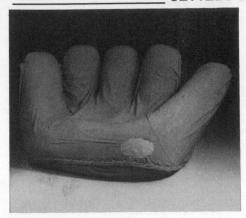

A giltwood daybed in the Theban style 79½in. wide. *(Christie's)* **$18,876**

A Denim Joe sofa, designed 1970, for Poltronova, the original denim upholstery on polyurethane form with tubular steel inner frame, marked with leather patch *Joe, Made in Italy.*

This design encapsulates the influence that the American Pop Art movement exerted on progressive Italian designers during the late 1960s and early 1970s; the oversize baseball glove in homage to baseball legend Joe DiMaggio, and alluding to the massive 'soft' sculptures of everyday objects by Claes Oldenburg. More often encountered with leather or vinyl upholstery, the choice of denim as a covering reinforces the allusion to American popular culture, and challenges preconceptions of 'good taste'.
(Christie's) **$4,000**

Man Ray for Ultramobile collection, Gavina 'Le Témoin', designed late 1960s, produced from 1971, white vinyl, perspex front, the eye is painted on the inner surface and the internal padding becomes its white, 27in high, 60in. wide.

The large eye, the witness insistently observes you in your home where your conscience cannot withstand then you turn it over, and it immediately turns into a sofa; this is Man Ray description of the new design for the Ultramobile series.
(Sotheby's) **$2,42**

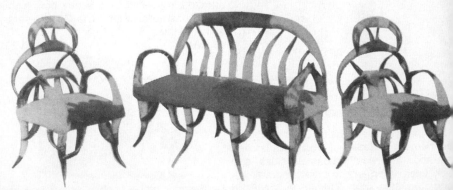

A Texas Steerhorn and hide-upholstered three piece suite comprising a settee and two matching armchairs, the settee 62in. wide. *(Christie's)* **$2,02**

Antique American Mammy's bench, with grain-painted and stencilled decoration, 48in. long. *(Eldred's)* **$660**

An impressive Black Forest carved and stained wood bench, circa 1880, the seat carved with bears, shown playing musical instruments and dancing beneath an oak tree, supported at either end by bears standing on their haunches, 37in. high. *(Christie's)* **$36,800**

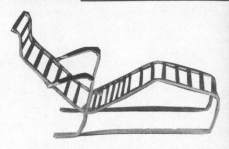

A 'lip' sofa, after a design by Salvador Dali, upholstered in red nylon stretch fabric. *(Christie's)* **$1,848**

An aluminum chaise longue, designed by Marcel Breuer, the seat, base and arms constructed from split and bent single strips of aluminum, circa 1935.
(Christie's) **$30,889**

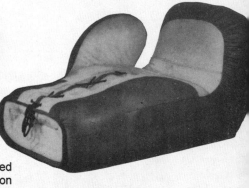

One of a pair of George III green-painted garden benches attributed to the Yealmpton chair-makers, each with waved serpentine toprail above a pierced strigil splat centered by an interwoven oval panel, 53¾in. wide. *(Christie's)* **$13,464**

A DeSede boxing glove chaise, the oversize form of light brown and pale cream leather, with cord laces, over foam and wood frame, circa 1970-75. *(Christie's)* **$8,000**

An amboyna and ivory inlaid boudoir canapé, the design attributed to Jules Leleu, circa 1920-25, the curved top inlaid with ivory with a design of swags, the front with small detailed ivory scrolls, 58½in. wide. *(Christie's)* **$10,281**

An Italian gray-painted settle, the arched back painted with putti and a winged angel with a horn supporting an armorial cartouche, late 17th century, 84in. wide. *(Christie's)* **$25,740**

wer pipe art is perhaps the archetypal
k art, produced as it was by workers in
wer pipe factories in their own time and
 their own pleasure and slipped into the
n along with the standard product.

As a practice it was widespread and
ng-lived in the American midwest from
ound 1890-1950, where it thrived despite
e attempts of the factory owners to stamp
ut.

Most of the items produced were
actical in nature, such as bookends and
orstops. Animals, and lions in particular,
re favorite subjects.

Eventually some factory owners
me to see realise the merit of what the
en were making and made the practice
ore official, themselves turning out pieces
 advertising and souvenir purposes.
like the originals, which were always
onymous, these would be stamped with
 company's name.

Unglazed recumbent lion, probably
American, late 19th/early 20th century,
resting on a rectangular base and looking
straight ahead with incised patterning on
mane and tail, 12 x 14in.
(Sotheby's) **$1,000**

e 19th century unglazed recumbent lion
ting on an ovoid base and looking
aight ahead. *(Sotheby's)* **$500**

A rare large 19th century molded sewer tile
lion doorstop, probably Ohio, in the half
round with head facing left, painted dark
brown. *(Sotheby's)* **$1,500**

A fine and large glazed
sewer tile lion, probably
Ohio, late 19th/early 20th
century, the recumbent
figure of a lion posed on a
rectangular base with
canted corners, the whole
covered in an iridescent
reddish-brown glaze.
(Sotheby's) **$3,450**

A rare American Clark's Foliage cha
stitch machine, lacking needle, circa 1859
(Auction Team Köln) **$4,675**

A Shaw & Clark ('Scinny Pillar') American
chain stitch machine by the Shaw & Clark
Sewing Machine Co., Biddeford, Maine,
USA, spool replaced, technically complete,
circa 1864. *(Auction Team Köln)*

$6,958

A rare McQuinn lockstitch sewing mach
with scalloped base, partial gilt transf
Britannia trade-marks, dated *October*
1878. *(Christie's)* **$7,**

A rare 'Mary' German chain stitch machir
by Müller, circa 1890.
(Auction Team Köln) **$1,56**

A rare 'Clown' sewing machine, German,
third quarter 19th century, marked with an
armored arm holding a balance, and also
patent number 6125, the cast iron clown,
enamelled in colors, sewing at a table,
20cm. high. *(Christie's)* **$6,004**

A Jacob L. Frey original US pate
machine, wooden, with brass mechanis
1865. *(Auction Team Köln)* **$4,5€**

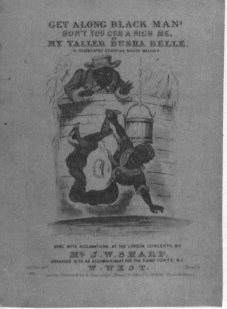

et Along Black Man! arranged by W. West, rca 1830. *(Lyle)* **$72**

I Bought Her a Sealskin Jacket by W. Bint, 1850. *(Lyle)* **$25**

e Jolly Dogs Polka, by C.H.R. Marriott, lored lithograph, 1870. *le)* **$32**

The Scientific Simpleton composed by Vincent Davies, 1850. *(Lyle)* **$65**

Dreaming Eyes Waltz by Thurley Beale, published by W. Paxton & Co. Ltd., London, circa 1904. *(Lyle)* **$25**

Song sheet for 'The Kiss on a Railway Train' by C.H. Mackney, dated *1866*. *(Lyle)* **$4**

The Daughter of the Regiment, as sung by Jenny Lind, colored lithograph, 1840. *(Lyle)* **$32**

Song sheet for Tom Matthews' 'Clown Songs', Hot Codlings, Tippitiwichet, The Life of a Clown, dated *1856*. *(Lyle)* **$4**

J.S. Sawyer pattern projectile, iron body covered by a lead jacket, missing use, 9⁵/₈in. long. *(Butterfield & Butterfield)* **$1,870**

Solid shot with metal banded wood sabot, 4in. in diameter. *(Butterfield & Butterfield)* **$1,760**

U.S. James bolt, missing sabot, 3.8in. caliber, 7in. long. *(Butterfield & Butterfield)* **$2,090**

J.S. 12-pound howitzer canister, for the howitzer cannon, wooden cylinder is longer than standard canister, 4.62 caliber. *Butterfield & Butterfield)* **$3,300**

U.S.N. 12-pound canister round, portion of tin side removed to expose canister shot, wooden sabot on base intact, 4.62in. caliber. *(Butterfield & Butterfield)* **$2,090**

U.S. 2.6in. canister round, portion of tin side cut away to expose the canister balls for display, wooden sabot intact, 6¼in. long. *(Butterfield & Butterfield)* **$3,575**

French rifled projectile, circa late 19th century, two rows of lead studs, missing fuse, ½in. long. *(Butterfield & Butterfield)* **$302**

British Whitworth rifled spherical solid shot, first appeared in 1867 Whitworth's manual, 5⁷/₁₆in. diameter. *(Butterfield & Butterfield)* **$1,650**

32-pound stand of grapeshot, complete with top and bottom plate 6.4in. caliber, 8½in. long. *(Butterfield & Butterfield)* **$2,200**

A shell veneered mirror, 20th century, the rectangular plate bordered by a profusion of shells, with a conforming cresting above, 51½ x 26in. wide. *(Christie's)* **$1,290**

Three Victorian graduated shellwork displays, modelled as trees, the wirework frames mounted with a profusion of shells and flowerheads and foliage, under glass domes, 24¾in., 22in., and 18in. high *(Christie's)* **$4,41..**

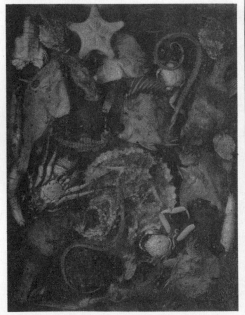

A cased display of crustacea and other marine life, 19th century, 18in. x 12in. *(Christie's)* **$645**

A shell encrusted stick stand, in the form a boot, circa 1975, 26in. high. *(Christie's)* **$1,84..**

A conch shell box in the 17th century style, the shell body with geometrically patterned neck mount, the silver-plated cap with chain, 7in. long. *(Christie's)* **$370**

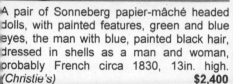

A pair of Sonneberg papier-mâché headed dolls, with painted features, green and blue eyes, the man with blue, painted black hair, dressed in shells as a man and woman, probably French circa 1830, 13in. high. *(Christie's)* **$2,400**

A shellwork valentine, mid 19th century, the parquetry rectangular box with canted angles inlaid with mother-of-pearl and ivory, the interior with various colored shells in a foliate pattern, 14in. wide. *(Christie's)* **$1,470**

A large shell encrusted composite bust of Neptune, last quarter 20th century, from the workshops of Anthony Redmile, the bust mounted with a spherical silvered dish, 46in. high. *(Christie's)* **$9,600**

Sailor's Valentine, 19th century, octagonal segmented cases various exotic shells, 'To One I Love', each case 9 x 9in.
(Skinner)   **$2,185**

An unusual carved wood and shell work frame, third quarter 19th century, the oval frame composed of a wood puzzle carving and mollusc shells, dated *1864*, 8in. x 6in.
(Sotheby's)   **$460**

An unusual sailor's valentine inscribed *Naval Review at Spithead*, dated *1895,* having a shellwork heartshaped frame surrounding a glass enclosed diorama, 8¾ x 7¾in.
(Sotheby's)   **$1,380**

Four late Victorian 'Sailor's Favours', all of octagonal form and mounted on stand with slender cabriole legs, each decorated with differing shells and coral beads forming heart, overall 30in. wide x 29in. high.
(Canterbury)   **$4,576**

A pair of late Victorian shellwork flower displays, each modelled as trees with a lady and gentleman seated beneath respectively under glass domes, 19¾in. high.
(Christie's)   **$1,920**

386

A pair of transparent yellow rubberized ankle boots, stamped with Mary Quant daisy in heels, with Mary Quant carrier bag. *(Christie's)* **$1,056**

A pair of white leather and beige suede brogues, made by Foot Loose and once owned by Ringo Starr, with a letter of authenticity. *(Bonhams)* **$474**

A pair of unusual court shoes, of multi-colored leather, the toe and vamp in the design of a Chinese dragon's head complete with eyes, nose, jagged teeth and topped with red flames, the ankle and toe with scale-like overlapping bands of silver and black leather and embellished with shaped green leather protruding like a crest, with 4¼in. heel, labelled *THEA CANDELABRA*, size 5.5. *(Christie's)* **$170**

A pair of Keith Moon's cowboy boots, 1970s, in tan leather and skin, size 9A, labelled *Sheplers Inc. The World's Largest Western Stores. (Sotheby's)* **$753**

Jean Harlow, a pair of size four black suede and cream leather dress shoes, the interior label of the open filigree style shoes reads *Walk Over, Cabana.*
(Christie's) **$1,955**

John Lennon's hiking boots, circa 1964-66, the pair of brown leather hiking boots labelled *Original Chippewa Shoe Company, USA,* size 6½ approx.
(Bonhams) **$2,611**

A pair of black kid leather high top boots worn by Audrey Hepburn as "Eliza Dolittle" in the film My Fair Lady, 1964.
(Christie's) **$1,610**

Elton John shoes, a pair of oxford platform shoes of beige canvas with metallic lime green covering the quarter.
(Butterfield & Butterfield) **$1,380**

A lady's mule of yellow and brown silk, brocade woven with abstract designs and cartouches, 2.5in. high, 10in. long, circa 1660. *(Christie's)* **$25,025**

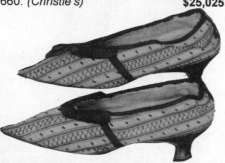

A pair of lady's shoes of blue and white ticking embroidered in pale blue and maroon silk with a fleck design and herringbone pattern, late 18th century.
(Christie's) **$6,950**

A pair of lady's boots of fine grosgrain crimson silk, embroidered in yellow silks with trailing flowers and strapwork, *F. Pinet, Paris*, the sole also stamped, *1867*.
(Christie's) **$2,375**

A pair of shoes, of green silk with white brocade with pointed upturned toe, white kid rands, and 2¼in. covered heel, 1730s.
(Christie's) **$4,329**

A superb pair of Michael Jackson's purple lace-up dancing shoes, heavily studded with purple glass stones.
(Phillips) **$7,500**

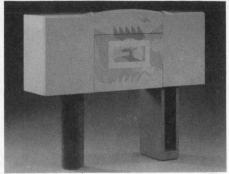

Alessandro Mendini for Nuova Alchimia, manufactured by Zabro, 'Cantaride' sideboard, 1984, limited production, gray and blue lacquered wood, 57¼in. wide. *(Sotheby's)* **$4,800**

A burr-maple Art Deco sideboard, the design attributed to Ray Hille, the rounded rectangular top above deep frieze with vertically fluted panel and two short drawers, 137cm. wide. *(Christie's)* **$1,181**

A large oak sideboard by Romney Green, the top with four open shelves flanked by two stepped compartments, on four bracket feet, 298cm. *(Christie's)* **$13,860**

A Hille sideboard, the rectangular superstructure with three sliding glass doors each enclosing single glass shelf, on four bowed carved legs, 167.5cm. wide. *(Christie's)* **$1,083**

Sideboard, designed 1985, inlaid wood, stained in various colors, black and natural shelf inside, double opening doors the underside with metal label *Zabro Divisione Nuova Alchimia 1985*, 33in. high by 52in. wide. *(Sotheby's)* **$1,280**

A burr maple Art Deco sideboard, the design attributed to Ray Hille, rectangular top above single fluted drawer, flanked by rectangular sides supporting single glass shelf, 113cm. wide. *(Christie's)* **$1,083**

An extremely fine, rare and important silk embroidered picture; The Tree of Life, Morris Family, Philadelphia, late 18th century, 13½ x 18in.
(Sotheby's) **$288,500**

A mid 17th century embroidered cushion worked in silk and metal threads on ivory satin silk ground, having a small tassel at each corner, English, 26.5 x 31cm., circa 1660. *(Phillips)* **$1,112**

A knitted silk pinball, signed *Sarah Hockey*, Pennsylvania, dated *1796*, the oval ball executed in red, yellow and white silk knitted stitches with a crown and hearts, 2in. long. *(Sotheby's)* **$690**

A pair of oval embroidered pictures in colored silks with sprays of naturalistic flowers and butterflies against a tobacco colored satin ground, 1780s, 14 x 17in. *(Christie's)* **$1,197**

A fine silk embroidered picture depicting Cymbelene, signed *Mehitable Neal at Mrs Saunders and Mrs Beach's Academy*, Dorchester, Massachusetts, circa 1807, 17 x 22½in.
(Sotheby's) **$23,000**

A pair of Beauvais tapestry cushions, the tapestry mid-18th century, woven in wools and silks, one depicting a pair of hounds in a wooded landscape, 24 x 26in. and 23 x 24in. *(Christie's)* **$7,921**

A late 19th/early 20th century Continental table centerpiece, modelled as a wolf, standing with his head to one side, in a fixed stare, the whole textured to simulate hair with colored glass eyes, the head detachable, circa 1900, lacquered, approximately 73cm. long, 138oz. *(Christie's)*
◄ **$11,408**

late 19th century Austro-Hungarian toothpick holder in the form of a sailor standing on a shaped oblong case with engraving next to a barrel and an anchor, circa 1880, 13cm. high, 2.25oz. *(Christie's)* **$499**

An Edwardian silver table bell, Birmingham 1001, maker's mark of S. and W. Smith Co. domed circular form, pierced foliate scroll decoration, with a Tudor rose mounted finial, the whole on four bracket feet, 7.3cm. high. *(Bonhams)* **$640**

A Chinese silver gift filigree dish modelled as a goldfish, set on four feet, pierced and decorated with fine scroll work simulating the fins and scales, 9½in. long, 19th century. *(Christie's)*
► **$440**

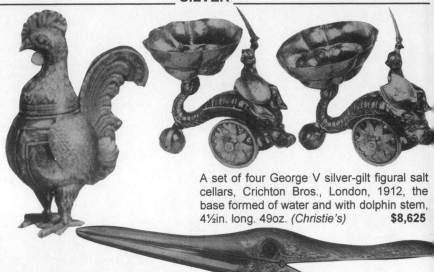

A set of four George V silver-gilt figural salt cellars, Crichton Bros., London, 1912, the base formed of water and with dolphin stem, 4½in. long. 49oz. *(Christie's)* **$8,625**

Rooster-form silver spice shaker, probably northern Europe, wings hinged for movement, lid rendered as rooster's head, pierced stopper within, chicken-form finial, 7in. approximately 11 troy oz. *(Skinner)* **$805**

A pair of late Victorian silver novelty glove stretchers, London 1887, maker's mark of George Heath, modelled as a duck's head, the duck's bill forming the stretchers, with glass eyes, engraved with realistically modelled feathers, 20.5cm. long. *(Bonhams)* **$480**

A late 19th century Continental table bell, in the form of a lady in 16th century dress, her costume elaborately chased and embossed with a foliate pattern, with English import marks for 1899, 9cm. high, 4oz. *(Christie's)* **$700**

A pair of German salt cellars, the bowls on wheeled dolphin supports with a child with sword and shield, late 19th century, 6cm. high, 200gm. total weight. *(Dorotheum)* **$330**

An egg cup and small spoon, designed by Joseph Hoffmann, manufactured by the Wiener Werkstätte, 1903-4, the egg cup on four cylindrical supports with bead brackets on a circular wire base, the spoon with four beads at the base of the handle, height of egg cup 2in. *(Christie's)* **$9,274**

A George III silver-gilt Sun Insurance Company badge, maker's mark of Peter and William Bateman, London, 1805, circular, cast and chased with a sun within a laurel wreath, above applied with text *Sun.Fire.Office*, on matted ground, the reverse with inventory no. *1805/6*, engraved 4, 7.5cm. high, 1.8oz.

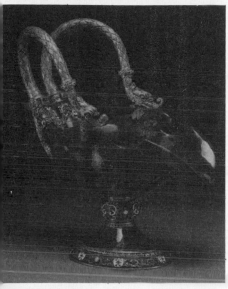

A German Renaissance style silver-mounted blood agate ewer, third quarter 19th century, by Herman Ratzendorfer, the shaped bowl applied with twin serpent handles over an oval spreading foot applied overall with semi-precious stones and natural pearls with maker's marks stamped *HR*, 9¾in. high. The firm Herman Ratzendorfer was founded in 1843, producing gold, silver, enamel and rock crystal in the Neo-Renaissance taste. He began showing his rock crystal and enamel pieces when he participated in the 1871 London Exhibition, and then went on to participate in the 1873 Exposition Universelle in Vienna, and the 1878 and 1889 Expositions de Paris.
(Christie's) **$12,650**

The earliest known references to insurance badges date from the very late 17th century. However, it was during the 18th century that the growth of insuring businesses and houses took place, with firms attaching their insurance marks to the exterior of the building they insured. They also issued insurance badges to their employees, by way of identification, in the way Watermen had worn badges on their sleeves for many years. The Sun Insurance Company who commissioned this badge from the Bateman's, whose business premises and houses they insured, was founded in 1710.
(Christie's) **$4,400**

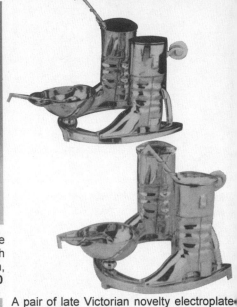

A Victorian electro-plated novelty preserve stand formed as two curling stones, with crossed broom handle and matching spoon, 7in. high. *(Christie's)* **$580**

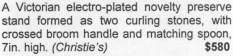

A pair of late Victorian novelty electroplate cruet sets, 1877 and 1884, maker's mark c Elkington and Co., the mustard pot an pepper pot modelled as a pair of ridin boots, the salt cellar modelled as a jockey' cap, the whole on a horseshoe base, th carrying handle modelled as a spur, th condiment spoons modelled as riding crop 9.5cm. *(Bonhams)* **$1,12C**

A rare pair of Old Sheffield plated candlesticks, commemorating four British Admirals and their naval victories over the French, formed to resemble telescopes with stepped, cylindrical columns, decorated with swirling garlands and oval cartouches below flared, stiff, papyrus leaf capitals, the base decorated in low relief with four shields, emblems of war and crossed Union flags, the shields inscribed with the names and dates of the following Admirals: *Nelson 1 Aug 1798, Jervis 14 Feb 1797, Duncan 11 Oct 1797 and Howe 1 June 1794*, circa 1800, 21.5cm. high. *(Christie's)* **$1,011**

Pair of Gorham pelican-form dishes, on pla oval base, the round dishes rendered as th body of a standing pelican, wings with strip of silver as stylized feathers head with lor beak, 8in. high, approximately 28 troy o. total. *(Skinner)* **$2,18**

A novelty parcel-gilt bon-bon dish, in the form of a wheelbarrow with lattice-work sides, a cast border of floral scrolls and a 'Tudor' rose wheel, by George Fox, 1896, 12.75cm. long, 3oz.
(Bearnes) **$1,083**

A late 19th century Dutch miniature novelty model of a bureau bookcase with a fall front, three drawers and a glazed upper section, the sides each with a hinged door, Leeuwarden, 1892, 14cm. high, 7.75oz. gross. (Christie's) **$1,100**

A silver gilt bezoar stone case in two sections, with bands of pierced scroll work and lined, each end with a double rosette rivet, with stone, probably Anglo-Indian or English, late 17th/18th century, 7.5cm. diameter.

Bezoar or Goa stones were more or less spherical concoctions of 'bezoar, ambergreece, pearl, Unicorn's Horn, Coral and such other of the greatest Cordial preservatives, Corroboraters and Renewers of Strength and Youth', which were devised by Gaspar Antonio, a Florentine lay-brother of the Jesuit monastery in Goa. Goa stones were imported into England in the last quarter of the 17th century and in the 18th century.
(Woolley & Wallis) **$9,164**

An Edwardian cast model of a leopard on an alabaster base, (the emblem of the Worshipful Company of Skinners) and engraved around the collar, King Edward VII Coronation 1902, 19cm. long overall. (Christie's) **$700**

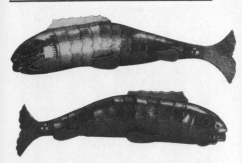

Two metalware flexible fishes with red and black glass eyes, hinged heads and a Hebrew inscription inside each one, bearing marks for Vienna, 1849, 33cm. and 35cm. long. *(Christie's)* **$2,200**

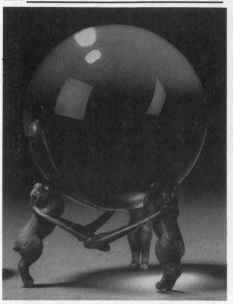

Three silver hares holding a glass ball, Meiji Period, 19th century, finely detailed, 6¾in. high. *(Christie's)* **$3,374**

A Victorian silver-gilt jug, maker's mark of John Samuel Hunt & Robert Roskell, London, 1865, cast and chased in the form of a seated satyr, draped with a lion's pelt, the covered spout formed as shell from which the satyr is drinking, with vine-tendril handle, the spout cover engraved with a coat-of-arms with baron's coronet above, 8¼in. high, 36oz.
(Christie's) **$23,900**

A chased vase with Surrealist bouquet by Cartier, 1936, of flared form, the rim and foot decorated with fronds of seaweed, the bouquet inspired by the sea, 30in. maximum height, stamped maker's marks, French poinçons. *(Christie's)* **$5,544**

A Victorian silver-gilt novelty nine-piece tea service, maker's mark of William Smith of Liverpool, Chester, 1870, comprising teapot, cream-jug, sugar-bowl, four nut dishes, with glass liners, pair of sugar-tongs and ladle, each piece entirely formed of overlapping vine leaves and tendrils, the swing handle to the sugar-bowl, sugar tongs and ladle incorporating bunches of grapes, the interior of the teapot cover engraved *Silver Wedding C.A & M.M.L. 30. May 1887*. fully marked, the teapot 11in. long, gross 57oz.

    William Smith was a Liverpool silversmith whose work was assayed by the Chester Assay Office. Their records list his address as 40 Mount Pleasant, Liverpool. The few pieces known to be by him are extremely unusual and appear to fall into two main catagories. A very distinctive Middle Eastern style with characteristic gold inlay on a second group, into which this service falls, consists of objects in the naturalistic style, the bodies of the vessels being formed from silver sheet chased to simulate leaves.

    Smith was apprenticed to James Wordley of Liverpool, whose other apprentice, with whom he went into partnership, was the Liverpool silversmith and native of Newcastle-Upon-Tyne, Joseph Mayer. Mayer was noted for his antiquarian interests and his large art collection. This reportedly stemmed from his discovery, at the age of 14, of a hoard of Roman coins. *(Christie's)* **$35,615**

An unusual parcel-gilt drinking cup, marked *Ovchinnikov* with Imperial warrant, Moscow, 1863, the cup tapering cylindrical, in imitation of a barrel, the parcel-gilt handle realistically chased and engraved as two wrestlers wearing rubashki, gilt interior, 9in. high, 1,090 gr. *(Christie's)* **$11,200**

A plated novelty, mounted red glass honey pot in the form of a bee with hinged wings forming the cover and six legs, by Mappin & Webb, 17cm. long. *(Christie's)* **$480**

A silver shell-form covered dish, Ball, Black & Co., New York, 1851-1876, oyster shaped, on openwork cattail and grass base, 3⁵/₈in. long, 4oz.
(Christie's) **$1,150**

Soft metal novelty dish, of a young girl gazing at two retrievers, immersed in an oval pond, pierced end lifts, 13in. wide.
(Woolley & Wallis) **$1,200**

German 800 standard silver table garniture as a pair of strutting peacocks, hollow bodies with detachable heads, 15½in. high, 92oz. 6dwt.
(Butterfield & Butterfield) **$2,300**

A pair of plated novelty knife rests, each formed as a jousting mouse and frog.
(Christie's') **$240**

A novelty silver stamp box, Birmingham 1910, maker's mark of K and S., modelled as a wheel barrow, the glazed hinged cover inset with a stamp, 6.5cm. long.
(Bonhams) **$192**

A silver miniature model depicting two fairies seated at a circular dining table, cutlery in their hands, complete with circular plates, covered tureen, wine bottle, cruet set and leg of meat, hallmarked Chester 1900, 1.25oz., length 2in.
(H.C. Chapman) **$430**

An Art Deco painted plaster group of a female skier and a large bird upon a rocky outcrop, impressed *Pecchioli*, 30½in. long.
(Bonhams) **$240**

'Skirolf' a clockwork tinplate figure by E.P. Lehmann, 18½cm. high.
(Lawrence) **$2,080**

The Skier, attributed to Manuel Felguerez Barra, signed *Felguerez* on the figure, painted steel, 10in. high.
(Skinner) **$300**

An undocumented handpainted papier mâché skier figure, with flannel and smooth cotton clothing and wooden legs, clockwork driven, 18cm. high, circa 1950.
(Auction Team Köln) **$187**

An Art Deco painted plaster figure of a female skier upon rectangular base, impressed *Boni.G,* 21in. long.
(Bonhams) **$192**

Copper slave tax badge, Charleston, South Carolina, mid-19th century, stamped *CHARLESTON 1851 SERVANT 2376.* *(Skinner)* **$1,840**

Copper slave tax badge, Charleston, South Carolina, early 19th century, stamped *CHARLESTON 1828 PORTER NO 254,* stamped on reverse *LA FAR* in a rectangle, 2¹/₈ x 2in.

John Joseph La Far (1781-1849) is on record as being a silversmith in Charleston, and also a city marshal.

The slave tax badge, commonly known as the slave badge, was worn by slaves in the southern United States when their owners allowed them to be hired out or self-employed. Each badge was stamped with the city, a number, and a specific trade or occupation and was worn suspended from the neck. The use of such tags arose as a means of controlling slave labor throughout the South, though mainly in the urban cities of Savannah, New Orleans, Mobile, and Norfolk, but Charleston is the only city for which badges still exist. This is hardly surprising when one realises that in 1830 Charleston was an African-American city: its 14,673 slaves and 1,558 free African Americans made up over 57% of the entire population. That almost one in 15 African Americans in the town was in fact a free man would have given the carrying of a slave badge considerable significance. Working arrangements of this type were mandated as early as 1722, but the badge ordinance was not adopted until 1783. After periodic repeal it was reinstated in 1800 and remained until the Civil War.

(Skinner) **$3,220**

Copper slave tax badge, Charleston, South Carolina, early 19th century, stamped *CHARLESTON 2083 SERVANT 1835.* *(Skinner)* **$1,840**

Copper slave tax badge, Charleston, South Carolina, mid 19th century, stamped *CHARLESTON 998 SERVANT 1857*, 1½ x 1½in. *(Skinner)* **$1,840**

A Dutch green painted and carved giltwood and decorated child's sleigh, 19th century, with foliate turned handle and pierced top-rail with hunting horn and scrolls, with a metal liner with pierced rococo foliate scroll sides with dogs and panels with cows and cottages in a Dutch landscape, with bird's heads and sleigh feet with wrought iron scrolls and spindle gallery, 29in. long. (Christie's)

$5,600

A Scandinavian child's painted wooden sleigh, with upholstered back seat and carved horse's head with facing seats for small children, the body painted with a goat, a horse and stars on a black ground, 45in. long. (Christie's) **$1,010**

Painted wooden sled, late 19th century, an olive green child's push sled with gold, black, and yellow striping, on runners, 24in. long. (Skinner) **$1,725**

19th century, an sled with gold, gold upholstery, without handle. **$1,725**

Painted wooden child's sled, late 19th century, 'Kelley' solid wood frame with iron runners, dark green, mustard and red paint, black letters and highlights, 34in. long. (Skinner) **$805**

An Arts and Crafts oak smoker's cabinet, the molded cornice above a glazed cabinet door fitted with a copper fretwork panel, opening to reveal a revolving pipe rack and shelf, the exterior flanked by assorted shaped shelves and racks, with cutout heart motifs, the lock stamped for Shapland and Petter, 50cm. wide. *(Bonhams)* **$700**

A Dunhill smoker's compendium, modelle as a leather bound armchair, the cushio houses a lighter, hinged arms, the base wit an ashtray, 17cm. high.
(Bonhams) **$48(**

A mid 19th century brass tavern tobacco box with central carrying handle flanked by two lidded compartments.
(Phillips) **$369**

A late Victorian oak smoker's cabinet English, circa 1900, with glazed doors an drawers, 42cm. wide.*(Bonhams)* **$418**

A portable tobacco set with a silver handle and six drawers decorated in gold hiramakie on clear lacquered wood with peonies and scrolling foliage, late 19th century, 25.8 x 26 x 19cm.
(Christie's) **$2,287**

An Art Deco chrome smoker's companior modelled as a propeller plane, comprisin two cigarette cases, tobacco holder, lighter cigar cutter and three ashtrays, 24cm diameter. *(Christie's)* **$3,20(**

A late Victorian novelty silver snuff box, London 1896, maker's mark of Henry Freeman, modelled as a Brazil nut, hinged cover, gilded interior, 5.5cm. long. *(Bonhams)* **$240**

treen shoe snuffbox, 18th century, in the rm of a ladies high heeled shoe inlaid in ngraved pewter with a lady and foliate esigns, the interior with a note stating *This hoe was made by the French Prisoners, onfined Sissinghurst near Cranbrooke in he year 1759*, 4¼in. long.
Bonhams) **$480**

An early 19th century Russian novelty snuff box, formed as the figure of a guard dog crouched and ready to pounce, Moscow, circa 1805, 7.25cm. long, 2oz. *(Phillips)* **$1,283**

A late Victorian novelty snuff box modelled as a walnut, London 1899, maker's mark of S. Mordan & Co. *(Bonhams)* **$160**

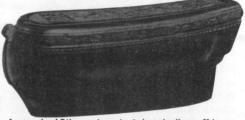

carved fruitwood snuff box in the form of a anding figure of Napoleon, English, early 9th century, his hinged back enclosing a rtoiseshell-lined interior, with the label of he *Antique Shop, Lion and Lamb Court, arnham Surrey*, the eyes inset with glass; e ankles repaired, 5in. high.
Christie's) **$960**

An early 19th century tortoiseshell snuff box, in the form of a ship's 'jolly boat' with pinchbeck mounts to the hinged cover, 3.75in. long. *(Woolley & Wallis)* **$1,200**

A novelty carved wooden snuff box modelled as a grotesque male head, with glass eyes and jagged bone teeth, with hinged cover, 6.9cm. high.
(Bonhams) **$400**

A Meissen gold-mounted snuff-box in the form of a mouse, circa 1750, the contemporary mounts with later 19th century control mark, naturally modelled with its tail curled up over its left hind leg, with a white coat and pale-pink ears, nose, mouth and claws, resting on a pale-yellow oval mound with indianische Blumen, the cover with flower-sprays and a loose bouquet, the interior of the cover with mice crawling all over eggs resting in hay, 2⅝in. long.
(Christie's) **$4,000**

A silver-gilt and niello-mounted shell snuff-box, probably Velikii Ustiug, circa 1768, the spiral shell body on three carved applied feet, the silver-gilt mount with two hinged covers, one nielloed with a maiden and winged Cupid in a arborial grove, the other with a crowned entwined initials *VM* dated *1768* within an rocaille and scroll border, 4¾in. long. *(Christie's)* **$9,600**

A Meissen gilt-metal mounted trefoil mining snuff-box, circa 1740, contemporary mounts painted by B.G. Häuer with a continuous landscape with miners sorting and grading ore and at various pursuits, the base with two miners at rest, the rounded triangular cover with three miners by a pile of ore, one with a pick and one with the gilt AF monogram on his hat, the interior of the cover with a master miner, a gentleman and a miner at discussion by a pile of ore before distant huts, 5.9cm. wide.
(Christie's) **$16,000**

ain Drops, Softens, eans, Blues, 1940s merican. *(Lyle)* **$25**

Rub-No-More, The Cleanser and Washing Powder, American. *(Lyle)* **$50**

Leda Washing Powder, 1943. *(Lyle)* **$25**

urf Lathers like Magic, 53. *(Lyle)* **$25**

Fun-To-Wash, Washing Powder, American packet. *(Lyle)* **$50**

Everest Soap Flakes, 1930s. *(Lyle)* **$40**

ozone, specially prepared washing machines, 1622. *le)* **$25**

Twink, Made by the makers of Lux, 1920s. *(Lyle)* **$40**

New Glee, For Everything You Wash, 1949. *(Lyle)* **$25**

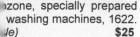

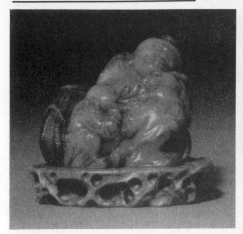

A fine soapstone of a man and boy, 18th century, the old man huddled and fast asleep on a rockwork, base, pipe in hand, the young boy cuddled up to him, a basket and straw hat behind them, their robes incised and gilt with cloud patterns, the stone of pale celadon-yellow tone with details incised and pigmented black, the basket tinted red, 6cm. high.
(Christie's) **$8,000**

A Chinese mottled russet and gr soapstone group of squirrels among fruiting vines, carved and pierced in gre detail, on a brown soapstone base carv and pierced as gnarled trunk and roo 12¼in. high, 19th century.
(Christie's) **$1,0**

An erotic soapstone carving of a reclining lady, late 18th/19th century, carved as reclining nude with calm expression, the hair elaborately tied in a high chignon, weari arm bangles and holding a flower in one hand, the other supporting the head and holding scarf, leaning on a pile of books and lying on drapery partially covering the waist and leg traces of black, red and green pigments, 8¼i. wide.

It is interesting to compare this recumbent figure, which is almost certain intended to be erotic, with the ivory recumbent ladies which have been known generations of Western collectors as 'medicine figures' to assist a prudish Chinese doc in his diagnosis, but may well also be erotically inspired.
(Christie's) **$4,0**

A pair of brass framed Chinese spectacles, with folding sides and quartz lenses. *(Christie's)* **$440**

A pair of tortoiseshell framed Nuremberg spectacles, German, 17th century, the tortoiseshell framed 3.5cm. lenses joined by lead rivet bridge with heart shaped mounts, in a pressed card and shagreen covered case, 7.5cm. wide. *(Bonhams)* **$1,153**

A pair of binocular spectacles with adjustable lenses. *(Lyle)* **$50**

Elvis Presley custom Grand Prix style sun glasses, circa mid 1970s, the center has 14ct white gold initials *'EP'* and a 14ct white gold *'TCB'* on each arm. *(Butterfield & Butterfield)* **$26,450**

A pair of 19th century brass and horn folding-sides spectacles with horn ear pieces and brown quartz lenses, in brown stained sharkskin case, 17.8cm. long. *(Christie's)* **$560**

An 'Erotic' spectacle case, Spanish, mid 19th century, painted pressed leather panels decorated with a young lady at her toilet, the reverse showing her deshabille clutching a champagne bottle and full glass, 11cm. wide. *(Bonhams)* **$280**

A rare pair of Ayscough-type rivet nose spectacles, with silver folding bridge stamped with maker's mark *SS*, with tortoiseshell frames, 2¾in. wide.
(Christie's) **$2,033**

A rare pair of 'Nuremburg' grooved single wire copper nose spectacles in fitted compartment located in front cover of book, Arndt, Johann., Sechs Bücher vom Wahren Christentum, Erfurt 1753.
(Christie's) **$19,088**

A pair of iron Martins Margins, arched bridge, folding sides with large ring ends, inserted horn vissuals, 1in. diameter lens, English, circa 1760.
(Christie's) **$604**

A rare pair of 'Nuremberg' single wire, round rim nose-spectacles. in flat-edged grooved copper wire with chamois leather fitted cover, German, 17th century.
(Christie's) **$8,203**

A pair of John Lennon's glasses, thin, gold-colored frames with oval, yellow-tinted prescription lenses.
(Sotheby's) **$6,638**

Elvis Presley's TCB sunglasses, circa 1972, with silver plated neo-style frames, the initials *EP* across the bridge in gold plate. *(Bonhams)* **$6,320**

Bono's 'Fly' sunglasses, worn by him as McPhisto on the U2 'Zooropa' tour, one-piece wraparound style in dark green plastic, with documents of provenance.
(Sotheby's) **$1,435**

A French spelter group, The Last of the Mohicans, late 19th century, depicting a gorilla with club carrying off a struggling maiden, the stepped base with plaque inscribed *The last of the Mohicans*, 32in. high. *(Christie's)* **$3,200**

A French Orientalist bronze-patinated and polychrome-decorated spelter figural vase, cast from a model by Arthur Waagen, circa 1880, of a young dancer holding a tambourine in her right hand, leaning on a double-headed elephant vase, on a semi-circular stepped base inscribed *A. WAAGEN,* 92.4cm. high.
(Christie's) **$11,000**

◄
A German bronze-patinated spelter mystery timepiece, early 20th century, modelled as an elephant on an oval ebonized wood base, the white enamel Arabic dial with integral gilt-brass gridiron pendulum suspended from the elephant's trunk, the single barrel movement with small internal bob pendulum, 11in. high.
(Christie's) **$1,195**

A rare George III large spoon, for marrow bone jelly with a long Old English pattern stem and an elongated oval bowl, crested and inscribed on the back of the stem *T. HOLT.TROJAN AND MUTTON-MONGER*, by Thomas Northcote, 1793, 30.5cm. long, 2.75oz. *(Christie's)* **$1,003**

Joseph Hoffmann for the Wiener Werkstätte, stylized bird and geometric motif spoon, 1905, silver-colored metal, inset with moonstone, martelé finish, the stem with two stylized birds, the reverse with *WW* monogram, 15.4cm. long.

This spoon was documented in the Wiener Werkstätte archive at the Austrian Museum of Decorative Art in Vienna. These records confirm that only two examples were made and that they were sold for 50 Kronen. *(Sotheby's)* **$12,975**

A Charles II hoof end spice spoon, maker's mark only of John King, circa 1665. *(Woolley & Wallis)* **$1,327**

A George III wavy-end or dog-nose strainer spoon, with a plain rat-tail and a drilled pattern of holes in the bowl, engraved with a cypher below a coronet, apparently by Paul Callard, circa 1760, 21cm. long. *(Christie's)* **$480**

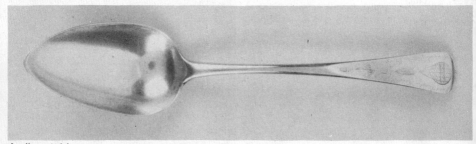

A silver table spoon commemorating the First Parachute Descent in England London 1802, maker's mark of Peter, Anne & William Bateman, engraved with André-Jacques Garnerin's balloon ascending with his parachute and basket, and his descent by parachute and *Sept 22 1802*.

André-Jacques Garnerin (1769-1823) became one of the most notable and fashionable aeronauts of his time chiefly because he was the first person to descend by parachute from a balloon. He was a pupil of Professor Charles and later became the official aeronaut of the French Government, in charge of all ascents for public festivities. He made the first recorded parachute jump on 22nd October 1797 in Paris. Installed in a parachute hanging below his gas balloon and made a successful landing at Clichy without injury. In spite of a Government ban on taking up 'young female persons in the name of morality and decency', Garnerin trained several young women as pilots. One, Jeanne-Genevieve Labrousse (1779-1847), became his wife and also the first woman parachutist, followed later by his niece Elisa. *(Bonhams)* **$1,760**

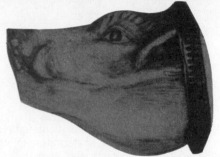

A rare Staffordshire boar's head bonbonnière, the cover painted with a seated figure of Zephyrus, 6.5cm. *(Phillips)* **$2,880**

extremely rare 19th century Staffordshire ttery group of the Blackheath Golfer and caddy, on an oval grassy knoll, Innes in red field marshal's uniform, his caddy rrying his clubs, 8in. tall.
onhams) **$4,800**

A Staffordshire pearlware satyr mask mug, circa 1830, the bearded mask cup and handle issuing a vessel of phallic form bearing the slogan 'No sport till I come', 11¾in. long. *(Christie's)* **$5,750**

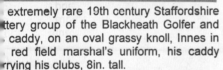

rare and large pair of Staffordshire arlware lop eared rabbits, each nibbles a en lettuce leaf, decorated with black tches, flesh tones to their ears and other amelled details, 1st half 19th century, n. wide.
oolley & Wallis) **$18,285**

A Staffordshire pearlware mug, circa 1790, molded as the head of a leering satyr and decorated in blue and white, 3⅞in. high. *(Christie's)* **$161**

A pair of Staffordshire pottery cat figures, primitively modelled in seated poses with sponged ocher markings and blue collars, 19th century, 21cm. *(Tennants)* **$800**

A Staffordshire cheese dish, the co modelled as a bullock's head. *(Greenslades)* **$2**

A pair of Staffordshire figures of smoking spaniels, seated in upright positions with raised front paws and each modelled with a clay pipe in its mouth, with tan markings, yellow painted eyes and with a yellow painted collar, 19th century, 35.5cm. *(Tennants)* **$3,850**

A fine pair of 19th century Staffordsh seated models of pug dogs with bla muzzles wearing collars, 11in. h *(Anderson & Garland* **$5**

A pair of Staffordshire creamware pottery realistic models of lions, each beast with a long tousled mane, standing with one foot on a ball, 23cm. *(Bearne's)* **$2,309**

A Staffordshire enamel circular box, cover modelled in relief, the ba decorated with floral sprigs and scrollwork, 4.5cm. *(Phillips)* **$1,5**

An attractive and rare Staffordshire enamel pug dog bonbonnière, the animal with pale straw-colored body, 5.5cm. *(Phillips)* **$956**

A pair of Staffordshire cow and calf figure groups, enamelled colors, coved base, 8in. high. *(Locke & England)* **$565**

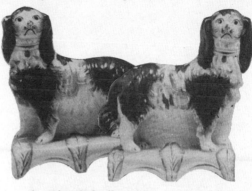

A pair of Staffordshire pottery figures of spaniels, second half 19th century, each molded with a shaggy coat painted in iron red, 7¾in. high. *(Sotheby's)* **$5,175**

A Staffordshire 'Drunken Night Watchman' jug. *(Bonhams)* **$480**

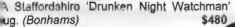

A rare Staffordshire pearlware ale bench group with figures of a lady and gentleman seated in yellow chairs and drinking, 21cm. high. *(Phillips)* **$3,520**

Two rare Staffordshire models of elephants, standing foursquare and with her calf at her side, 14.5 and 13.5cm. high. *(Phillips)* **$918**

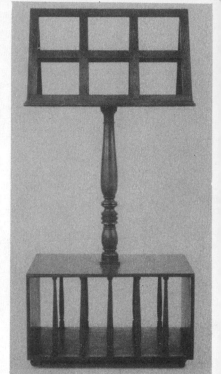

Federal mahogany reading stand wi canterbury, Albany, New York, early 19 century, the stand above a ring-turne tapering post on a rectangular shape canterbury with turned tapering spindles, c castors, 47½in. high.
(Skinner) **$3,10**

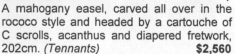

A mahogany easel, carved all over in the rococo style and headed by a cartouche of C scrolls, acanthus and diapered fretwork, 202cm. *(Tennants)* **$2,560**

A rare chromium-plated stand, probably for an Ekco Model AC74 radio (designed by Chermayeff), in chromium-plated steel tubing of simple, counterbalanced design, 26in. high.

Few examples of this stand are known; this one was bought, with its receiver, late in 1932 to celebrate the birth of a son. The set was subsequently disposed of separately, but the stand has remained in the original owner's family.
(Christie's) **$800 ▶**

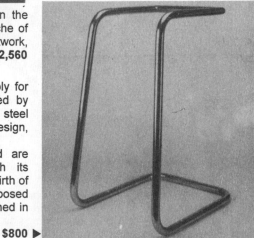

An ebonized and boxwood portfolio, Napoleon III, circa 1855, the carved panel centered by an allegory of Painting, on an easel stand, with ball and claw feet, 153cm. high. *(Sotheby's)* **$10,670**

mannequin figure of Marilyn Monroe, in a tticoat dress, on stand base, 1.62m. high. *uction Team Köln)* **$112**

A William IV rosewood folio stand, the ratcheted pierced slatted sides on end supports and lobed bun feet, 67cm. wide. *(Phillips)* **$4,920**

A polished chromium hat stand made fo[r] Bazzi in Milan, 51.6cm. high.
(Christie's) **$65[0]**

A pair of painted and ebonized walnut stands, Venetian, circa 1880, each in the form of a young blackamoor crouching on a pillow and supporting a circular seat, each 55.5cm. high. *(Sotheby's)* **$11,960**

A draughtsman's easel, 19th century, with an adjustable leather stand inset with the points of the compass, on a brass tripod rising and falling on a ratchet, with a quadripartite base, 92cm. wide.
(Phillips) **$6,450**

A novelty mahogany pedestal or plant stan[d] or recent manufacture, modelled in th[e] round as a woman's legs, the oval platfor[m] with folded skirt fringe, on a circular mold[ed] base, 38in. high. *(Christie's)* **$1,65[0]**

A good and unusual silver double-ended stirrup cup relating to Richard Daft's cricket and baseball tour to North America, 1879, Henry William Dee, London, 1879, finely modelled as a British bulldog biting the rear of an American baseball player, the buckle of whose belt displays crossed cricket bats and a ball, the bulldog's collar inscribed *J.C. Wordie*, both cups with gilt interiors, 4¾in. long, weight 170gms.

Richard Daft, the Nottinghamshire captain, selected and led a side of professional cricketers on a tour of North America in the summer of 1879. The program began in Canada with three matches in Toronto, followed by games in Hamilton and London, Ontario. The team then travelled to Detroit, before playing two matches in New York. The most important fixture of the tour was in Philadelphia, which attracted 25,000 spectators over three days and ensured that the tour was a financial success. Daft's team then returned to New York for two matches in Brooklyn – one of cricket and the other baseball. The English players were as inexpert at baseball as the New Yorkers were at cricket, resulting in overwhelming victories/defeats accordingly. It is possible that several of these stirrup cups may have been made and presented to players and officials from England and their North American opponents, hence the unusual double-ended construction allowing the holder to choose from which symbolic end to drink. *(Sotheby's)* **$5,382**

▶

A Victorian cast stirrup cup, realistically modelled as the mask of a deerhound, possibly an Irish wolfhound, with textured hair in high relief, mouth slightly open and tongue protruding through his front teeth, panting, by John S. Hunt, 1851, 18cm. long, 26oz. *(Christie's)* **$19,861**

A boar mask stirrup cup, with textured hair and snarling mouth, the rim, plain and slightly tapering with a molded band, by Messrs Slater, Slater & Holland, 1896. 14cm. long. *(Christie's)* **$6,499**

A Stevenson & Hancock Derby fox mask stirrup cup, with pricked ears and bared teeth, inscribed in gilt *Tally Ho*, painted mark in lilac, circa 1880, 12cm. *(Tennants)* **$480**

A rare English porcelain trout's head stirrup cup, possibly Derby, naturalistically modelled and colored, the rim inscribed *The Fisher's Delight*, circa 1820. *(Woolley & Wallis)* **$2,320**

A silver stirrup cup in the form of a stag's head, by Samuel Arnd, St. Petersburg, 1863, 8cm. high, 134.5gr. gross. *(Christie's)* **$2,974**

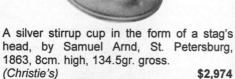

A pearlware hound's head stirrup cup, possibly Portobello, typically modelled as a fox hound with black markings with a pink and black collar, circa 1820, 13cm. long. *(Christie's)* **$885**

A Scottish cast hare-mask stirrup cup, with textured fur and erect ears, the rim flared and plain with an applied molded band, maker's mark *S.S. & S?*, Edinburgh 1899. *(Christie's)* **$7,222**

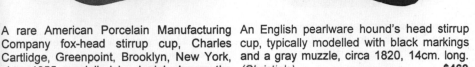

A rare American Porcelain Manufacturing Company fox-head stirrup cup, Charles Cartlidge, Greenpoint, Brooklyn, New York, circa 1855, modelled by Josiah Jones, the pricked ears, eyes, nose, mouth and coat picked out in gilding, the rim around his neck inscribed in gilding *American Porcelain Green Point*, 11.8cm. long.
(Sotheby's) **$7,475**

An English pearlware hound's head stirrup cup, typically modelled with black markings and a gray muzzle, circa 1820, 14cm. long. *(Christie's)* **$460**

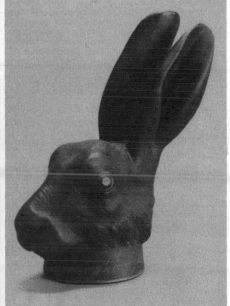

A Wedgwood black basalt hare's head stirrup-cup, naturalistically modelled, the collar inscribed in iron-red enamel *Success to bowl away & the merry Harriers of Newton*, circa 1785, 17cm. high. *(Christie's)* **$1,472**

A pair of George III silver stirrup cups, Tudor and Leader, Sheffield, 1786, each formed as a fox's mask, realistically chased, 4¾in. long, 8oz. *(Christie's)* **$6,900**

A Victorian stirrup cup, finely modelled as a fox's head, also engraved with a presentation inscription, 1864, by George Fox, approximate weight 7oz. *(Bonhams)* **$4,000**

A stoneware frog and mouse group by George Tinworth with frogs riding mice over a water jump, circa 1875, 4½in. high. *(Lyle)* **$4,480**

A saltglazed stoneware baluster shaped character jug, 4¾in. high, circa 1800. *(Dreweatt Neate)* **$234**

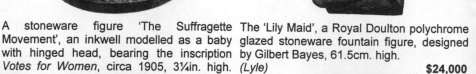

A stoneware figure 'The Suffragette Movement', an inkwell modelled as a baby with hinged head, bearing the inscription *Votes for Women*, circa 1905, 3¼in. high. *(Lyle)* **$1,520**

The 'Lily Maid', a Royal Doulton polychrome glazed stoneware fountain figure, designed by Gilbert Bayes, 61.5cm. high. *(Lyle)* **$24,000**

A stoneware monkey group by George Tinworth, inscribed *A United Family*, sitting on a bench and sheltering under an ocher umbrella, circa 1892, 5in. high. *(Lyle)* **$2,880**

A small stoneware vase of hexagonal section inscribed on either side *The Waning of the Honeymoon*, supported on an oval base with two hares sitting defiantly at either end, 1880, 4¾in. high. *(Lyle)* **$1,920**

A salt glazed stoneware inkwell, circa 1800, possibly Lambeth, modelled as the head·of Walpole, his mouth open wide, his hair with fleur-de-lys garland, 3in.

The image is probably taken from a print titled 'The Late Prime Minister' (Anon) published in 1743.
(Bonhams) **$240**

A salt glazed stoneware snuff-taking toby jug, circa 1800, Fulham, well modelled holding an open snuff box in his left hand, wearing a waistcoat, jacket and breeches beneath a tricorn hat, 8in., incised *Fulham*.
(Bonhams) **$560**

A luster glazed stoneware vase, by Zsolnay Pecs, circa 1900, modelled in full relief with a mermaid and a merman draped over the squat body, 8in. high.
(Christie's) **$2,570**

Salt glazed stoneware 'Wellington' jug, circa 1830, by Stephen Green, well modelled as the head of the Duke, with a scrolling handle, 7½in. *(Bonhams)* **$320**

A model stoneware owl with detachable head, the feathers formed by applied motifs in shades of blue, ocher and brown, circa 1880, 8in. high. *(Lyle)* **$640**

A set of six bronze and fruitwood stools, 20th century, in the neo-classical style, the X frame supports cast with ibis heads, the seats of square form, with applied moldings, 18¼in. high.
(Christie's) **$9,600**

An original clogger's stool, complete with a paring knife, a hollowing knife and a gripper.
(Tool Shop Auctions) **$480** ▶

A pair of ebonized and gilt highlighted elephant seats, 20in. high.
(George Kidner) **$1,120**

A French giltwood ropetwist stool, in the manner of A.M.E. Fournier, circa 1860, the rectangular bead work seat depicting flowers within a border, on rope twist legs tied by a conforming 'X' stretcher.

(Bonhams) **$3,200**

An oak stool, designed by Le Corbusier for the Maison du Brésil at the Cité Universitaire, Paris 1957-59, oak, cut out grip handles, 17 x 13 x 10in.

(Christie's) **$7,079**

A suite of four stools, early 20th century, in carved painted wood and braided leather, metal and turquoise pearls, the base decorated with Indian feathers, the sides in the form of medallions centered by an Indian mask, with leopard and cheetah skin upholstery, 29in. high. *(Christie's)* **$47,760**

A chromium plated tubular steel revolving stool, model no.B304, designed by Le Corbusier, P. Jeanneret and Charlotte Perriand, 1929, manufactured by Thonet, France, the circular revolving green leather upholstered top on four chrome tubular legs, 20in. high.
(Christie's) **$4,475**

A Huanghuali folding stool, jiaowu, late 17th/early 18th century, of slender proportions, the 'eight piece' stool with two pairs of round legs wider at the ends and mid-point, the hinge a continuous rod through each pivot-point, the top and bottom horizontal members forming the upper framework and the stretcher feet, 13¼in. wide. *(Christie's)* **$12,000**

A Regency mahogany chamber horse, wit brown leather and brass studded adjustabl seat with scroll arms and ring turne tapering supports raised on short turne legs, with brass plate *Pococks Paten Warehouse, Southampton St., Cover Garden, London*, 103cm. wide.

The chamber horse was th precursor of today's exercise machines inasmuch as it duplicated the effect of riding without having to leave the comfort of you own home!

It became popular (mainly, on assumes, with overweight gentlemen) in th second half of the 18th century, an consisted of a leather covered seat whic had a concertina movement created b boards supported on blocks, with wir twisted around. When the seat was in us the weight of the sitter compressed the ai allowing him to move up and down.

Sheraton, in his Drawing Book c 1791-4, provides a detailed set c instructions for making chamber horses, th top board to be stuffed with hair and th leather fixed to each board with brass nail tacked all round. Some known examples b him are of stool form, with arms at each en to provide a grip. *(Cheffins)* **$4,800**

An elm and ash cobbler's bench, English, 19th century, the shaped top with divided work surface, on splayed legs, formerly with a drawer, 39in. long. *(Christie's)* **$1,120**

polychrome-painted stool and dog bed, late 20th century, the padded top covered in green, white, pink and orange gros point needlework, the sides painted in white with peach velvet close-nailed panels, the interior with peach velvet cushion, above a waved apron, 19in. high. *(Christie's)* **$1,280**

A cherrywood three-legged stool, designed by Adolf Loos, circa 1903, the bowed shaped seat in two sections, on three scrolled legs, 15½in. high.

This design took a piece of English furniture as its inspiration, although Liberty's three-legged stool was itself based on an ancient Egyptian stool seen by Leonard Wyburd in the British Museum.

Loos' version differed from this by virtue of its tighter proportions. It was produced by his famous carpenter Josef Veillich in mahogany, oak and cherrywood and proved extremely popular - Loos himself had one - by virtue of its lightness and utility. *(Christie's)* **$5,960**

French giltwood stool after a design by .C.M. Fournier, the four legs and X-shaped stretcher carved in the form of knotted rope, 9in. diameter. *(Christie's)* **$4,462**

A George II walnut close stool, the hinged oval top above a shaped apron, on cabriole legs with pad feet, one back foot tipped, formerly with pot, 18½in. high. *(Christie's)* **$4,410**

A pair of unusual Victorian Irish sugar nips, the arms terminating to form an eagle's head, the central part of scallop form, by John Smyth, Dublin, 1844.
(Phillips) **$819**

A pair of Edwardian novelty silver suga tongs, London 1904, maker's mark of Hen Stewart Brown, modelled as wishbone approximate weight 0.5oz, length 8.5cr
(Bonhams) **$9**

A pair of William IV cast naturalistic sugar nips, oak bough decorated, William Theobalds, London 1834.
(Woolley & Wallis) **$252**

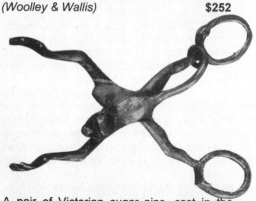

A pair of Victorian sugar nips, cast in the form of a spider monkey with his tail curled around the right leg, realistically textured to simulate hair, the grips formed by his cupped hands, by William Leuchars, 1884, 13.75cm. long, 2.75oz.
(Christie's) **$1,425**

An unusual pair of sugar nips formed as 'Dutch doll', the head enamelled with a fac and hair, London 1911, 3.6in. hig
(Christie's) **$84**

A pair of Victorian cast sugar nips, of leaf and floral design with butterfly, one either side at junction of arms, by Yapp & Woodward, Birmingham, 1847, 2.75oz.
(Phillips) **$420**

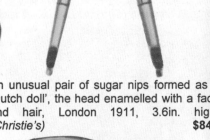

A pair of Edwardian novelty silver sugar nip London 1906, maker's mark of Hen Brown, modelled as a crab's claw, retaile by Barrett and Sons, length 8.4cr
(Bonhams) **$32**

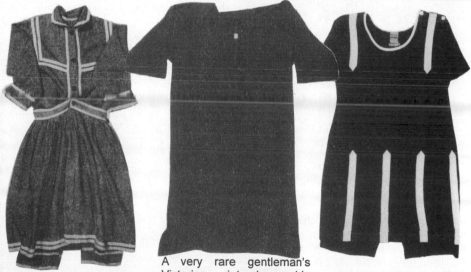

One of the first two-piece lady's costumes in elasticated linen from the late 40s, early 50s.
(Lyle) **$50**

Lady's late Victorian red flannel bathing dress with detachable skirt.
(Lyle) **$280**

Gentleman's black woollen trunks from the late 1930s.
(Lyle) **$50**

Late 1940s lady's linen beach play-suit.
(Lyle) **$65**

Lady's grey flannel Victorian bathing dress with detachable skirt.
(Lyle) **$320**

A very rare gentleman's Victorian interchangeable three-piece set in matching cotton jersey, marked *A.S.A. regulation costume.*
(Lyle) **$400**

Lady's one piece interlock cotton bathing suit with built-in skirt by Meridian, 1908.
(Lyle) **$160**

A rectangular center table with plain hardwood top supported by two First World War French laminated hardwood four-bladed propellers, probably by Renault, top 60 x 35in. *(Canterbury)* **$5,977**

A gilt-metal, quartz-mounted and glass coffee table, last quarter 20th century, by Antony Redmile, the rectangular plate glass table top supported by the model of a quartz crystal encrusted grass hopper, with gilt-metal legs and antenna, the eyes inset with malachite cabochons, on a rectangular ebonized wood stepped plinth, 40½in. long. *(Christie's)* **$4,400**

An Empire burr-elm and ormolu-mounted vide-poche, early 19th century, the rectangular well top with a thin leaf band above a single mahogany lined frieze drawer, on turned legs with ormolu leaf capitals and joined by a shaped box stretcher, stamped *JACOB D./R. MESLEE*, 75.5cm. high. The stamp refers to François-Honoré-Georges Jacob Desmalter and was adopted by him in 1803.
(Sotheby's) **$19,200**

A North Italian carved wood occasional table, late 19th century, the rectangular silvered shell shaped top on scroll legs with dolphin feet and X-frame stretcher, 29½in. high. *(Christie's)* **$29,980**

A pair of giltwood console tables of recent manufacture, in the mid-Georgian manner, each with maroon variegated marble top with an egg-and-dart, waterleaf and textured frieze supported on dolphin modelled supports, on a rock-work base, each 24½in. wide. *(Skinner)* **$12,800**

A George IV mahogany drum table, possibly Irish, the circular top inlaid with ebonized lines and with green leather lining above four frieze drawers and four simulated drawers, on a lotus leaf shaft and tripartite base with animalistic legs headed by foliate knees, on claw feet with sunken brass castors, restorations, 29¼in. high, 47½in. diameter. *(Christie's)* **$16,000**

A thuya work table, Austrian, the top with scrolled sides headed by ebonized eagles heads above a small fitted drawer, on saber supports of square section ending in hoof feet, with a plinth base, 90cm. high. *(Sotheby's)* **$19,682**

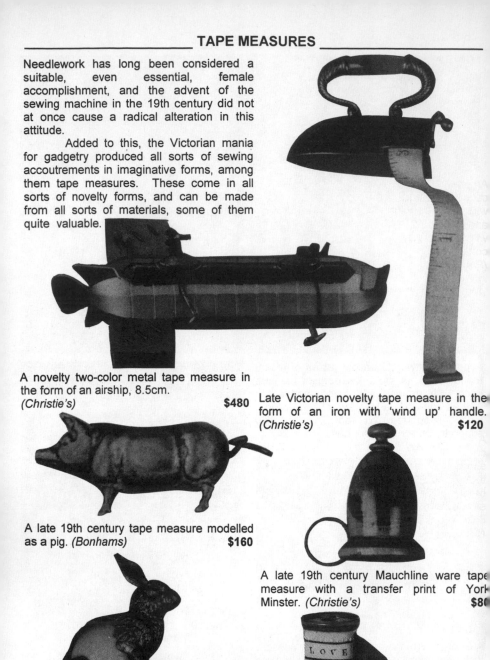

Needlework has long been considered a suitable, even essential, female accomplishment, and the advent of the sewing machine in the 19th century did not at once cause a radical alteration in this attitude.

Added to this, the Victorian mania for gadgetry produced all sorts of sewing accoutrements in imaginative forms, among them tape measures. These come in all sorts of novelty forms, and can be made from all sorts of materials, some of them quite valuable.

A novelty two-color metal tape measure in the form of an airship, 8.5cm. *(Christie's)* **$480**

Late Victorian novelty tape measure in the form of an iron with 'wind up' handle. *(Christie's)* **$120**

A late 19th century tape measure modelled as a pig. *(Bonhams)* **$160**

A late 19th century Mauchline ware tape measure with a transfer print of York Minster. *(Christie's)* **$80**

Late 19th century novelty tape measure in the shape of a rabbit with a 'wind up' tail. *(Christie's)* **$160**

An English enamel tape measure of drum shape, inscribed *A Token of Love* in black on a white band, 2cm. *(Phillips)* **$306**

An early 19th century tea caddy in the form of a house with two dormer windows and chimney, the interior with two lidded compartments, 17cm. high. *(Phillips)* **$950**

A Regency painted caddy in the form of a country cottage, inscribed on the base *from Mr Alice (?) to LHM, August 16th 1809...Tenby SW,* 5½in. wide. *(Hy. Duke & Son)* **$3,337**

A mahogany veneered miniature sideboard tea chest, inlaid brass stringing with a fitted interior, 13in. wide. *(Woolley & Wallis)* **$1,265**

A Regency painted and carved tea caddy, in the shape of a house with turrets and chimneys, the breakfront door flanked by semi-detached columns, 8½in. wide. *(Christie's)* **$5,088**

A George III amaranth, rosewood and marquetry tea caddy of rectangular shape with stepped top surmounted by an ormolu Classical urn within a spotted circle of friendship, the interior fitted, circa 1820, 13½in. wide. *(Christie's)* **$32,912**

A Chinese Export silvered metal-mounted mother of pearl tea caddy, decorated overall with pierced foliate panels with scallop shells, late 18th/early 19th century, 11½in. wide. *(Christie's)* **$3,972**

A George III fruitwood tea caddy formed as an apple, 5in. high. *(Christie's)* **$1,179**

An unusual painted metal figural, box, American, late 19th century, 9¾in. high. *(Sotheby's)* **$3,220**

An early Victorian mother of pearl and abalone shell bowfront tea caddy, decorated all-over with a geometric pattern, 9in. wide. *(Christie's)* **$2,100**

Late 19th century Fabergé silver tea caddy in the form of a large tea packet, Moscow, 13cm. wide. **$11,320**

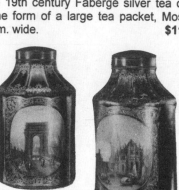

A Böttger red stoneware hexagonal baluster teacaddy, circa 1715, each recessed panel molded in low relief with birds of paradise in flight or perched among branches of flowering shrubs issuing from rockwork, the angles incised with hatching, 12.4cm. high. (Christie's) **$8,000**

A pair of early Victorian japanned metal tea canisters, the black ground cylindrical bodies heightened in gilt and each painted with oval panels, 18¹/8in. high. (Christie's) **$1,033**

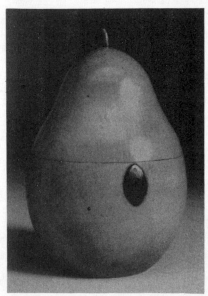

A 19th century flame mahogany tea caddy in the form of a serpentine front sideboard, with hinged lid enclosing two mixing bowls and central well, 42cm. wide. (Bristol) **$924**

Turned fruitwood tea caddy, England, late 18th century, in the form of a pear, 6¼in. high. (Skinner) **$5,750**

An early 19th century curl work paper tea caddy of hexagonal form, with an inset painted panel of a girl holding a garland of flowers, 18.5cm. wide.
(Phillips) **$951**

A Ralph Cahoon antique tea bin decorated with a gentleman toasting a lady, oil on wood, 24¹/₈in. high. *(Skinner)* **$2,530**

Anglo-Indian antler and sandalwood tea caddy, 19th century, with serpentine sides, the interior with two ivory covered wells, 11in. long. *(Skinner)* **$2,185**

A George III fruitwood tea-caddy in the form of a Cantaloupe melon, 4½in. wide.
(Christie's) **$6,864**

A Meissen blue and white tea caddy, painted with the fisherman pattern in rounded panels, circa 1725, 10.5cm.
(Tennants) **$1,440**

An American silver and other metals Japanese style tea caddy, Gorham Mfg. Co., Providence, RI, 1879, of crumpled sack form with spot-hammered surface, 9oz. gross, 4¼in. high.
(Sotheby's) **$3,737**

A Victorian mahogany three tier buffet, each tier with gallery supported by reeded columns raised on turned supports terminating in castors.
(Academy)   **$1,136**

A late Victorian ebonized and ivory two-tier trolley by Howard & Sons, the rectangular top with balustrade gallery and ring-turned finials, 30½in. wide.
(Christie's)   **$7,438**

Ludwig Mies van der Rohe, for Bamberg Metallwerkstätten, serving trolley, designed 1927-29, manufactured circa 1930, nickel plated steel, wood handle, glass, 28⅞in. high. *(Sotheby's)*   **$27,180**

Tapio Wirkkala; Finland, a birch and laminated birch serving trolley, designed circa 1955, for Asko, the two removeable trays with conforming laminated surfaces, on solid birch frame, on castors, with metal label to the underside, 35½in. wide.
(Christie's)   **$1,920**

Alvar Aalto for Artek, tea trolley, 1930s, blondewood on castors, the underside stamped *'Aalto Design', ARTEK*, 65cm. wide. *(Sotheby's)*   **$1,472**

Alvar Aalto, bentwood trolley, circa 1936-37, bent and laminated wood with painted wheels, 33½in. wide.
(Sotheby's)   **$3,546**

A mahogany and plate glass two-tier trolley, by Cesare Lacca, Italy, circa 1955, 40in. wide. *(Christie's)* **$337**

Alvar Aalto, a birch tea trolley model no. 90, designed 1936-37, manufactured by Oy Huonekalu-ja Rakennustyötehdas AB, for Artek, the rectangular top with yellow linoleum surface, on laminated birch frame with wicker basket attached, the white enamelled disk wheels with black rubber tires, 36in. wide. *(Christie's)* **$6,861**

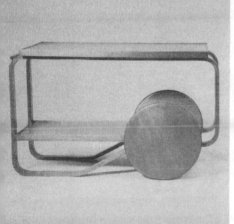

Bent plywood tea cart, mid 20th century, top fitted with beverage holder, centering tray, bent wood legs joined by lower median shelf, 20in. wide. *(Skinner)* **$320**

Alvar Aalto, Finland, tea trolley model no.98, designed 1936-37 manufactured by Oy Huonekalu-ja Rakennustyotehdas AB, for Artek, retailed and imported into U.K. by Finmar Ltd. Birch laminated frame of ribbon form supporting two birch veneered shelves, with rod shaped handle, the whole raised on two wheels, 555mm. high. *(Bonhams)* **$2,674**

An Art Deco bentwood serving trolley, in the style of Alvar Aalto, on shaped supports, disk wheels with rubber tires, 28½in. wide. *(Christie's)* **$1,298**

A Minton majolica monkey teapot and cover, the smiling creature's head forming the detachable cover and its curling tail forming the handle, date code for 1874, 6in. high. *(Christie's)* **$2,000**

Racing car teapot by Sadler & Co. in green and silver, 1930s *(Muir Hewitt)* **$210**

A Staffordshire pearlware 'Bear Baitin' teapot formed with the figure of a standin' bear holding a hound, the cover forming removable head, the whole textured bo decorated in brown and blue glaze, 9i high. *(Canterbury)* **$2,4**

A Minton teapot and cover modelled as a Japanese dwarf, wearing a pale-blue robe molded with flowers, seated holding a Noh theater mask, the spout issuing from its mouth, the handle formed from a plait of his hair, shape 1838, year cypher for 1875, 19.5cm. wide. *(Christie's)* **$2,400**

A George Jones teapot and cover modell as a rooster, its tail forming the handle, open beak the spout, on shaped oval ba molded with blades of grass, with bro plumage and pink comb and watt impressed *10*, circa 1876, 29cm. wi *(Christie's)* **$7,0**

Quimper pottery teapot and cover with a snake handle and spout, 7in., decorated with Breton figures and flowers.
(Woolley & Wallis) **$240**

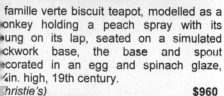

famille verte biscuit teapot, modelled as a
onkey holding a peach spray with its
oung on its lap, seated on a simulated
ockwork base, the base and spout
ecorated in an egg and spinach glaze,
4in. high, 19th century.
hristie's) **$960**

Royal Doulton Old Charley teapot, D6017, produced in 1939, 7in. high.
(Lyle) **$1,360**

famille verte biscuit Cadogan teapot,
odelled as phoenix seated on a lotus petal
se, well molded to simulate the plumage,
4in. high, 18th/19th century.
hristie's) **$1,840**

A very rare Minton majolica ware teapot and cover, dated *1877*, the cobalt blue pot of egg shape, the handle formed by a monkey, the spout by a cockerel, 15cm. high.
(Phillips) **$6,720**

Staffordshire Rooster teapot, 1930s. *(Muir Hewitt)* **$125**

Colclough bone china Sabu teapot in blu circa 1939. *(Muir Hewitt)* **$3,**

Clarice Cliff 1951 Teepee teapot with *Greetings from Canada* on underside. *(Muir Hewitt)* **$1,140**

A Victorian silver-gilt naturalistic teapot, the form of a stylized cabbage, on four c tendril feet with an ivory insulated han and a flower bud finial, by John S. Hu 1852, 10.5cm. high, 12oz. *(Christie's)* **$2,4**

A Holdcroft majolica teapot, circa 1875, in the form of a brown coconut with green stock handle and spout molded with a Chinese boy wearing blue and yellow robes climbing over the vessel, his head and shoulders forming the cover and finial, 13.5cm. *(Phillips)* **$1,280**

A Staffordshire creamware teapot a cover, circa 1785, of Ralph Wood ty modelled as a brown elephant surmoun by a monkey seated in a green crenella howdah, 11in. high. *(Christie's)* **$28,6**

A Makazu Kozan blue and white ewer and cover, modelled as an exotic bird, molded and painted with panels of ho-o, peony sprays, scrolling foliage and geometric designs, 6¾in. high, signed to interior of cover. *(Christie's)* **$460**

A Minton teapot and cover, designed by H.H. Crealock, modelled as a vulture attacking a serpent, painted in colored glazes, the raptor with pink neck and brown plumage with black wing tips, the green serpent mottled with dark-green spots, on rocky-molded base, impressed marks and date code for 1874, 22cm. high. *(Christie's)* **$55,200**

A Royal Worcester 'Aesthetic' teapot and cover, circa 1882, polychrome decorated in 'Greenery Yallery' colors, the obverse molded showing a lady in typical Aesthetic costume, a lily on her chest, the reverse molded with an 'Oscar Wilde Figure' in similar pose, with a sunflower across his chest, puce printed factory marks and inscription *Fearful consequences-through the laws of natural selection and evolution-living up to one's teapot, Budge*, 15.5cm. *(Sotheby's)* **$4,785**

A.J. Roth teapot and cover modelled as a monkey clinging to a green coconut molded with leaves, with a branch handle and spout, bud finial, impressed mark, circa 1880, 26cm. long. *(Christie's)* **$800**

Humpty Dumpty teapot, 1930s.
(Christie's) **$180**

Peggoty teapot by Beswick Pottery, 6in. high, introduced 1948.
(Lyle) **$165**

A creamware Royal portrait teapot, molded in relief with portraits of George III and Charlotte, the rim inscribed *GOD SAVE THE KING AND GOD SAVE THE QEE*, enriched in brown, pale-blue, green and ocher glazes, late 18th century, 15cm. high.
(Christie's) **$1,065**

Unusual Japanese Satsuma teapot, the handle and spout modelled as a dragon and elaborately painted in colors with humorous scenes of tribal robber bands, the cover with handle modelled as praying devout man, 19th century, 9½in. high.
(G.A. Key) **$528**

Bunnykins teapot, in the form of a bunny with ivy handle, painted in shades of brown, black and green, printed factory mark, 12cm. high. *(Christie's)* **$935**

A Beswick Pottery teapot featuring Sairey Gamp, 5¾in. high, introduced 1939.
(Lyle) **$165**

440

A Hermann teddy bear, with shaggy brown tipped cream mohair, deep amber and black glass eyes, clipped plush cut muzzle, inner ears and pads, black stitched nose, cream felt open mouth, red felt tongue, swivel head, unjointed bendable limbs and flat card lined feet, 16in. tall, circa 1955. *(Christie's)* **$143**

▶

An Edwardian articulated silver teddy bear pin cushion, Birmingham 1908, by H.V. Pithey Co. *(Lawrence Fine Art)* **$826**

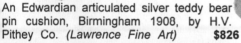

Gold plush teddy bear purse, the teddy bear with brown eyes, black stitched snout, his back in the form of a purse with handle, having jointed body, 10in. long. *(Cotswold Auction Co.)* **$650**

A rare Steiff 'Petsy' bear with brown tipped cream mohair, comical blue and black moveable glass eyes, large ears, center seam to face, beige stitched nose, mouth and claws, swivel head, long jointed shaped limbs, felt pads, hump and button in ear with hint of white label, 18in. tall, circa 1928.

The Steiff Petsy began life as 'Buschy' and Registered at the Patent Office in January 7, 1928. However the name 'Buschy' did not win favor with consumers and in November of the same year his name changed to 'Petsy', his comical eyes were designed so they would be moved into any position and expression. *(Christie's)* **$8,970**

A pair of very unusual Steiff muzzled teddy bears, 18in. high. *(Lyle)* **$26,400**

A fine Steiff black mohair plush teddy bear with wide apart rounded ears, black boot button eyes mounted on red felt disks, cut stitched snout, on an excelsior filled body with swivel joints, hump back and elongated felt pads, 19in., button in ear marked Steiff, circa 1912. 494 of this type, serial no. 5335 were produced, for the English market and available in five sizes ranging from 14in. to 19in. *(Phillips)* **$12,800**

A dark golden plush covered teddy handbag, with black button eyes, pronounced snout, and moveable joints, 8in. long, pads replaced, possibly by Schuco. *(Christie's)* **$1,270**

A pair of Steiff rod jointed blonde plush teddy bears, German, 1904, with sealing wax noses and boot button eyes, swivel and metal rod jointed with excelsior stuffing, 17¾in. and 18½in. *(Sotheby's)* **$20,165**

A dual-plush teddy bear, German, circa 1920. The bear was bought by Jack Wilson, Chairman of The House of Nisbit, teddy bear manufacturers, on behalf of a private friend in the U.S.A. *(Sotheby's)* **$90,000**

collection of teeth extracted from 19th
ntury Royalty & Other Worthies, dated
tween 1830-1859, each contained in an
velope or wrap of paper with manuscript
notation as follows:

ctoria's 24th tooth taken out on the 1st
ne 1832.

ctoria's tooth taken out on the 10th July
*30.

ctoria's 23rd Tooth was taken out on the
*th Octr: 1832.

wer Molar & Upper Dend Sap Extracted
*m H.R.H. The Duchess of Kent

*oth of Saide Pacha, Son of Mehemet Ali
*Viceroy of Egypt ext. July 3rd 1852

tracted from H.R.H. Princess Mary of
*mbridge March 5th 1855.

*rence Nightingale March 31 1859.

contained in a red morocco leather satin
d plush lined box. These teeth were
tracted by Dr. Charles DuMergues, who
*s Queen Victoria's dentist throughout
*ich of her life. The earliest examples in
*s collection date from Queen Victoria's
*ildhood (between the ages of 11 and 13)
*en she was living at Kensington Palace
*h her mother the Duchess of Kent.
*een Victoria was to have a lifelong history
problems with her teeth and became so
ached to her second dentist, Dr. Edward
*unders, that he became the first dentist to
*ceive a knighthood.

*onhams)   **$2,636**

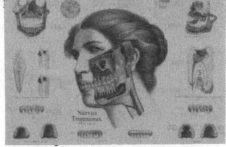

The Teeth of Man. Dents Humaines.
Lithographed in colors, printed and
published by Meyer, Hofer, Fries & Cie,
Winterthur, 24 x 30½in.
(Christie's)   **$360**

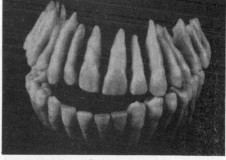

A complete set of upper lower human teeth,
bound with brass wire to a shaped back
frame, with plastic container, 4¼in. wide.
(Christie's)   **$800**

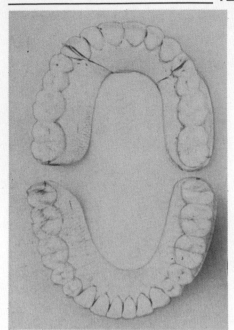

A set of bone false teeth, English, early 19th century, upper and lower jaw.
(Bonhams) **$313**

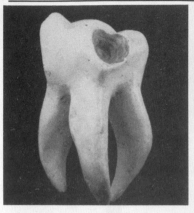

A model tooth, with cavity, showing ro system, 6½in. high.
(Christie's) **$4**

A part-sectioned model of the human skull, showing the jaw with teeth, nerves and blood vessels, mounted on an ebonized circular stand with embossed brass label for *C. Ash. Sons & Co. Ltd., Broad St., Golden Square London.W.England*, the base, 10in. diameter. *(Christie's)* **$515**

Two anatomical models, circa 1910, the fi 'The Major Dental Diseases', black wood demonstration box by the Ber Lehrmittelwerke Verlagsanstalt, with 25 w models of diseased teeth, 32 x 26 x 4.5cr the second a painted plaster model of 1 left lower jaw, demonstrating various der diseases, the gums can be folded back expose the tooth roots, the corner too removable, on well-turned wooden base, x 26 x 10cm.
(Auction Team Köln) **$96**

An alabaster System Bailleux wall telephone, with key, circa 1900. *(Auction Team Köln)* **$1,072**

n English Stanley hand telephone of wood
d brass, circa 1880.
uction Team Köln)   **$640**

A telephone doll with brocade dress and china head and arms, 50cm., circa 1900. *(Auction Team Köln)* **$978**

mahogany telephone, Système crophonique, M & M, Paris, the turned eaker with bell at rear, on baluster support tapered rectangular base with maker's aque and sprung knob at rear, 9½in. high, th century. *(Christie's)*   **$1,011**

A B Mk V field telephone with handset and buzzer, together with an L M Ericsson mouthpiece, circa 1942. *(Auction Team Köln)* **$169**

An Austrian terracotta figure of a negro boy, late 19th or early 20th century, shown three-quarter length, the polychrome figure modelled with a straw hat and playing a banjo, stamped to the reverse of the plinth *4195*, 26¾in. high.
(Christie's) **$3,680**

Albert-Ernest Carrier-Belleuse, Frenc 1824-1887, 'Le Sommeil', a fantasy bus signed: *A. Carrier-Belleuse*, terracotta, on a ebonized wooden socle, 60cm.

Commissioned around 1854 by th newly-appointed director of the Limoge Porcelain factory, Henri Ardant, Carrie Belleuse's Sommeil and its pendant Reve echo the mild eroticism of L'Automne, one c the first of his series of fantasy busts.

The use of terracotta both enhance the warmth and sensuality of the subject an follows the eighteenth century tradition c terracotta busts. The spontaneous and ric detailing achieved in this terracotta however, could not be mistaken for a eighteenth century work and embodie Carrier-Belleuse's originality and innovatior
(Sotheby's) **$14,72**

◄

An Austrian glazed terracotta bust of a African gentleman, circa 1890, wearing a tc hat, a cravat, a white dress sh and a cummerbund, stamped to th underside *Vervielfaltigung Vorbehalte Gesetz...Erschützt,* on a stepped spreadir canted rectangular socle numbered *57* 27in. high. *(Christie's)* **$3,8C**

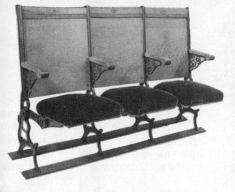

A 'Manhattan' row of theater seats, with three fold-up upholstered seats from the new York Theater, the frame of richly decorated cast iron with wooden armrests and backs, mounted on a wooden frame for stability, with program storage under the seats, and a wooden bracket on the back of the center seat, with nickelled original seat numbers, 1886.
(Auction Team Köln)   **$1,339**

An Edwardian mahogany marquetry and upholstered theater seat, the two linked seats each with curved backs, the top-rails with satinwood crossbanding and an oval medallion inlaid with a crown and *R & H Gaiety*, with lotus-scroll arm terminals, upholstered in close-studded red covers, on square tapering legs with a shelf behind, 49½in. wide. *(Christie's)*   **$800**

Oak Ecclesiastical two seater settle with quatrefoil pierced back, trefoil pierced arms, 0in. wide. *(G.A. Key)*   **$400**

A large Flemish oak choir stall, late 15th/early 16th century, the three seats divided and flanked by differing grotesque masks, 105¾in. wide.
(Sotheby's)   **$10,925**

Two oak choir stalls, each with individual seats, flanked by Ionic style columns and carved with figures and animals, French, late 19th century, 129in. wide and 159in. wide.
(Christie's)   (Two)   **$4,620**

A gold thimble of domed design, the border applied with a twisted wire-work design, Turkish, possibly 16th century.
(Christie's) **$6,750**

An enamel thimble, with applied brass top and rim, English, South Staffordshire, circa 1760, 1.9cm.
(Christie's) **$1,350**

A Meissen chinoiserie thimble painted in the manner of J.G. Höroldt with a continuous band of Orientals at various pursuits, circa 1735, 1.7cm. high.
(Christie's) **$15,800**

A silver thimble, in the form of a thistle, stamped with a Registration number 222445, English, maker's mark indistinct, Birmingham, 1893, 2.5cm.
(Christie's) **$1,855**

A silver combination thimble and seal, the thimble unscrewing from its seal base to reveal a clear cut glass scent bottle and stopper, probably Thomas Bartleet, early 19th century, 2.9cm.
(Christie's) **$878**

A gold thimble, the border applied with alternat flowerheads and garne settings, French, maker' mark for Michel Veyder early 19th century, 2.3cm.
(Christie's) **$1,012**

A gold and tortoiseshell Piercy's Patent thimble, the tortoiseshell body applied with a gold tip, rim and the Royal coat of arms, English, circa 1825, 2.7cm.
(Christie's) **$2,362**

A gold and enamel combined thimble/scent bottle holder, unmarked, English, late 18th century, the tapering body decorated with a broad translucent red enamel band, ¾in.
(Sotheby's) **$5,762**

A silver gilt thimble, th sides cloisonné enamelle with strapwork, flowers foliage and spot work maker Ovchinniko Russian, circa 1910, 2.3cm.
(Christie's) **$6,750**

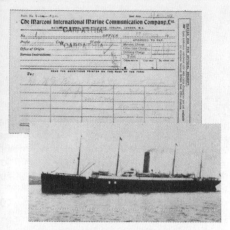

A copper two-handled wine cooler or ice bucket by Elkington & Co., stamped *White Star Line Restaurant*, 23cm. diameter. *(Onslow's)* **$942**

S.S. Carpathia post-disaster messages, 17th April 1912, messages sent by survivors of the Titanic to New York, two album pages, 5½ x 8½in. each. *(Christie's)* **$2,576**

A sterling silver mug inscribed *To Captain Rostron As A Token of Grateful Appreciation of His Kindness on the Carpathia after the sinking of the Titanic April 15th 1912 from John B Thayer Jr*, 6.5cm. high. *(Onslow's)* **$6,594**

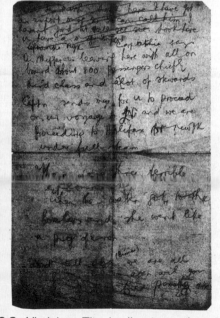

S.S. Virginian: Titanic disaster and post-disaster messages, 14th April 1912. Twelve messages starting (11.15pm*) Hear MGY call CQD SOS has struck iceberg oos. 41.46N 50.14W.* The signals in pencil on Marconi headed service paper, 8½ x 5½in. *(Christie's)* **$18,400**

A White Star Line circular cut glass crystal fruit bowl, engraved with company burgee, 21cm. diameter. *(Onslow's)* **$1,334**

White Star Line Fleet Includes 'Olympic' 45,000 Tons 'Titanic' 45,000 Tons Largest Steamers in the World, a hanging calendar on card for 1912, 30 x 50cm.
(Onslow's) **$3,680**

White Star Line TSS 'Titanic' color art postcard from Thomas Mudd to his mother, *'Dear Mother, Arrived at Southampton safe The Titanic is a splendid boat…'*
(Onslow's) **$5,760**

The key and brass identity tag to the Chart Room on RMS Titanic, the mortice lock key attached to the rectangular shaped brass tag with brass ring, the tag stamped on one side *Chart Room.*
(Onslow's) **$18,840**

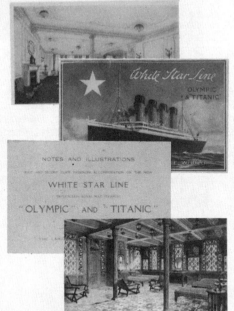

White Star Line 'Olympic' & 'Titanic' Largest Steamers in the World, a publicity booklet entitled Notes and Illustrations of the First and Second Class Passenger Accommodation, 1912.
(Onslow's) **$8,000**

A White Star Line tartan deck rug from RMS 'Titanic' recovered from a 'Titanic' lifeboat circa 1912, woven in a green/brown/moss tartan with a bold red check, the reverse navy blue with bold cream and pale red check and embroidered with White Star Line Logo in one corner, approximately 150 150cm. square.*(Bonhams)* **$15,01**

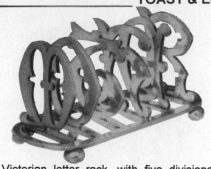

A Victorian letter rack, with five divisions, each separated by a gothic letter spelling *Mother*, on flattened bun feet, 6¼in. *(Woolley & Wallis)* **$269**

An electroplated four-division toast rack, the divisions modelled as crossed golf clubs, 5½in. wide. *(Christie's)* **$473**

An unusual silver-gilt toast rack, the five divisions formed from crossed apostle spoons, and surmounted by a coronet handle, London, 1910. *(Bonhams)* **$251**

An Edwardian novelty five bar toast rack by Heath & Middleton, the wire work rack forming the letters 'Toast', Birmingham 1906, 94grammes, 12.5cm. wide. *(Phillips)* **$282**

A novelty seven bar toast rack, London, 1920, Holland Aldwinckle and Slater, modelled as the letters of the name Dorothy, 4oz. approximately, 11cm. long. *(Bonhams)* **$320**

Christopher Dresser for Hukin & Heath, toast rack, 1878, electroplated metal, rectangular base with upright prongs and 'T' shaped handle, 5½in. *(Sotheby's)* **$3,749**

A Royal Doulton 'Paddy' tobacco jar designed by Harry Fenton, issued 1938-1941, 5½in. high. *(Lyle)* **$1,280**

A Victorian treen tobacco jar, circa 1850, carved in the form of a boxer dog's head, with a collar at its neck and a brass plaque stamped *Lieut Col Elington*, 8¼in. high. *(Bonhams)* **$1,920**

Small fox, head down, a Royal Doulton Kingsware tobacco jar with hallmarked silver rim, circa 1912, 7¾in. high. *(Lyle)* **$610**

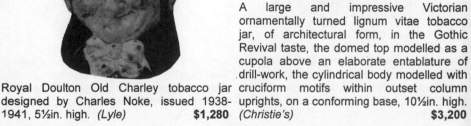

Royal Doulton Old Charley tobacco jar designed by Charles Noke, issued 1938-1941, 5½in. high. *(Lyle)* **$1,280**

A large and impressive Victorian ornamentally turned lignum vitae tobacco jar, of architectural form, in the Gothic Revival taste, the domed top modelled as a cupola above an elaborate entablature of drill-work, the cylindrical body modelled with cruciform motifs within outset column uprights, on a conforming base, 10½in. high. *(Christie's)* **$3,200**

Continental pottery and terracotta character tobacco jars and covers, a racing driver, early 20th century. *(Christie's)* **$56**

A Japanese carved boxwood tobacco jar, set with a carved hardwood octopus lid, and the matching pipe holder, pouch and holder with inlaid ivory signature, ivory ojime. *(Academy)* **$170**

A bisque Bonzo tobacco jar, probably German, 1920s, flesh colored jar of Bonzo seated with arms crossed, molded and painted features including one eye wide open and a slight grin, wearing a black hat and remains of collar, removable head, 6¼in. tall. *(Bonhams)* **$560**

An Austrian painted terracotta tobacco box, late 19th century, modelled as a dog's head, 7½in. high. *(Christie's)* **$1,104**

A Continental terracotta tobacco jar and cover, modelled as the head of a man wearing a red cap, late 19th century, 16cm. high. *(Christie's)* **$56**

A Continental earthenware tobacco jar and cover, modelled as a boy mounted on a dog, 11¼in. *(Bonhams)* **$240**

19th century German pottery tobacco jar and cover modelled as a native American warrior, 15cm. high. *(Christie's)* **$240**

A pair of treacle glaze pottery tobacco jars and covers in the form of pug dogs, 22cm. high. *(Phillips)* **$438**

Mid 19th century tobacco jar and cover, modelled as the head of a spotted dog, 6¾in. high. *(Lyle)* **$640**

A Royal Doulton Kingsware tobacco jar and cover, modelled as a large pipe with a scene of two gentlemen smoking beneath a fox's head, 12½in. *(Bonhams)* **$240**

A German pottery tobacco jar and cover modelled as the head of a servant boy, 15cm. high. *(Christie's)* **$240**

Greers Scotch Whisky, Age & Quality Guaranteed, pub jug, 15cm. high. *(Lyle)* **$320**

A Wilkinson, Royal Staffordshire, pottery 'Winston Churchill' Toby jug, modelled as First Sea Lord of the Admiralty, seated on a bulldog draped with a Union Jack, a model of a warship on his lap and inscribed around the base, 31cm. high, printed *Clarice Cliff* and painted *No.12. (Bearnes)* **$1,150**

Corbetts Irish Whiskey water jug by D.A. Campbell, Belfast, 20cm. high. *(Lyle)* **$400**

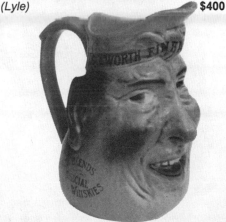

A papier mâché ventriloquist headed toby jug, English, probably 1920s, the hand painted toby jug face with glass eyes, and leather upper and lower lips, handle to back with three metal levers operating eyes and lips, 8in. high. *(Bonhams)* **$480**

Isleworth Special Old Whiskies water jug, 17cm. high. *(Lyle)* **$400**

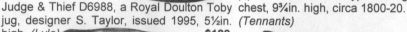

Judge & Thief D6988, a Royal Doulton Toby jug, designer S. Taylor, issued 1995, 5½in. high. *(Lyle)*   **$128**

A fine Prattware toby jug, the ruddy-faced toper firmly grasping his jug and goblet, his pipe of coiled snake type resting against his chest, 9¾in. high, circa 1800-20. *(Tennants)*   **$1,395**

The Best Is Not Too Good D6107, a Royal Doulton Toby jug, designer H. Fenton, issued 1939-1960, 4½in. high. *(Lyle)*   **$392**

Charlie Chaplin, a Royal Doulton Toby jug, designer unknown, issued circa 1918, 11in. high. *(Lyle)*   **$3,600**

King & Queen of Clubs D6999, a Royal Doulton two faced Toby jug, designer S. Taylor, issued 1995 in a limited edition of 2,500, 5¾in. high. *(Lyle)*   **$160**

A 14in. Georgian carved wooden Toby jug figure of a seated auctioneer holding a gavel, in the form of a money box. *(R.H. Ellis)*   **$4,800**

A rare black man ordinary toby jug with a black face and gray wig, seated in chair and holding a pink lustered frothing jug of ale, 25cm. high. *(Phillips)* **$1,360**

Jolly Toby D6109, a Royal Doulton Toby jug, designer H. Fenton, issued 1939-1991, 6½in. high. *(Lyle)* **$152**

Dr. Jekyll & Mr. Hyde D7024, a Royal Doulton two faced Toby jug, designer S. Taylor, issued 1996, 15in. high. *(Lyle)* **$128**

Burkes Green Label Whiskey jug by Fieldings, Stoke on Trent, 29cm. high. *(Lyle)* **$1,000**

A Staffordshire creamware toby jug of conventional type, seated holding a jug of frothing ale and with a pipe by his side, 25.5cm. high. *(Phillips)* **$768**

A rare red-painted tinware cookie box, Pennsylvania, circa 1825, the front painted in yellow and green with paired 'love birds', 8¾in. high. *(Sotheby's)*   **$23,000**

A pair of tôle chestnut covered urns, on stepped feet, with serpentine handles, the tapered cover with octagonal gilt finials, paint decorated with foliage in gold and siena on black ground, 12in. high. *(Skinner)*   **$2,300**

Painted tin and glass light refractor, New England, early 19th century, painted floral decorated tin frame surrounding a blown flattened globular glass font and mounted on a painted wooden base, 11½in. high. *(Skinner)*   **$5,463**

A pair of tôle peinte cache pots and liners, early 19th century, each of flaring square section, gilt with trophies, 7¾in. high. *(Sotheby's)*   **$1,840**

A pair of tôle peinte ormolu and patinated bronze palm trees, mid 20th century, each with a rectangular base with an Egyptian winged motif with confronting eagle monopodiae centered by a starred circular motif, on ring-turned supports headed by a ball motif and on toupie feet, issuing palm trees finishing in a fruited cone, one of the bases of the palm trees stamped *K.D Paris*, 28½in. high.

The ormolu bas reliefs of the falcon winged and cobra-protected sun-disk derive from the Theban Apollo Temple illustrated in Vivant Denon's Voyage dans la Basse et la Haute Egypt of 1802. Furniture mounts of this pattern were brought back from Paris early in the 19th century by Thomas Bruce, 7th Earl of Elgin. *(Christie's)*   **$8,000**

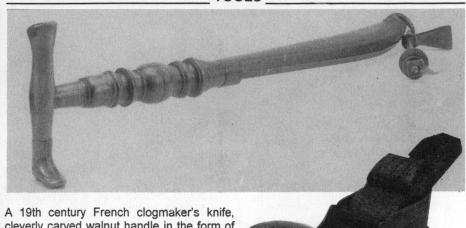

A 19th century French clogmaker's knife, cleverly carved walnut handle in the form of a booted leg, small brass pins form eyelets on the boot. *(Tool Shop Auctions)* **$530**

A unique 16 x 2¾in. steel soled gun metal Norris No. 54G panel plane, over 2in. of original iron remaining.
(Tony Murland) **$6,300**

A pair of French shears stamped A. Noyers. *(Tool Shop Auctions)* **$135**

A most unusual boxwood handled saw with deeply cast decorative floral plate. *(Tool Shop Auctions)* **$225**

A late 16th, early 17th century European musical instrument maker's plane, front tote repaired with smith-made rivets, with a band of decoration around the top. *(Tool Shop Auctions)* **$913**

An incredibly rare example of a double handled stairsaw in Brazilian rosewood. *(Tool Shop Auctions)* **$332**

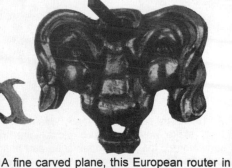

A fine carved plane, this European router in oak, 7 x 6in. is elaborately carved into the face of a ram, 17th/18th century. *(Tool Shop Auctions)* **$2,393**

A 16/17th century musical-instrument maker's plane, 6 x 2³/16in., complete with toothing iron and conceivably original wedge, *(Tool Shop Auctions)* **$2,021**

A rosewood handled center wheel plow plane with ivory tips by The Ohio Tool Company. *(Tool Shop Auctions)* **$10,043**

A fine example of the elusive double socketed French beheading ax, unhandled. *(Tool Shop Auctions)* **$450**

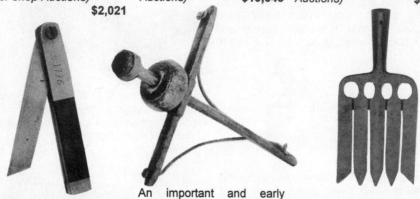

An 18th century rosewood and brass bevel, dated 1776. *(Tool Shop Auctions)* **$647**

An important and early stonemason's pump drill, the boss hewn from solid stone and interestingly decorated. *(Tool Shop Auctions)* **$225**

An attractive wide 5 tine eel gleave. *(Tool Shop Auctions)* **$564**

A 16th/17th century, 13 x 10in. stake anvil. Classic early form, the hexagonal stake thickens at the bottom to form an elegant buttress. *(Tool Shop Auctions)* **$299**

A Mathieson 9b handled plow plane, the white beech crisp and unfinished and the boxwood arms with a slight polished appearance. *(Tool Shop Auctions)* **$465**

A pair of 4¼in. early 19th century dancing-master calipers with detailed boots and seductive frilly garters. *(Tool Shop Auctions)* **$299**

A German carved torchère, 19th century, in the form of a stooping elf, hands aloft supporting a cornucopia, on a plinth base, 44in. high. *(Christie's)* **$3,634**

A Continental majolica torchère, the circular top supported by a female terminal figure bust on a tapered column and four hoof feet with a square base, gray and brown coloring, circa 1880, 94cm. *(Tennants)* **$1,280**

A pair of Venetian polychrome-painted blackamoor torchères, one 18th century, the other of later date, each holding a spirally gadrooned cornucopia, wearing a feather hat, feather tunic and red boots, standing on a rocky plinth with lion claw feet and blocks, 50in. high. *(Christie's)* **$7,544**

Consul, The Educated Monkey, a rare tinplate calculating toy by the Educational Toy Mfg Co. Ltd. USA, in original box, circa 1918. *(Auction Team Köln)* **$462**

A German pull-along toy, the composition-headed trainer with cloth clothing, the stick and the plush bear's head nodding when pulled along, circa 1900, 31cm. high. *(Bristol)* **$951**

Carved wood and wrought iron jig toy, America, late 19th century, the articulate figures with period clothing and remnants of hair wigs, 38½in. high. *(Skinner)* **$805**

Paint decorated child's wheelbarrow, American, 19th century, the red and green painted wheelbarrow with gilt and black decorations and painted landscapes on the sides, 33in. long. *(Skinner)* **$517**

An automaton picture of a young girl and dog, French, last quarter 19th century, the lithographed picture showing a seated child wearing a checked dress, shawl and bonnet cuddling a puppy, with movement to child's head and arm, puppy's head and paw. *(Bonhams)* **$2,560**

Painted tin rowing scull, America, circa 1920, with painted wood and composition articulated rowers, scull 40in. long. *(Skinner)* **$2,300**

Painted wood four-piece toy floor train, late 19th century, black locomotive with red and yellow details and striping, black flat car with red and yellow striping, red '200' Pullman car with black and yellow details, dark green Pennsylvania R.R. no. 20 baggage car with yellow and black details, total 54³/₈in. *(Skinner)* **$6,900**

Painted wood horse-drawn baby vehicle, early 20th century, blue seat and base with red striping, rubber rimmed spoked rear wheels, small cast iron front wheel, mohair covered horse mounted on front of base, 39in. long. *(Skinner)* **$690**

Painted and metal brass 'braker' electric car, American, circa 1896, the black painted working model with a spindle backseat, 10in. long.
(Butterfield & Butterfield) **$2,750**

A fine early Doll and Cie ferris wheel ride entirely hand-painted, consisting of six swinging gondolas, each with two passengers, 13½in. high.
(Christie's) **$4,000**

1920s fretwork model of a bus.
$480

A painted and lacquered tinplate side-wheel steam gunboat carpet toy, mounted on four revolving spoked wheels, with cannon, probably French, 1880s, 12in. long. *(Christie's)* **$533**

A 'Fox and Goose' rare clockwork tinplate toy by Schuco, Nürnberg, with lithographed suitcase, the fox with plush head, glass eyes and felt clothing, in working order, post 1956. *(Auktion Team Köln)* **$468**

A unusual Kobi toy, Chinese, late 19th century, comprising four characters on a log, carved from nuts with faces with extending eyes and tongues, the figures holding a stick in each hand, figures 4cm. *(Sotheby's)* **$360**

A carved and painted wood large toy figure of a camel, 19th century, possibly American, realistically modelled with two humps, fitted with leather ears and a rope tail, painted in tones of tan and cream, 23½in. long. *(Sotheby's)* **$287**

English butcher's shop, mid 19th century, 26½in. high. *(Christie's)* **$8,000**

An extraordinary Märklin tinplate fire set, circa 1919, consisting of three keywind matched fire trucks; each hand painted in red, black and yellow with rubber tires, all three bear the Märklin metal embossed shield on the front panel, firehouse 21in. wide. *(Christie's)* **$79,200**

The style of decoration which characterizes Tramp Art has its origins in the carving of the European medieval period. It was brought over to America by German and Scandinavian immigrants, many of whom settled in New York and Pennsylvania.

These states also produced, around the 1850s, when cigar smoking was especially popular, cedar or mahogany cigar boxes; when the boxes were empty, they would be sold very cheaply or given away, and they became the basic recycled material for Tramp Art.

Although some pieces may have been made by tramps or hobos, most were the work of lumberjacks, miners or rural craftsmen, in fact anyone who had a penknife and enjoyed whittling. They were made for the personal satisfaction or pleasure of the maker, and not with any idea of commercial gain.

The earliest known piece of Tramp Art is dated 1862, but because so few were signed or dated, the tradition is likely to be quite a bit older than that. It began to decline after 1925, as cigar smoking became less popular, and thus the production of cigar boxes also dried up. However, some craftsmen continue producing pieces to this day, still mainly for their own enjoyment, though Tramp Art is becoming increasingly sought after by collectors.

Tramp Art is characterized by its geometric shapes and layering and notch carving - various layers are added on top of each other and then small V or Z shaped notches are carved out to create patterned surfaces. It also features an abundance, even a superfluity, of decoration, whereby, in addition to elaborate chip carving, some pieces have applied decoration such as paper pictures or photographs, inlaid bits of mirror, colored glass or stones.

Generally speaking, more modern pieces, consisting mainly of small boxes or picture or mirror frames, fetch less than older examples, which can often be distinguished by the fact that they are darker, whether from age or shellacking.

White painted Tramp Art cabinet, America, late 19th century, the rectangular cabinet with peaked mirrored crest and sides with applied decorative details flanking the rectangular mirrored door, all on four applied feet, 34in. high. *(Skinner)* **$800**

Tramp Art carved side table, New England or New York, late 19th/early 20th century, the projecting square top and medial shelf on square legs all with applied multi-layered shaped and chip carved decorations, 26in. high. *(Skinner)* **$690**

A sycamore serving platter, in an early style, of rectangular outline with rounded angles, 0 x 43.2cm. *(Christie's)* **$3,680**

An Austrian polychrome carved wood model of a monkey, late 19th or early 20th century, shown standing in costume and holding a tray to the fore, the plinth with retail label to the underside *A.PESSE, 9 & 11 BRD. DE LA MADELAINE,* 18in. high. *(Christie's)* **$1,920**

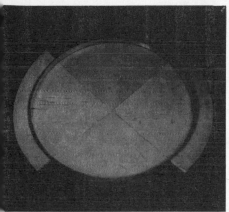

oris Lacroix, two-handled tray, circa 1930, arnished vellum surface on oak within ickel-plated metal band, the circular tray onsisting of four quadrants, two extending form the handles, 50cm. wide over andles. *(Sotheby's)* **$4,865**

Pope Joan board, early 19th century, the shed board with divisions painted with ards, with checker stringing to the borders, ½in. diameter. *(Christie's)* **$800**

An early Victorian mahogany lazy susan, attributed to William Harrison, the lobed circular top with eight molded circular recesses separated by spandrels each containing a five-petalled flower, supported by a rotating base with a shaped pierced frieze and curved feet, 23¾in. diameter. *(Christie's)* **$4,629**

As its name suggests, Trench Art is the name given to the souvenirs that serving soldiers in the two World Wars made in their spare time from the debris and fragments they picked up around them on the battlefield. These could take many forms, such as lighters, made from shrapnel or bullet cases, knives or ashtrays, often carved with messages or initials. Sometimes, more ambitiously, they produced superb models of ships, planes, tanks or field guns, and these are particularly highly prized by collectors.

Brass Trench Art World War 1 aeroplane made from bullet cases.
(Lyle) $12●

An early 20th century French metalware 'trench art' condiment set and spoon in the form of a First World War howitzer shell which takes apart to form an egg cup and reveal a condiment shaker together with a spoon, enamelled on the terminal with crossed flags and 'Gloire aux Allies', 4oz weighable silver. *(Christie's)* **$400**

Trench Art, World War 1 German aircraft
(Lyle) $16●

Combined lighter and ashtray dated *1944*.
(Lyle) **$50**

First World War Trench Art aeroplane
(Lyle) $19●

Chinese Export aubergine-glazed tortoise-rm tureen and cover, late 18th century, alistically modelled as a tortoise with its ead raised, 9in. long.
Christie's) **$4,370**

A Chelsea asparagus tureen and a cover, naturally modelled as a bunch of asparagus enriched in puce and green tied with chocolate-brown ribbon, circa 1755, 18.5cm. wide. **$5,790**

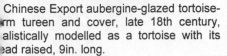

Volkstedt hen tureen and cover, circa ʼ80, with pale-brown, dark-brown, black nd white plumage, red comb and brown nd yellow crown, nestling on an oval dish plied with grass with a chick on her back ɑ two chicks either side of her, 47½cm. ng. *(Christie's)* **$4,800**

A Strasbourg faience cauliflower tureen and cover, circa 1750. *(Christie's)* **$9,190**

Chelsea fish tureen and cover, circa 1755, rmed as a perch fish, finely molded with ales picked out in yellow with brown ɡes and brown fins, the cover formed as e upper body and tail, 37.5cm.
ʻhillips) **$3,040**

A Chelsea Red Anchor period cauliflower tureen and cover, decorated in shades of green, 4½in. high, circa 1755.
(Tennants) **$2,511**

A Worcester partridge-tureen and cover, the bird on an oval nest to the right, its plumage enriched in shades of brown, the edge of the cover with stylized entwined straw, circa 1765, 17.5cm. long.
(Christie's) **$15,169**

A Sceaux faience cabbage-tureen and cov naturally modelled, the outer overlappi gray-green leaves with pale-green midri and veins, circa 1755, 32cm. wid *(Christie's)* **$12,5**

A mid 18th century Brussels faience boar's head tureen, cover and stand, the stand 40cm. long. *(Christie's)* **$7,668**

A pair of Longton Hall pigeon-tureens a covers, the naturally modelled birds to l and right with purple feather markings, cir 1755, 22cm. long.
(Christie's) **$13,0**

Two Chelsea eel tureens and covers naturally modelled with their bodies curled, their tails forming the handles, circa 1755, 18.5cm. wide. *(Christie's)* **$35,420**

A Chelsea melon-tureen and cover natura modelled and enriched in yellow and gre the cover with curled branch finial w foliage and flower terminals, circa 17 17cm. long. *(Christie's)* **$7,4**

A pair of 'carp' tureens and covers, 18th/19th century, each modelled poised in a position to attack with upturned tail and raised head, fiercely baring its teeth, a wang character dividing the bulging eyes, with two sets of horns, the domed cover shaped as the beast's back with raised dorsal fins, overall enamelled in iron-red with brown and gilt details, 8¼in. long.
(Christie's) **$8,000**

A Worcester partridge tureen and cover sitting on a rest, with natural colored plumage in shades of brown, red and black, the head in red, 14.5cm.
(Phillips) **$2,639**

A famille rose export tureen and cover, modelled as a chicken, painted in colored enamels and gilt and molded to simulate the plumage, 7½in. long, 18th century. *(Christie's)* **$7,360**

A Minton majolica pigeon-pie tureen and cover, the circular body moulded and colored to simulate yellow wicker-work, impressed date code for 1859, 12½in. diameter. *(Christie's)* **$3,809**

Hammonia typewriter produced by Guhl & Harbeck, Hamburg, the first mass produced German machine, circa 1882. *(Auction Team Köln)*
$19,179

◄

An Edison Mimeograph Typewriter No. 1 1894. At the end of 1875 Thomas Edison developed and wax stencil copier, which he called the Edison Mimeograph. Because the wax matrices still had to be written by hand there were often an unacceptable difference in quality, particularly in the case of the late copies. To correct this, Edison produced his Mimeograph Typewriter, an understrike machine which was produced in three models, each with a greater number of characters. It was produced, as the Mimeograph had been, by A. B. Dick & Co of Chicago. Other typewriter manufacturers however, decided to boycott the Mimeograph Copier, and because of this Dick decided to concentrate purely on producing typewriters, so that only a few of the Mimeograph Typewriters were produced Edison later sold the patents of both the copier and typewriter, reportedly at a very low price, to Dick, who went on to become one of the largest manufacturers of office equipment in the US.
(Auction Team Köln) **$13,398**

A Malling Hansen writing ball typewriter, the first mass produced writing machine in the world, circa 1867.
(Auction Team Köln) **$57,538**

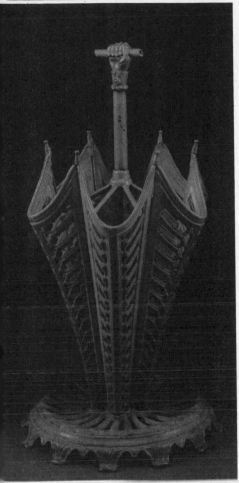

A Continental beechwood umbrella stand, late 19th century, possibly German, in the form of a begging hound holding an oval ring and above a metal tray, 38in. high. *(Christie's)* **$1,120**

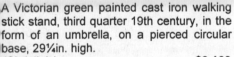

A Victorian green painted cast iron walking stick stand, third quarter 19th century, in the form of an umbrella, on a pierced circular base, 29¼in. high.
(Christie's) **$3,160**

▶

A patinated iron umbrella stand, mid 20th century, with two hippopotamus feet fitted with circular drip pans and bound with copper piping, the twin looped stand with a foliate backed hippopotamus mask bearing a faded paper label *The Gallery of Natural History & Artistic Treatment of Trophies and Products. Rowland Ward Ltd. The Jungle, 167. Picadilly. London.*
(Christie's) **$2,049**

A French cream and green-painted umbrella stand, of semi-elliptical outline with laurel leaf cresting and caned back, 27½in. wide. *(Christie's)* **$1,036**

Unusual Pontipool two-section umbrella stand, 19th century, copper colored with gold highlights surrounding landscape reserves, 26in. high. *(Eldred's)* **$385**

A T C Brown-Westhead Moore and Co Pottery figural umbrella stand, late 19th century, decorated in majolica type glazes, modelled as a bearded trapper dressed in furs, holding a seal in both hands, an axe at his feet, impressed factory marks, *30* and *1340*, 94cm. high. *(Bonhams)* **$7,680**

A late Victorian figural umbrella stand, 58cm. *(Bonhams)* **$300**

lady's linen corset, probably American, id 19th century, inscribed *Julia A. Hudson* ℈. 7 with a sterling silver boat pin and an igraved baleen busk.
otheby's) **$1,610**

Late 19th century ladies padded corset, edged with lace. *(Lyle)* **$130**

pair of rare young girl's hoops composed f an oval hoop with two supporting bands, overed with padded glazed linen, mld 18th entury. *(Christie's)* **$8,800**

Dimity bustle, with hide and fabric covered steel springs, circa 1880.
(Lyle) **$320**

composition, leather and fabric corset, th straps and buckles, 29.5cm. high. *hristie's)* **$45**

Victorian open gusset linen 'drawers' with broderie anglais lace edge.
(Lyle) **$65**

A devore corset of white cotton, the sides and back corded, with lacing over hips, 1820s. *(Christie's)* **$734**

A black satin and lycra bustier with front hook closure, ribbed back and elastic straps, made for Madonna, with a letter of provenance. *(Christie's)* **$6,900**

Gone With The Wind, 1939, a pair of undergarment pantaloons worn by several actresses before and during the filming of Gone With The Wind, with four black and white photographs from the film, 8 x 10in. *(Christie's)* **$4,025**

A baby's corset of wadded cotton, 18th century. *(Christie's)* **$952**

A silk stocking belonging to Queen Victoria, English, 19th century, the white stocking embroidered crown and V.R. near the top, with further embroidery above the ankle. *(Bonhams)* **$428**

A boned corset of brown canvas lined with white linen, with tabbed waist, circa 1770. *(Christie's)* **$4,620**

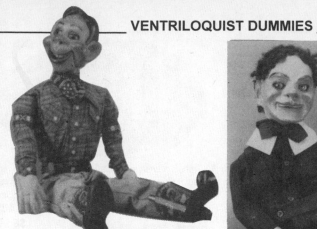

The Howdy Doody Show, a Howdy Doody puppet constructed in the image of Buffalo Bob's best friend Howdy, dressed in the familiar red painted shirt, faded jeans and red cowboy boots.
(Christie's) **$23,000**

A ventriloquist's dummy modelled as a boy, with jaw, eye and hand movement and dressed in contemporary green tweed suit with Eton collar, 33in. high.
(Christie's) **$405**

A papier mâché sailor ventriloquist doll, French, circa 1890, the painted face with glass eyes, hinged mouth, black mohair wig, in a hollow body with composition hands and feet, 35in. tall. *(Bonhams)* **$640**

A good ventriloquist's dummy, nattily dressed in tuxedo and black Oxford shoes, with tousled brown hair, together with two spare heads and a spare hand.
(Academy) **$740**

A fish, silver, realistically stamped an
chased to resemble a fish, S Blanckense
and Son Ltd, Birmingham, 1891, 6.5cm
(Christie's) **$85:**

Mr. Punch, silver vesta case, formed as a
bust study of Mr. Punch, maker's mark
indistinct, Birmingham 1890, 5.8cm.
(Christie's) **$560**

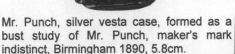

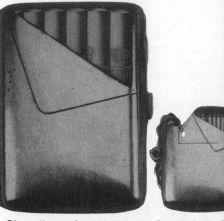

A railway ticket vesta case, silver,
rectangular, the front enamelled with a first
class return ticket from St. Pancras to
Newmarket on the Great Eastern Railway,
the reverse engraved with entwined initials,
Sampson Mordan, London 1889, 5.6cm.
(Christie's) **$1,280**

Cigarette and vesta case, the rectangula
cigarette case cast to incorporate a 'fla
revealing a row of enamelled cigarettes, th
vesta similarly cast and incorporating a wic
holder, the flap revealing a row of enamelle
vestas, both Austro-Hungarian, late 19
century, 8.8cm. and 4.4cm. respectivel
(Christie's) **$1,70**

A football and leg, silver vesta case formed
as the lower leg of a footballer, a ball
balanced on his foot, the lid stamped *C. &
M. Patent*, Birmingham 1884, 5.05cm.
(Christie's) **$690**

A vesta case, formed as a mussel shell, or
side with applied initials, *H.M.M.B.A.*, th
reverse chased with the legen
*Compliments. Gorham Mfg. Co. New Yor
American, Gorham, late 19th centur
6.2cm. (Christie's)* **$56**

A pig, 9ct gold, formed as a seated pig, one side engraved with an inscription and date, Continental, import marks for London 1905, 4.9cm. *(Christie's)* **$1,518**

A brass rectangular box-type vesta case, the cover with applied enamel plaque depicting a lady relieving herself into a river, French, late 19th century, 4.5cm. *(Christie's)* **$400**

An Edwardian silver vesta case, the fascia repoussé with a golfer about to strike the ball, London 1903, by H. Matthews, 32 grms. *(Phillips)* **$290**

Amorous ladies, silver, rectangular box-type vesta case, the cover enamelled with two ladies exchanging a kiss, Austro-Hungarian, late 19th century, 4.4cm. *(Christie's)* **$3,036**

A football and rugby ball, both silver and both chased and engraved to resemble the above, H.W. Ltd., Birmingham marks, the rugby ball 5.5cm. *(Christie's)* **$1,612**

A late 19th century American silver and yellow metal vesta case, circa 1890, modelled as a wrapped mailing newspaper, the yellow metal address label with blue enamel stamp and addressed to *Mrs Jaffrey, 7 Sloane Street, London*, 5.9cm. *(Bonhams)* **$960**

Man Stealing into Bedroom, silver, rectangular with sloping cover, the front enamelled with a scene of a man climbing through a bedroom window, French, late 19th century, 4.9cm. *(Christie's)* **$1,422**

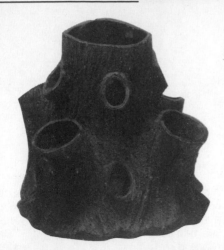

An English Doulton stoneware stick stand, late 19th/early 20th century, modelled naturalistically as a hollow tree stump with various hollow branches and apertures, 17in. high. *(Christie's)* **$640**

A large brass mounted mahogany hall stand, early 20th century, the openwork frame of rectangular form with domed tops and ends, with two shelves and twin walking stick retainers to the sides. *(Christie's)* **$5,520**

A brass bound barrel shaped walking stick stand, early 20th century, of coopered construction, the top with divisions, with retractable drip trays to the interior, 25in. high. *(Christie's)* **$1,472**

A Victorian antler stickstand formed from a arrangement of interlocking antlers, on turned oak base with bun feet, 20in. diameter. *(Christie's)* **$1,92**

Victorian painted iron stick stand and door stop of a boy holding a serpent.
(Lyle) **$640**

Black Forest carved wood stick and hat tand, of a bear with glass eyes clasping a ranch of a tree, a baby bear seated on the op above a mirror, the base with a zinc well, ft.5in. high.
Woolley & Wallis) **$3,680**

A late 19th century Black Forest wood bear stick stand, realistically carved with outstretched arms holding an oval stick support frame, 30in.
(Christie's) **$4,050**

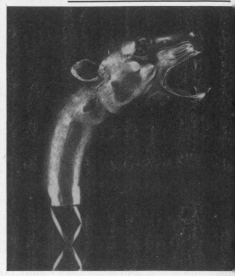

An ivory handled walking stick, late 19th or early 20th century, the handle as a double sided head, with Christ to the front and a skull to the reverse, on a weighted ivory shaft with ebony banding, 36¾in. *(Christie's)* **$2,400**

A silver mounted walking stick, the handle modelled as a jaguar's head with open jaw and mounted with garnet eyes, upper applied with silver trellis decoration above a plain collar, 34¾in. *(Christie's)* **$1,56**

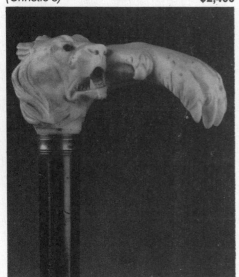

An ivory handled walking stick, late 19th or early 20th century, the 'L' shaped grip carved with a lion's head and extending paw, with white metal collar and yew wood shaft. *(Christie's)* **$1,747**

An ivory handled walking stick, late 19th or early 20th century, the grip carved as dog's head with inset glass eyes, with g metal collar to the malacca sha *(Christie's)* **$84**

A Victorian novelty walking stick, the boxwood handle carved with an ebonized stag beetle clutching a field mouse in its claws. *(Woolley & Wallis)* **$721**

An ivory handled walking stick, late 19th or early 20th century, the grip carved as a snarling dog's head, with inset glass eyes, the bamboo shaft with white metal wirework collar. *(Christie's)* **$1,288**

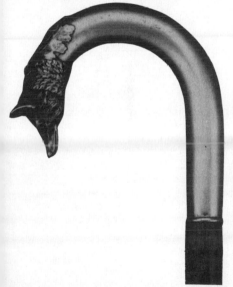

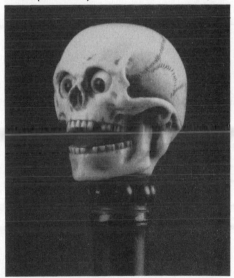

A silver mounted bamboo walking stick, the crooked handle with tip modelled as an oak-leaf crested fox's head mounted with garnet eyes, and engraved with monogram of initials *FC*, horn ferrule, 37¼in. *(Christie's)* **$1,195**

A Victorian ivory handled automaton walking stick, late 19th century, the grip amusingly modelled as a human skull, a button to the white metal studded collar operating the articulated eyes and jaw, with stained wood bamboo shaft. *(Christie's)* **$7,728**

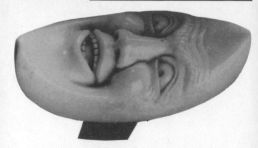

A George V ivory handled walking stick, the grip carved as a man in the crescent-shaped moon, the tapering ebony shaft with silver collar, with assay marks for Birmingham 1912. *(Christie's)* **$1,011**

Continental silver, enamel, and gilt wash hippo-form cane handle, modern, with foliate cast body and band of blue engine-turned enamel, mounted with stones, 5¾in. high. *(Skinner)* **$2,530**

An ivory handled walking stick, early 20th century, the grip amusingly modelled as a smiling moon-faced man, the rosewood shaft with gold collar, incised with the dates and initials *1885, A.B. 1935 Kendall*, and with assay mark. *(Christie's)* **$883**

An ivory handled walking stick, late 19th or early 20th century, the handle as a hound's head, on a malacca shaft, 35½in. *(Christie's)* **$1,475**

A novelty walking stick, the ivory handle carved with a pelican grasping an egg in his mouth, with an ebonized shaft. *(Bonhams)* **$480**

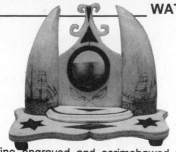

A fine engraved and scrimshawed whale ivory, baleen and whale teeth watch stand, probably American, third quarter 19th century, 7in. high
(Sotheby's) **$14,950**

A large Staffordshire pottery treacle glazed watch stand, 19th century, formed as two columns with sunburst arched pediment with rectangular slab base and on six ball feet, the back-board sprigged with baskets of fruit trees and a putto. *(Bonhams)* **$960**

Prisoner of War carved whale ivory, whale bone and ebonized wood watch hutch, America, 19th century, the extended back of three pierced and carved staves with round window cut out beneath a shaped crest 14in. high. *(Skinner)* **$2,500**

▶

An unusual walnut and pine watch hutch, probably American, mid 19th century, in the form of a tall case clock with elaborately chip-carved details and inlaid with bone, the arched pediment above a circular oculus and a Gothic-style window; mounted on a chip-carved base, 9½in. high.
(Sotheby's) **$1,035**

Unusual pocket watch holder, 19th century, in the form of a pig fashioned from molded brass, with a pocket watch, 3in. high x 5in. long. *(Sotheby's)* **$1,380**

A Doulton Punch and Judy clockcase, the buff stoneware with a bright blue glaze, circa 1905, 11½in. high. *(Lyle)* **$3,200**

A fine inlaid mahogany, bone and églomisé hearth-form watch stand, American, late 18th/early 19th century, the carved bone fireplace with an églomisé mantel and surround set into an architectural wood case, surmounted by a triangular églomisé panel below a circular watch holder and flanked by bone flame-form finials, 21¼in. high. *(Sotheby's)* **$1,035**

A Pratt type watch holder, modelled as a long case clock, flanked by loosely-draped putti beside plinths on a rectangular base, enriched in blue, ocher, yellow and green glazes, circa 1800, 27cm. high. *(Christie's)* **$885**

Swiss watch decorated in Neoclassical manner with enamelled decoration and pearls inset in gold, the back opens to reveal a scene of love-making, circa 1800. *(Christie's)* **$8,000**

A late 19th century quarter repeater with automated erotic scene in a silver full hunter case. Later added erotic automaton scene of a chef and kitchen maid in polychrome enamel on an engraved background. The man keeps time with the striking of the hour hammer when the repeat is sounded. *(Pieces of Time)* **$3,680**

An 18ct. gold and turquoise-set helmet with concealed watch, signed *Tiffany & Co.*, movement signed *Movado*, circa 1960, 43mm. high. *(Christie's)* **$4,345**

A silvered metal pocket watch with circular white enamel dial in a golf ball shaped case, 1½in. diameter. *(Christie's)* **$295**

An early 19th century French gold and enamel ball watch, the verge movement with pierced bridge cock signed *L'Epine A Paris*, 23mm. diameter. *(Phillips)* **$1,380**

A pink gold self-winding water resistant wristwatch with center seconds, signed *Rolex, model no. 14238*, 1950s, with self-winding movement, the associated painted enamel dial depicting a peacock, pink gold hands, in circular case with chamfered bezel, screw down winder and screwed back, case and movement signed, 34mm. diameter. *(Christie's)* **$9,163**

An early 19th century Swiss quarter repeating automaton verge with concealed erotic scene in a gold open face case, as the watch strikes the hours and quarters the arms of the figures move as though striking the bells between them, below the dial a parcel gilt cover which can be slid aside to reveal a couple embracing on a couch above a blue steel background. As the watch strikes the man springs into action, continuing until the repeating train stops. Circa 1810, 57mm. diameter.
(Pieces of Time) **$19,500**

A rare 18 carat gold asymmetric wristwatch, signed *Cartier, model Crash*, 1980s, the nickel plated movement signed *LeCoultre* with gold alloy balance, the white dial with stylized Roman numerals, in unusual shaped case, the back secured by four screws to the band, cabochon winder, screwed bar lugs with leather strap, maker's gold deployant clasp, maker's mark *J.C* on case, 43 x 23mm.
(Christie's) **$24,518**

An 18ct. Swiss gold and enamel quarter repeating musical automaton keywound openface watch with erotic scene, unsigned, early 19th century, 58mm. diameter.
(Christie's) **$48,300**

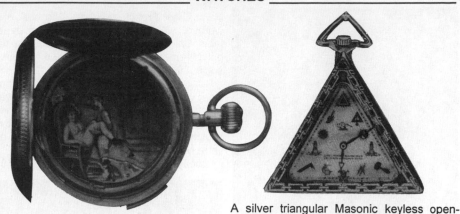

A silver triangular Masonic keyless open-face pocket watch, the movement signed *Tempor W. Co.*, 55mm.
(Christie's) **$2,250**

A gold hunter cased quarter repeating watch with concealed erotic automaton, circa 1890, 18k, three quarter plate gilt lever movement, gold cuvette fitted with a panel depicting a lady and a gentleman within a boudoir moving in unison with the repeating work, silvered dial applied with gold foliage and scrolls, the case engraved with foliage inhabited by griffins and an urn, 53mm. diameter. *(Sotheby's)* **$5,750**

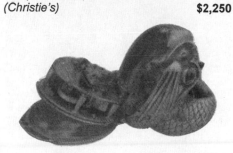

An extraordinary silver verge watch in the form of a dolphin by J. Sermand [Geneva], the hinged mouth opening to reveal the dial, circa 1640, 40mm. long.
(Christie's) **$132,000**

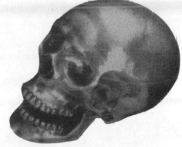

A rare silver erotic pocket watch by Joseph Georg in Graz, 1810-20, the case in two parts, with incised edges and decorated with painted enamels depicting a gallant under Cupid's guard and three allegorical figures. Inside the lid is a scene of Venus and Cupid in a garden, and behind the works an erotic bedroom scene, 45mm. diameter. *(Finarte)* **$3,875**

A finely modelled silver skull watch opening to reveal the engraved silver chapter ring with Roman numerals and Arabic five-minute divisions, signed Pete. Garon, London, 75mm. long. *(Christie's)* **$2,798**

Henri Cros, French, 1840-1907, a bust of a woman, signed *H Cros* and with a paper label *Chenue Emballeur/Mme Leon Heuzel*, polychromed wax, on a gilded wooden socle, 20cm. 8in.

Cros is a fascinating sculptor whose work rarely appears on the market. He was both a sculptor and accomplished draughtsman. His most innovative sculptural works are his wax and pâte de verre busts and reliefs.
(Sotheby's) **$4,400**

Two red wax figures of gentlemen in period costume, possibly 17th century, each shown standing with hands clasped to the front, on stepped square section plinths, 16in. and 20in. high respectively.
(Christie's) **$2,400**

A fine poured wax doll of Queen Victoria as a child, English, circa 1830, the well molded head with blue glass eyes, down turned mouth, inserted blonde hair, shoulder plate leading to cloth body with wax lower arms and legs, wearing elaborate gray silk dress with cerise trim and sewn on rosebuds, 22in. tall.

It is said that Queen Victoria's court dressmaker made the dress for the Duke and Duchess of Hamilton in their racing colors of cerise and green.
(Bonhams) **$2,400**

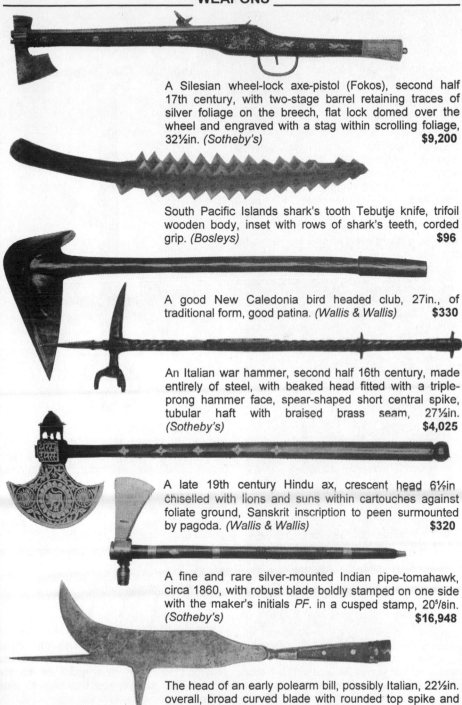

A Silesian wheel-lock axe-pistol (Fokos), second half 17th century, with two-stage barrel retaining traces of silver foliage on the breech, flat lock domed over the wheel and engraved with a stag within scrolling foliage, 32½in. *(Sotheby's)* **$9,200**

South Pacific Islands shark's tooth Tebutje knife, trifoil wooden body, inset with rows of shark's teeth, corded grip. *(Bosleys)* **$96**

A good New Caledonia bird headed club, 27in., of traditional form, good patina. *(Wallis & Wallis)* **$330**

An Italian war hammer, second half 16th century, made entirely of steel, with beaked head fitted with a triple-prong hammer face, spear-shaped short central spike, tubular haft with braised brass seam, 27½in. *(Sotheby's)* **$4,025**

A late 19th century Hindu ax, crescent head 6½in chiselled with lions and suns within cartouches against foliate ground, Sanskrit inscription to peen surmounted by pagoda. *(Wallis & Wallis)* **$320**

A fine and rare silver-mounted Indian pipe-tomahawk, circa 1860, with robust blade boldly stamped on one side with the maker's initials *PF.* in a cusped stamp, 20⁵/8in. *(Sotheby's)* **$16,948**

The head of an early polearm bill, possibly Italian, 22½in. overall, broad curved blade with rounded top spike and flattened backspike. *(Wallis & Wallis)* **$493**

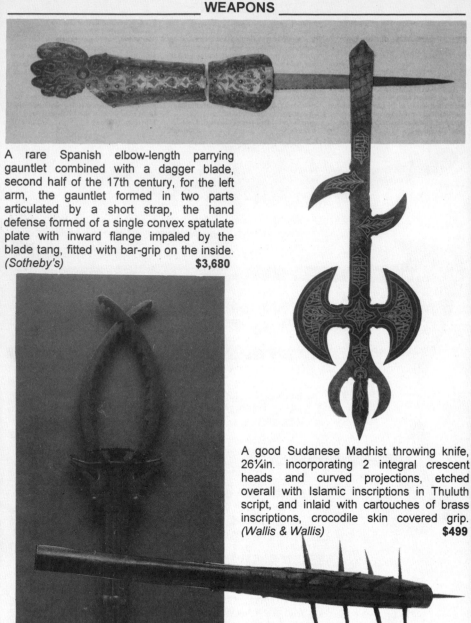

A rare Spanish elbow-length parrying gauntlet combined with a dagger blade, second half of the 17th century, for the left arm, the gauntlet formed in two parts articulated by a short strap, the hand defense formed of a single convex spatulate plate with inward flange impaled by the blade tang, fitted with bar-grip on the inside. *(Sotheby's)* **$3,680**

A good Sudanese Madhist throwing knife, 26¼in. incorporating 2 integral crescent heads and curved projections, etched overall with Islamic inscriptions in Thuluth script, and inlaid with cartouches of brass inscriptions, crocodile skin covered grip. *(Wallis & Wallis)* **$499**

A Japanese iron man-catcher, the mechanism designed as two serrated claws with spring release, mounted upon a two-part pole with brass juncture, 7ft.10in. *(Christie's)* **$2,300**

European spiked club, 14th century style, the 42in. haft swelling toward the top and mounted with 6in. top spike of square section and side straps retaining 16 side spikes. *(Butterfield & Butterfield)* **$1,100**

Gilded and silver painted sheet copper American flag weather vane, New England, third quarter 19th century, the silhouetted American flag with molded arm and hand holding a hammer, old weathered surface with gilt and later silver paint, 65in. long. *(Skinner)* **$35,650**

A molded and gilded copper pig weathervane, American, late 19th century, the profile form depicting a pig with intaglio eyes and mouth and applied ears, snout and curling tail standing on a rod, with rectangular base, stamped indistinguishably at tail, *J NIELD* and *000/91*, 12in. high, 17½in. wide. *(Christie's)* **$5,000**

Eagle gilt molded copper weathervane, A.L. Jewell & Co., Waltham, Massachusetts, 1855-67, areas of verdigris, 25½in. long. *(Skinner)* **$3,738**

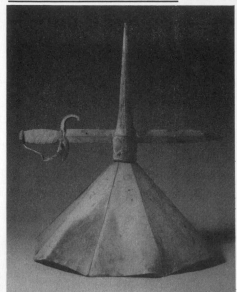

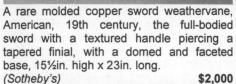

A rare molded copper sword weathervane, American, 19th century, the full-bodied sword with a textured handle piercing a tapered finial, with a domed and faceted base, 15½in. high x 23in. long.
(Sotheby's) **$2,000**

An unusual carved and painted rattlesnake weathervane, American, late 19th century, carved from a single thickness of pine in the form of a curled serpent painted red with yellow markings, 35½in. long.
(Sotheby's) **$6,612**

A painted sheet-iron weathervane, 20th century, silhouette form depicting a cow jumping over the moon, the whole rusty-orange-painted, on a rectangular stand, 23½in. high, 22in. wide.
(Christie's) **$800**

A green-painted sheet-iron locomotive weathervane, American, late 19th century, the green-painted profile silhouette form depicting an engine car with one large stack issuing steam and two smaller stacks behind, the engineer driving at the rear, 21in. high, 23in. wide.
(Christie's) **$1,200**

A molded and gilded copper Indian weathervane, American, 19th century, the frontal figure holding a bow in one hand and an arrow in the other, with articulated head-dress, hair, eyes, nose, mouth, wearing a fringed tunic, pendant necklace, and dagger, standing on a directional, 44½in. high, 45in. long. *(Christie's)* **$60,000**

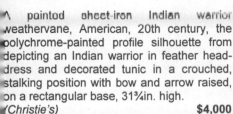

A painted sheet-iron Indian warrior weathervane, American, 20th century, the polychrome-painted profile silhouette from depicting an Indian warrior in feather head-dress and decorated tunic in a crouched, stalking position with bow and arrow raised, on a rectangular base, 31¾in. high. *(Christie's)* **$4,000**

▶

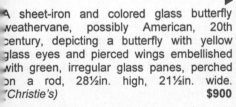

A sheet-iron and colored glass butterfly weathervane, possibly American, 20th century, depicting a butterfly with yellow glass eyes and pierced wings embellished with green, irregular glass panes, perched on a rod, 28½in. high, 21½in. wide. *(Christie's)* **$900**

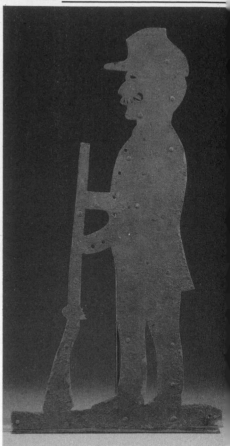

A red, white and blue-painted sheet-iron flag with metal star weathervane, American, mid-20th century, in the form of a waving American flag, mounted on a cylindrical support with square base and surmounted by a sheet metal star.
(Christie's) **$500**

A black-painted sheet iron Civil War soldier weathervane, American, 19th century silhouetted in profile leaning on a shot gun with punched details of eye, mouth and coat buttons, 35in. high, 18½in. long.
(Christie's) **$6,000**

◀

Molded and painted William Tell weather vane, America, 19th century, the full-bodied figure of the archer with raised arms wearing a plumed hat with red and blue feathers, his ruffled shirt of blue with red and yellow designs and red pantaloons, old weathered surface, 32in. high.
(Skinner) **$18,400**

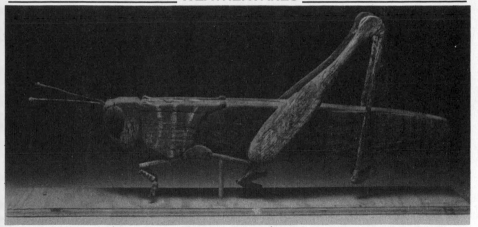

A carved and painted pine grasshopper weathervane, American, late 19th/early 20th century, the grasshopper formed from several pieces of pine with metal antennae and joints, retains original green, brown and white paint, 14in. high x 32in. long. *(Sotheby's)* **$10,000**

An extremely rare American locomotive and tender copper weathervane, circa 1882, 61in. long. *(Skinner)* **$185,000**

Jumping horse gilt molded and applied copper weathervane, probably A.L. Jewell & Co., Waltham, Massachusetts, second half 19th century, old painted surface, 36½in. long. *(Skinner)*

$23,000

A carved and painted pine sailor boy whirligig, American late 19th/early 20th century, the flattened bearded figure with rotating arms held straight out from his sides, wearing a blue shirt with a white collar, and white trousers with a red belt, 14¼in. high. *(Sotheby's)* **$517**

A carved and painted pine Hussar whirligig, American, 19th century, the mustached figure dressed in full uniform, fitted with rotating paddle arms, painted black, blue, white and gold, 13½in. high.
(Sotheby's) **$3,450**

▶

Rare Christianized Indian whirligig, 19th century, found in Maine, bearing its original paint, the stylized Indian squaw on a painted floor, her hair made of horse hair, depicted with wide open eyes and slightly parted lips showing carved and painted teeth, dressed in leather bustier, skirt and boots, with zinc cuff protecting her arm joints and a copper cross around her neck, carved with defined bicep and calf muscles, 24in. high.
(Skinner) **$27,600**

'Happy Jack' whirligig, in red, white, and blue paint, 13in. high. *(Eldred's)* **$605**

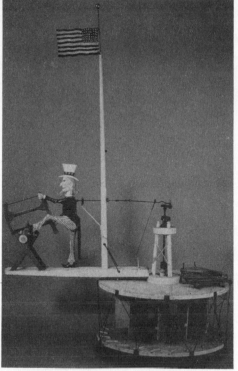

Polychrome carved wood and sheet metal 'Uncle Sam' figural whirligig, Henry Wilson Sargent, 'Henny Penny', Wilmington, Massachusetts, dated *1900*, depicting Uncle Sam sawing a log, 72in. high.

Henry Sargent, known as 'Henny Penny', lived and worked in Wilmington, Massachusetts all his life. Sargent operated a bicycle repair shop on Woburn Street where he charged 1¢ a minute for his work. This was apparently his standard charge for repairs he knew would be successful. For more difficult tasks he charged 15¢ if he fixed the problem 10¢ if he did not. In his spare time Sargent made mechanical models. *(Skinner)* **$12,650**

◄

A carved and painted whirligig, American, late 19th century, depicting a negro soldier in Civil War uniform, with copper kepi, dark blue coat with raised buttons, yellow belt and red pants, the swinging arms terminating in red-painted paddle baffles, 33in. high, 9in. wide.
(Christie's) **$8,000**

A George V rattle/whistle, the collar stamped *darling* on a mother of pearl teething stick, Birmingham 1920. *(Phillips)* **$120**

A salt glazed stoneware whistle, early 19th century, realistically modelled as a hound's head, 2¾in. *(Bonhams)* **$190**

Rare George II bosun's whistle, London 1740, 4¼in. long. *(Lyle)* **$3,200**

A Victorian silver novelty whistle vinaigrette, marks for 1870, S. Mordan & Co., modelled as a bugle, the other end with a whistle, 5cm. long. *(Bonhams)* **$320**

A late Victorian silver whistle vesta case, Birmingham, date letter rubbed, maker's mark of Levi and Salaman, compressed cylindrical form, spot hammered body with classical busts and Greek writing, hinged cover, with a dependant loop, 6.5cm. long. *(Bonhams)* **$480**

A Royal Irish Rifles officer's silver (J. & Co. Birmingham, 1893) whistle with holder, chains and chain boss. *(Christie's)* **$32**

A 19th century sheep's horn sheepdog whistle, 5in. long. *(Lyle)* **$50**

Silver bosun's whistle, unmarked, 19th century, English or American, cylindrical tube ending in a ball form hollow chamber with cut scrolling strut below, 6¼in. long, 1oz. 16dwt. *(Butterfield & Butterfield)* **$31**

Victorian silver whistle and penknife, London 1879. *(Lyle)* **$480**

Antique silver whistle/rattle/teether with mother of pearl end, Birmingham hallmarked. *(G.A. Key)* **$63**

late Victorian silver whistle cum vesta se, Birmingham 1898, maker's mark rtially worn, shaped rounded rectangular m, hinged cover, with a ring, crested and scribed, 7cm. long.
onhams) **$800**

A Derby dog head whistle, modelled as a pointer-like hound with black and white markings, yellow eyes, pink tongue and droopy ears, gilt lined mouthpiece, 19th century, 5cm. *(Tennants)* **$689**

he silver referee's whistle used by Mr. .P. Harper of Stourbridge in the 1932 A Cup final at Wembley, with ring uspension and inscribed, in case, 4.5cm. ng. *(Sotheby's)* **$1,886**

brass 'Canary songster' photographer's die in maker's original box by the Risden g. Co., Naugatuck, U.S.A.
hristie's) **$861**

A 'Griesbaum' whistling figure, German, mid 20th century, whistling and turning his head, 34cm. high. *(Bonhams)* **$640**

Victorian cast whistle formed as the head a dog, by Sampson Mordan, London, 36, 2½in. long. *(Christie's)* **$739**

A cast lion whistle, the lion with one front paw raised, unmarked, probably Italian, 18th century. *(Phillips)* **$699**

A pair of 19th century treacle glazed earthenware window stops modelled as a female bust wearing a curly wig, 4½in. high. *(Sotheby's)* **$250**

A rare set of four early 19th centu Sunderland luster sash window stops in th form of King Charles caricatures, purp luster bodies, 4in. wide. *(H.C. Chapman & Son)* **$1,4**

A pair of late 19th century glazed dark brown stoneware window stops modelled as a monkey clutching her young, 6½in. high. *(Lyle)* **$800**

A pair of hollow molded treacle glaz earthenware window stops in the form of lion's head with full mane, 5in. hig *(Sotheby's)* **$2**

An early 19th century brass bound mahogany bottle carrier, with domed lid revealing fitted interior, brass campaign handles, 17¼in. high.
(Andrew Hartley) **$1,042**

A George III brass bound wine cooler, late 18th century, of oval outline with brass loop handle, the cover hinged to either side over twin cylindrical liners inside the lead lined interior, 10¼in. high.
(Christie's) **$8,175**

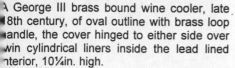

A pair of George III ormolu mounted mahogany wine coolers, each of oval shape with a gadrooned rim above a guilloche frieze, 30in. wide.
(Christie's) **$45,816**

George II mahogany wine cooler on stand, possibly Irish, of oval tapering form with carrying handles and brass band, on a conforming stand with club legs joined by a turned stretcher and pad feet, 31½in. high.
(Christie's) **$8,000**

An early Victorian oak and brown oak cellaret, the top with stepped center with beaded edge and a ribbon-tied laurel edge, 35in. wide. *(Christie's)* **$5,814**

A Berlin woolwork rectangular picture depicting a figure in a red coat and cap in an Arcadian landscape with Lord Byron's dogs, 19th century, 29 x 37in. overall.
(Christie's) **$1,319**

A needlework casket, worked in colored silks against an ivory silk ground, depicting the story of Joseph, 5½ x 14 x 10in., with key and wooden case, English, 1660.
(Christie's) **$160,000**

A high relief woolwork panel depicting a brace of partridge, 19th century, inscribed *Mr Wilcockson Spalding, Lincolnshire*, in a glazed giltwood circular frame, 17½in. diameter. *(Christie's)* **$640**

A rare slave sampler, worked in colored wools with The African Slave, and embroidered *Thou God Seest Me*, 13in. square, circa 1836.
(Christie's) **$3,200**

A Charles II wool and silk raised-work picture, worked in polychrome wools and silks, on an ivory silk ground, in a later concave molded and beaded giltwood frame, 15¾ x 19½in.
(Christie's) **$20,746**

A Victorian woolwork picture of HMS Warrior, the three-masted steam assisted vessel depicted under reduced sail in a heavy sea, 16 x 19in.
(Bearne's) **$1,200**

504

Index